MIDDLE-CLASS

WAIFS

The Psychodynamic
Treatment of Affectively
Disturbed Children

T0383393

MIDDLE-CLASS

WAIFS

The Psychodynamic Treatment of Affectively Disturbed Children

ELAINE V. SIEGEL

CRC Press
Taylor & Francis Group
Boca Raton London New York

CRC Press is an imprint of the
Taylor & Francis Group, an **informa** business

First published 1991 by The Analytic Press, Inc.

Published 2018 by CRC Press
Taylor & Francis Group
6000 Broken Sound Parkway NW, Suite 300
Boca Raton, FL 33487-2742

First issued in paperback 2018

© 1991 by Taylor & Francis Group, LLC
CRC Press is an imprint of Taylor & Francis Group, an Informa business

No claim to original U.S. Government works

ISBN 13: 978-1-138-88153-2 (pbk)
ISBN 13: 978-0-88163-098-5 (hbk)

Library of Congress Cataloging-in-Publication Data

Siegel, Elaine V.
    Middle-class waifs : the psychodynamic treatment of affectively
disturbed children / Elaine V. Siegel.
        p. cm. –
    Includes bibliographical references.
    Includes index.
    ISBN 0-88163-098-5
    1. Affective disorders in children.   2. Child psychotherapy.
I. Title. II. Series.
    [DNLM: 1. Affective Disorders – in infancy & childhood.
    2. Affective Disorders – therapy.   3. Psychotherapy.   W1 PS427F v.
12 / WS 350.6 S571m]
RJ506.D4S54   1991
618.92'8914 – dc20
DNLM/DLC
for Library of Congress   90-1226
                                                              CIP

On Phillips Court
Houses stood in an open circle
Like sentries guarding the familiar world
Bright clean windows stared at driveways
Leading to the pavement mouth of street
That gathered children in its belly
As they screeched bicycle bells in tumbled crying laughter
Running endless races of hopscotched frozen tag
In hot sweet afternoons
When clouds sat low
Over skinny man-placed trees
And mothers hung curtains
Drank coffee
Sounded children's names
In long-drawn efforts to recall them
To life they would remember
With a timeless earlier sense
When the humid summer days
Passed into hotter nights
Of rain and storm and sweat.

A poem by Melanie,
whose life enriched mine.

This book is dedicated
to the spirit alive
in the children I treated
and to my family,
including Dr. Robert C. Lane

Acknowledgments

Many thanks go to Dr. Paul E. Stepansky for his steadfast support and to Eleanor Starke Kobrin for her painstaking work in manuscript editing, and special thanks to Louella Levine for her help in clarifying the children's pictures.

Contents

MIDDLE-CLASS

WAIFS

The Psychodynamic
Treatment of Affectively
Disturbed Children

𝕫𝕫𝕫

Introduction

This book is about a group of children who live in middle-class homes, have parents who look after their physical well-being, and go to school. Their outward appearances even make them seem fortunate to others less wealthy than they. Yet these children, in a very real sense, are waifs. They have no emotional home, no person who is concerned with their inner being. Obviously, they are children in trouble. Their troubles are manifest in many ways, almost universally as low grades in school or as outright academic failure. Academic failure is recorded with monotonous regularity in the case histories I am about to present. These children have no friends; indeed, they do not get along with anybody. Their behavior is often destructive, always inappropriate; and they are subject to strong mood swings. Their parents see them as doomed to failure and are angry with them. "As a last resort," and often after many warnings by school officials and sometimes pediatricians, the children finally wind up in psychotherapeutic treatment. But after years of living in the lonely world of misperceptions among people they feel they cannot trust, they view therapy and the therapist as yet another intrusion by the adult, dangerous, incomprehensible, and, to them, unfair world. They have no hope for themselves and are mired in self-justification and angry denial. As reported in the *American Psychologist*, a prestigious and widely read journal, "there is compelling evidence from a variety of sources that affective disorders among children and adolescents are more persistent than hitherto thought and have numerous negative associated features and consequences. . . . school-aged children and adolescents do experience depression" (Kovacs, 1989, p. 209).

To parents who have sad or passively rebellious kids hanging around the house, this revelation is nothing new. Neither is it a startling discovery to teachers and others who work with children. But how did children, from relatively affluent homes, come to exhibit the symptoms of sorely underprivileged children? And why was no one able to help them before they became disaffected? There are many reasons. Not the least of which is the myth of the invariably happy childhood, which is only now loosening its hold on many influential behavioral scientists and researchers.

Other reasons for disaffection are purely personal, having to do with the unique life history of the individual. In the case histories that follow I speak a great deal about personal fates, but it will become clear that there is a unifying thread in what I am talking about. These children, true waifs, were emotional outcasts. They were unable to share the standards of their surroundings. Again, how did such a sad state of affairs come about in a country where everyone is entitled to schooling and remediation?

In 1975, Public Law 94.142 was passed. It stipulated that every handicapped child in the United States must receive, in the least restrictive environment, a free and appropriate education and remediation of the handicap. In 1981, this law was severely curtailed but the essential message remained: children with difficulties were to be treated and educated in their home districts if possible. School boards and local legislators groaned under this new burden but valiantly rose to the challenge. Testing procedures, individual education plans, special classes, and a host of other devices were instituted to deal with the nation's handicapped children. Some of these children were funneled to special schools, but most remained in their own school districts, which, for better or worse, tried to cope with these students' special needs. Objective tests were favored. Officials wanted to know, is this child progressing? But how was progress to be measured? By intelligence rating scales? Behavioral tests? There are many of those. But how do they serve the individual child? Nobody seemed inclined to ask that question.

It was assumed that if a diagnosis of a handicapping condition could be made, remediation would automatically follow. That many conflicts and conditions cannot be addressed as though they were faulty spare parts in a person's mental apparatus was simply denied. In the so-called developmental lags the missing part, be it cognitive or social failure or both, was to be eradicated simply by teaching the child to behave differently. When this attempt failed, reward and punishment systems were instituted. When a child's behavior was extra bad, the child was banished from school altogether. Since often the child in question did not want to go to school anyway, such actions by responsible adults tended to confirm the child's belief that all adults were "nuts." In other words, the worst punishment that could be meted out was also the relief from experiential and inner pressures sought by the child who wanted to be "lazy" in the first place.

Faulty parts to be expunged from the psychic economy of children were called handicaps. The word "handicap" soon became a catch-all for all sorts of difficulties. Culturally deprived children often ended up in the same classrooms as learning disabled children. Streetwise kids with behavior disorders rubbed elbows with schizophrenic and psychotic children, and minimally brain damaged ones with emotionally disturbed ones. The list of untoward combinations of students who have only behavior rating scales and low academic grades in common is endless. If the same parts of a child's educational or psychological profiles matched, then it was assumed they should be grouped together, even if it was crystal clear to everyone involved that Max couldn't learn because of anxiety and John couldn't integrate information owing to retardation.

Special education teachers were supposed to be able to deal with this conglomerate of despair and helplessness but often failed, despite their dedication. Usually nothing in their training had prepared them to handle 10 or 15 disturbed children at once, especially if each child required different handling.

School psychologists and school social workers also have incredible burdens. Often their caseloads are enormous. Because parents must give their consent, the most severely handicapped children on occasion do not receive the treatment and education they need.

Sometimes their parents are poorly informed or simply ignore or deny their children's difficulties. Faced with such mental health problems, unable to provide family therapy or counseling to persuade such recalcitrant families to avail themselves of the resources that do exist, school officials and teachers retrench. Most simply do the best they can under horrendously difficult circumstances, throw up their hands in despair, and go about their daily tasks, resigned or angry, eventually hardened to situations they cannot remediate.

Disruptive behaviors were harder to classify as "parts." But here, too, objective solutions could be found. For instance, hyperactivity caused by minimal brain damage could go a long way to explain aggressive behavior and, in the opinion of objective behavioral scientists, obviated the need for psychodynamic treatment. That hyperactivity can also be caused by extreme anxiety is hardly ever acknowledged by behaviorists. The cognitive approaches seemed to carry the day despite the fact that children learn best in an environment that includes warm relationships with significant adults. The question really becomes why so many grown-ups are afraid to look at emotions and positive interpersonal relationships as a matrix for learning. In my opinion, everyone is entitled to the courtesy of psychodynamic treatment.

I had the good fortune to work with a fairly high functioning boy who had Down Syndrome. At the beginning of treatment he managed an IQ score of 38-40 "depending on how he felt," as the testing psychologist reported. At the end of treatment, the boy obtained a score of 70 (Siegel, 1972). Others with whom I worked learned self-help skills and gained sufficient independence to stay out of institutions. Some educators and behaviorists would say that my work was wasted on such people. But was it really? To meet those nay-sayers on their ground, the very fact that these former patients can now live in the community instead of taking up space and tax dollars in mental hospitals should be enough of an argument for psychodynamic treatment of "boring" patients.

But this is a side issue in the much larger one of how to deal with the vast group of children who cannot learn and who do not adapt to society despite rigorous educational measures. Without minimizing cognitive and rational approaches, I want to point out that a humane environment enhances learning and that close interaction with empathic adults enables children to grow up with purpose, motivation, and joy. Where families have been unable for whatever reasons to provide such a background for growing up, psychodynamic treatment can facilitate renewed growth.

Stimulant medication is currently thought to be the most efficient way to deal with children who cannot control their aggressive behavior. Various studies with parents and teachers of such children show that "medication-related behavioral improvements in hyperactive children are accompanied by what might be called 'normalization' in the adults who interact with these youngsters, reflected most clearly in more positive and less controlling interchanges" (Henker and Whalen, 1989, p. 219). One cannot help but wonder if in this research the adults were not revealing more about themselves than about the children, for Henker and Whalen state on the same page that it is important to note the possibility of adverse effects of medication on mood and sociability. Medication-related decreases in the quantity of social interactions have been noted by several researchers, as have emotional changes such as flattened affect or mild dysphoria (e.g. Barkley, 1985; Cunningham, Siegel, Offord, 1985; Pelham et al., 1985)

The picture I am drawing is a frightening one: Ill children, powerless officials, and poorly informed or emotionally disinterested parents add to society's burden. I am not speaking of inner city schools, nor of children of the ghetto. The problems I am describing exist in middle-class settings everywhere. Nor am I speaking of the severely handicapped child or only of the dysfunctional family. I am talking of that curious phenomenon, the middle-class waif, who does not belong anywhere emotionally and feels betrayed.

I wish I had a sweeping hypothesis to reform and undo all the evils I have alluded to. I don't have one. But as a middle-class therapist and sometime administrator in a school for special—but middle-class—children I did learn important lessons. The vast majority of the children and adolescents I dealt with on one level or another had received a good many services and still did not improve. They *seemed* not to have been neglected. These youngsters by and large had been sluiced through every form of remediation available in their districts: special education, speech pathology, physical therapy, art therapy, dance therapy, occupational therapy. But nothing touched them sufficiently to make a real difference. Most had dedicated teachers and well-educated parents. They had been placed here and there and received this or that service, to little or no effect. Oh, their reading scores improved perhaps, or they passed math or managed not to provoke their peers; but not much else happened to them. They stayed locked in their various diagnostic categories, doomed to failed lives before they left grade school.

It finally became clear to me that what had taken place was a failure to recognize these children as whole human beings. Each well-trained specialist worked on his or her speciality, recorded progress and failure, and then went on his or her merry way. The children's emotional hunger was rarely if ever addressed, and the potentially healing effects of strong interpersonal ties were disavowed. In many instances teachers were warned not to become too attached to a child because they would have to leave the pupil in a year; or, conversely, if children became attached to a teacher, steps were taken to help them see the error of their ways. Rather than using an unfolding interpersonal dynamic to guide an ill child back to mental health, this "defective part" was unplugged in the service of staying within a budget or of being objective. Test scores counted, but not much else. Even where social workers and psychologists were psychoanalytically informed, they often were prohibited from using, or were afraid to apply, their knowledge and skills. There simply is no way to measure a transference[1] or to talk about dawning object relationships when the entire cumbersome system is based on the assumption that only test scores are valid. So-called objective tests, especially those where "the tester's personality is washed out," remained the favorite tool with which to look at a child. Many ways of testing were devised and widely used in the name of scientific accuracy.

But did they serve the children? After all, handicaps from neurosis to psychosis (descriptive words that were not favored) or any organic difficulty do not go away merely by being tested or by being identified. Because parents must give their consent for testing and treatment, the most severely handicapped children on occasion do not receive the treatment and education they need. Parents blindly hope their children will outgrow their handicaps or should try harder. Or else they

---

[1]Transferences are the displacement of feelings and behaviors that were originally experienced toward significant others in one's environment. These significant others are also called objects. Thus, a dawning object relationship is the beginning of an important interpersonal relationship that may be reminiscent of the relationship to mother, father, siblings, or whoever else was important in the past.

believe that recognizing and acting upon the child's needs is somehow weak and will spoil the child.

The problems they confront are often too much for school officials and teachers to deal with. Many correctly begin to doubt the efficacy of their tools. Their own self-images become weakened by the recognition that they, like the children, are helpless. They, along with their charges, become locked in a cycle of trying to control situations that are already deadlocked and can be resolved only by psychodynamic interventions. When their methods fail, they feel as helpless as their charges; but, being adult and professional, they seek a way out, which all too often consists of applying more pressure and more control. Their students do not respond, or they become more resistant, implying to the adult involved, "You're no good. I don't need you." The adult, understandably, withdraws, and thus the same cycle starts over again.

At the other end of the spectrum of parental beliefs is the assumption that in order to grow up a child must be denied nothing. Neither this stance nor the idea that to meet the child's needs is to spoil the child recognizes the child as an individual but, rather, reflects the parents' inner needs. Both sets of beliefs create disaffected, churlish children who act out their fantasies and have little impulse control, making their parents feel like total failures also. To repeat, I am not speaking of inner city schools, nor of children of the ghetto. The problems I am describing exist in middle-class settings everywhere. Despite all efforts failures are to be expected. Twenty-minute sessions once every other week simply are not enough. This is a norm I have heard described in many school districts. The schools alone cannot be blamed. Certain services, such as speech therapy for autistic youngsters, have been mandated. However, because of budget cutbacks and insufficient personnel, often such mandated services are delivered at the expense of those children who need just as much but must fall at the wayside because what they need is simply not available. The kind of treatment they need—psychodynamic intervention, which deals with interpersonal communication and uses transferences to undo or to distance from past trauma and developmental lag—is often simply dismissed as too idealistic or impractical or as too time consuming.

The children's emotional hunger is rarely if ever addressed, and the potentially healing effects of strong interpersonal ties are disavowed. Child Guidance Team meetings are most often devoted to comparing notes and to devising strategies for eradicating the behavior of troublesome pupils and to apply the latest gimmick in educational hardware. Test scores are counted; possibly anecdotal material is collected to prove that this or that child should be in a special class or receive extra educational help. That the child might be crying out to be seen as a person is all too often felt to be the weak-kneed reaction of unenlightened but well-meaning newcomers. Psychoanalytically informed social workers and psychologists are all too often dismissed—in every sense of the word. Other than by the *results* of their work, they cannot "prove" what they are talking about. The entire system operates on the assumption that only test scores are valid. This concrete, linear kind of thinking permeates our whole culture. It is not surprising, then, that educators and mental health professionals fall into the same trap of assuming themselves to be objective when they are in reality disavowing the inner world of human beings.

So instead of offering learned treatises proving or disproving that any or all of the many systems being applied in our schools work or do not work, I would like to offer a far simpler suggestion: Let all of us, educators and mental health professionals, offer our expertise with the recognition that we are emotionally significant to our charges! Let us understand that they are driven by inner forces they do not understand and that even the most obstreperous among them needs us to guide them emotionally as well as cognitively out of their inner fragmentation and despair.

Many of the youngsters I treated came from apparently intact homes. They appeared to have concerned parents and devoted teachers. Yet something had gone terribly wrong. Most had been in trouble for years before they reached my treatment room. They had been remediated and therapized and scolded until their resistances[2] were so solid they did not want to talk to me or to play in my presence. Before training as a psychotherapist and then as a psychoanalyst, I was a dance therapist and so did not experience a person who did not want

---

[2]The inner equilibrium of all people rests on a balance of inner forces that allows them to function without anxiety. When anything disturbs this balance, people feel anxious and, consciously or unconsciously, ward off even "what is good for them," such as psychotherapeutic treatment.

to talk to me as particularly strange. The language of the body and of expressive movement were my forté, or so I thought. Unfortunately, many of my young patients thought the idea of moving about in a rhythmic fashion "definitely uncool" and sneered at the mere thought of dancing. Drawing was something they thought was for kindergartners. The younger children did not know how to play (Klein, 1955). They were not by any means autistic but viewed toys as something to avoid, and the thought of playing in front of someone or with someone was too frightening. Perhaps they unconsciously recognized play as too revealing. Some of the teenagers reluctantly decided it might be okay to bring in their records to show me just how far removed I was from their world. They were convinced that I could not begin to imagine their terror and despair, which they thought they were hiding so cleverly under smooth talk and fashionable disguises.

Therefore, the beginning phases of each treatment were excruciatingly difficult. Working alliances[3] had to be painstakingly developed and did not spring up in the spontaneous fashion to which one is accustomed in psychoanalytic work. That the children had not come for treatment of their own free will and had no conception of what psychotherapy might entail added to the initial difficulties. The concept of a conflict-free ego sphere (Hartmann, 1939) helped me here. This is a construct used by psychoanalysts to describe the areas of functioning that are not involved in conflict. For instance, such ego functions as motility, perception, memory, and thought have from the beginning of life a relative freedom to develop outside of conflict. Those areas of ego functioning that are impaired can be seen in psychoanalytic theory to be conflict ridden. The vast majority of our remedial and educational measures address themselves to the conflict-ridden areas in a given person. Thus, students are constantly made aware of how deficient and troubled they are. Using the concept of the conflict-free ego sphere, however, one can zero in on those aspects of a person's life that are still healthy. This kind of interaction is popularly known as "stroking." A newer school of psychoanalysis, self psychology, makes a virtue of "empathically holding" a patient as well (Kohut, 1971). Whatever one calls it, making patients aware of their strengths builds a conscious working alliance and bypasses much

---

[3]As the term implies, a working alliance is the conscious decision of the patient to work with the therapist toward change.

anxiety until the time comes to focus safely on what needs to be changed. In the case histories that follow there are many examples of how I approached seemingly unapproachable youngsters by keeping in mind that somewhere there had to be an avenue by which I could reach them.

Finding those avenues was difficult because not only the school system had failed these children. Although their parents looked after their physical well being, paid their bills, and were concerned for their education, emotional closeness and intimacy, and, in particular, respect for the child, were often missing. I had to step gingerly indeed in order to establish an interpersonal pattern that would allow these children to relate to me as a safe person who could be used as a model but who was also strong enough to withstand their aggression and despair. I often had to devise "tricks" to approach my young patients emotionally. Some of these tricks have become accepted treatment techniques particularly among dance movement therapists (Siegel, 1984a). I think that some of them will be helpful to other mental health professionals as well. The case histories described in this book delineate what I mean.

INSTINCTUAL OVERSTIMULATION

All children need help and protection. The waifs I am talking about here need a double dose of what is usually called the milk of human kindness and a firm conviction that understanding their unconscious dynamic will help to calm and soothe them so that they eventually can become productive and law-abiding citizens. I view their often inappropriate behavior as a manifestation of so-called instinctual overstimulation. They have not been able to digest appropriately what they have cognitively and affectively experienced. Their egos and their fragile sense of self have been overwhelmed by the magnitude of what they have seen, heard, or felt. But how is it that these human beings can be so overwrought and still function, albeit on a lower level than might be expected? That these youngsters can still function has to do with the motivational forces of human behavior that Freud (1915a) called instincts. The most cogent definition he offered was that "an instinct . . . appears to us as a concept on the frontier between the mental and the somatic, as the psychical representative of the stimuli originating from within the organism and reaching the mind, as a measure of the demand made upon the mind for work in consequence of its connection with the body" (pp. 121–122).

The mental work that has to be accomplished has to do with both the aim and the object of the instinct that is aroused. The aim of an instinct is always to find satisfaction by the removal of the stimulation at the source of the instinct. It was just such a lack of basic satisfaction that landed my young patients in trouble. When children wish to love their parents (when they libidinally cathect their parents, as the psychoanalytic jargon has it) and the parents turn away from them at each step of the way, love is thwarted and can turn into its opposite — hate.

Another often ignored instinctual wish of children is to be identified with one or both parents. But if the children are laughed at, shamed, or ignored, this wish turns into frustration and rage, leaving them alone with their wish to grow up. One of the most potent difficulties can arise when a child identifies with a parent and then sees this parent engage in behavior that cannot be readily understood. Sexual intercourse and violent rages are the most destructive examples. Seeing, or being subjected to, sexual overtures or excessively punitive measures arouses children's instincts. But because they are still children, they cannot cope with such arousal and become difficult to educate. Their instincts have been overstimulated and force them into chaotic behavior. For parents and therapists alike it is not always easy to recognize the source of such overstimulation. Often schools or social situations are blamed for the children's troubles. The question is always how to make it better for the child. But, at the same time, love alone is not enough. It is not only the uncomprehending and cold world out there that produces troubled children; clearly, some responsibility falls at the doorstep of the parents. Some colleagues and friends who have read my case histories have yelled, Child abuse! Yet the children I am speaking of had parents who were committed enough to bring their children for treatment and to pay for it. With the exception of the children who were actually sexually abused, there was no *conscious* intent on the part of the parents to hurt their children. As a matter of fact, the concept of conscious intent of a parent or adult to hurt a child might be important only legally. In a psychoanalytic or psychodynamic setting, it has little or no meaning.

By pointing an accusing finger one can easily drive a family from treatment. Although it is often difficult to do so, it is better to bite one's tongue and look for an avenue of approach to the problem. For the therapist wishing to rescue the young patient, this is often a major problem. Later I will enlarge on this issue. Suffice it to say now that parents, like their children, are driven by inner needs and past traumas. They need to be offered the same chances as the children to reconstitute their inner selves. Having been misused or mistreated in one form or another themselves, they often are merely passing on what happened to them.

For example, Loretta's father was the son of immigrants who thought he was lucky because he had enough to eat. They beat him and his 10 siblings routinely. He did not beat his little girl, but in his own brutalization he had not learned that intrusion and overstimulation can cause havoc with the inner life of a child. He himself had found an outlet for his aggressive drives in stock car racing. Or take Gino. His parents, immigrants themselves, were insecure and came from a culture that assumed unquestioning filial obedience as an ideal. They had no tools for understanding their sensitive child. Then there is Ted, whose parents were so unhappy themselves that they did not have sufficient loving energy left for perhaps the most talented of their children. The list goes on.

Yes, there were sadistic components in the inner life of the parents I dealt with. But this is not to say that they did not have their own, albeit abbreviated or unevolved, forms of loving their children. Confronting them would have scared many of them away. Many were afraid of losing their children altogether, and this fear made them act in a hostile manner toward, first, their children, who had placed them in such a vulnerable position, then the referring school officials, and finally the therapist. But except for the fathers of Saul, Nick, and Tommie, I really cannot accuse any of the parents of being perverts or of being totally devoid of love for their children. They sometimes seemed like emotional toddlers to me; they had grown up without understanding their own inner lives and could not soothe and comfort themselves, let alone their children, who were striving for independence.

Although these parents demonstrated that their inner lives were impoverished, unevolved, or primitive, they had enough awareness and reality perception to adapt to their environments appropriately. By and large they earned more than sufficient income to support their families; they had friends and related in some form or another to the world at large. Not so for their children. Instinctual flooding is even more serious than instinctual overstimulation. For instance, if children have been physically punished but can still think, "I am very angry," or even fantasize, "I want to kill the old man," they may show poorly adapted behavior but not act on all of their rage. During instinctual flooding, however, all impulse control is lost, and the child becomes an agitated warrior or incorrigible masturbator, or the like. The enormous instinctual flooding these children experienced rendered them incapable of trusting, assimilating information, and learning. It is as though these children hold up an enormous magnifying glass to the emotional needs of their parents, showing the parents that they have been inadequate. The unconscious of the parents reads the message loudly and clearly but must deny it in order to preserve self-esteem. Thus, the children must cope for themselves and by themselves.

Often, they give up learning because learning is a form of assimilating and processing material that is at first foreign. Dire experience has shown these children that the taking-in process is full of dangers for them. To look at their misdeeds and their lack of academic achievement would mean that they are achieving cognitive acceptance, or cognitive taking-in, of another's perceptions. And this they are unable and unwilling to do. To acquiesce, to use their intelligence as their parents and teachers want them to do, would also mean understanding how much these significant others have let them down. So the children close themselves off and continue to stagnate. Appealing to their intelligence alone simply does not work. A significant other has to be there to soothe their ruffled feathers without overgratifying them. Their injured and arrested inner selves have to be given another chance to evolve out of the overgrowth of distrust, apathy, and lack of caring, which, on the affective level, also mirrors aspects of the distrusting, apathetic, uncaring parts of their parents. In psychodynamic psychotherapy, which not only includes but emphasizes the affective process between therapist and child, a second chance for renewed development exists. In this approach, educative and cognitive tools are not discarded but, rather, take their place along with other treatment tools. But, it must be stressed, the interpersonal relatedness between therapist and child is the bridge that makes all growth possible.

Growth was originally stunted within the parent to child interaction; for instance, some parents believe that young children do not understand the significance of what is happening during sexual intercourse, or they believe that it is "modern" to let a child be present when they are nude, or defecating or urinating. Others are simply oblivious of their children's presence and vent their rage on each other while the children deal with that form of overstimulation as best they can. Yet another group feels that bringing up children without corporal punishment will spoil them. Whatever the manifest behavior of the parents, those who are able to bring their children to a therapist realize that something has gone wrong. However much they want to ward off their own guilt and dismay, they want to take care of their children. Having been prey to either sexual or punitive overstimulation themselves, they have never learned to mediate their own needs appropriately. Many of them do not see themselves, nor does society view them, as being abusive to their children. If we accept Gill's (1975) definition of child abuse as any parental act that interferes with a child's optimal development, even errors made by well-meaning parents are child abuse. Gill's definition leaves the door open for much mud slinging, indeed. Within its openendedness and lack of specificity many parents would be villains. Were the parents I am talking about villains? Some were, and some were not. Most had many psychological difficulties of their own and did not understand that their inner turmoil affected their children. The majority thought of themselves as good-enough parents. When they realized they were not, some were able to change their behavior toward their children. Yet the majority exhibited a chilling similarity to more abusive parents in their perhaps neurotic, certainly psychologically ill-informed assumption that the children were their property to do with as they saw fit. Regard for the children as human beings was typically lacking. This lack, in some cases, like Tommie's and Ted's, did lead to physical abuse. Despite such abuse the parents "bought" the cloak of normalcy for their behavior. They never once asked themselves, what am I contributing to my child's behavior? They simply saw their children as their chattels and were puzzled by the children's profound sense of disenfranchisement and worthlessness. After all, the parents did provide toys and the usual gadgets assumed to make for happiness. TVs, mini motorbikes, snowbuggies, and other accessories of middle-class life were given to these children. Therefore, the parents saw their children as ungrateful brats and themselves as good-enough parents.

On phenomonologic and social levels, these parental attitudes raise questions of what constitutes child neglect or child abuse. On psychodynamic and treatment levels, they demand examination of their inferred and actual unconscious meanings. Other researchers and clinicians offer some insights and observations. Despite a fervent desire for reforms in some quarters and the new recognition that child abuse has been occurring at a staggering rate (Gelles, 1975), society has not for long tried to protect its most innocent and helpless citizens. The term "battered child syndrome" was first introduced in 1962 by Kempe and his colleagues when they presented radiologic evidence of the scarring, broken bones, bruises, rectal and vaginal ruptures, gonococcal infections, failure to thrive, and even death, all of which until then had too often been labeled and reported as "unrecognized trauma." The psychiatric symptoms that are also part and parcel of this syndrome only recently received validation (Weil, 1989). My case studies corroborate his findings. In statistically examining the frequency of occurrence of certain defined symptomatic behaviors in 100 children seen in psychotherapy, Weil was able to show that specific symptoms were linked to particular erotic or punitive behavior of parents. He identified types of overstimulation and their resultant symptoms. The symptomatic reactions investigated in relation to children's instinctual overstimulation include 22 reactions occurring as components of children's neurotic, psychotic, and delinquent behavior and in their dreams. Only the most important ones are cited. For instance, Weil considers sharing a bed with an adult a source of stimulation that a child cannot cope with unless the child just quietly rests in bed with the adult or cuddles in an affectionate way. According to him, of the children exhibiting separation phobias, including school phobias, 54% shared a bed with an adult at least once a week, either to induce sleep in the child or to please the adult (p. 33).

Weil defines erotic, genital, visual or tactile contact with an adult as follows: child wrestles or is very physical with adult in bed; child shares bed with a nude adult; child shares bed with adults who are preparing for or performing sexual intercourse; child shares bed with adult who is masturbating; child contacts nude adult's genitalia in a shower or bath; child observes adult penis during partial or complete erection; child observes adults copulating or masturbating; child observes adult's genitalia, breasts, or buttocks during overt invitation for sexual play; child is exposed to sexual contact by adults fondling the child's genitalia; child observes hard-core pornography (pp. 14–15).

The symptoms that beset children after repeated exposure to such adult behaviors are equally well-defined and consist, in broad outline, of separation hysterics, with noisy, fearful, and agitated display of emotions; irrational fears and phobias; night terrors or other hysterical twilight states, including sleepwalking and phobic hallucinations during periods of waking; irrational temper, hysterics, and anger manifested in agitated, angry screaming, thrashing, or disorganized, nondirected hitting or screaming; and such sexual activities as compulsive masturbation, driven sexual activity of either homo- or heterosexual nature, antisocial sexual activities, sexual activities with animals, and sexual fetishism (pp. 16–17). Witnessing an adult dressing or undressing, or taking a shower or bath, without genital contact is not seen as detrimental to the child (p. 52).

Interestingly, many children who have been exposed to adult erotic behavior show symptoms that include dreams that pertain in one form or another to eyes. Concomitantly, there can be psychogenic disturbances of the eyes, including blurring, tics, difficulty in seeing, even psychogenic blindness, psychogenic reading problems,[4] poking self or others in the eye, and dreams and symptoms involving staring or looking (p. 66).

Actually, Weil's pioneering efforts are a substantiation of Freud's hypothesis that exposure to sexual contact with adults, other children, or adolescents overstimulates children and plays a role in symptom formation (Breuer and Freud, 1893–1895; Freud, 1900, 1905). By 1906, Freud had shifted his opinion about his now famous seduction theory. He began to believe that he had overestimated the role of actual sexual seduction of children. He felt that it was more accurate and more therapeutic to pay close attention to patients' sexual fantasies. Much has been written and speculated about this change in his opinion. Some writers (e.g., Masson, 1984) believe that

---

[4]Psychogenic reading problems are seldom, if ever, recognized by testers and reading specialists as having originated in trauma. They are usually assumed to be a perceptual or cognitive deficit.

it was the influence of his Victorian culture that persuaded Freud to abandon the idea that fathers and other family members could regularly commit incest. But Freud never gave up the idea completely. He often referred to it (Freud, 1916, 1931) and in his "Outline of Psychoanalysis" (1938) concluded that neurotic symptoms often stem from sexual abuse of children by adults (p. 187).

Punitive contacts with parents are obviously just as, or even more, detrimental to a child's development as is sexual stimulation. Punishment received equally detailed study and definition by Weil, who found that a child's symptoms can be used as an accurate diagnostic tool even if the abuse took place years earlier. Indeed, often the traumatization of a child does not show itself until much later, when what actually took place is difficult to document. Repression is at work and prevents even the victimized children themselves from reporting what happened to them. Besides this often profound amnesia, there is the need of children for their parents — they will go to great lengths to keep intact the picture of their parents as loving and helpful.

It has long been clear to child care workers and mental health professionals that parental lack of empathy affects children adversely. They become morose, withdrawn, and stubborn or agitated, nervous, and unmanageable. Lack of empathy often shows itself in arbitrary and senseless prohibitions. It also manifests itself in extreme parental negativism, which includes parents' frequently screaming to correct and punish the child or screaming at each other; corporal punishment with a strap, belt, or utensil; hitting, kicking, and other painful punishments in which the parent is out of control (Weil, 1989, pp. 16–17). Occasional hitting with one hand without loss of control by the adult and without violence, leaving no marks, is considered within the normal range of expectable parent–child interaction.

Weil has research data to show that long-term exposure to beatings

> would be expected to prime the children's destructive behavior and in turn accentuate the rewarding aspects of the children's discharging destructive behavior upon others or upon themselves. Furthermore, if the excessively activated destructive reactions cannot be discharged overtly, the likelihood arises that these destructive reactions will alternatively permeate the children's fantasies, dreams and symptoms [p. 93].

Fifty-nine percent of children who suffered beatings had learning problems (p. 94). This finding, of course, does not show up in the objective testing devices used in schools. It does show up in the children's symbolizations,[5] dreams, and symptoms, as Weil's and my own case histories show over and over again. Weil investigated 100 cases. I can add to these experiences another 125 cases both from my private practice and from my work in a day school for atypical children. I did not go to the lengths that Weil did to define statistically and analyze the many cases I supervised and those I conducted myself. Suffice it to say that my experiences corroborate his findings. Interestingly, failure in school was usually the most important symptom cited by parents and was the reason for referral. Unruly behavior placed as a distant second in the complaints voiced by the parents.

In this book I give examples of children who were diagnosed as either retarded or learning disabled; as having attention deficit disorders, behavior disorders, mutism; or as falling within a host of other diagnostic categories, none of which took into account their having been instinctually overstimulated. I have separated their cases into categories of my own: children who do not accept their gender and its functions; children who have been exposed to adults' sex play; children who have been severely punished; children who have been sexually abused; and children who are socially withdrawn. Very often sexual and punitive interactions overlapped, yet one or the other type of overstimulation seemed specifically to stamp the individual children's behaviors.

I hope that by my sharing what I learned with other therapists and educators of all persuasions, more children and their parents will find each other again emotionally.

SOME IMPORTANT THEORETICAL ISSUES: PREOEDIPALITY, THE OEDIPAL PHASE, AND CASTRATION ANXIETY

The oedipal phase is unlike any other that precedes it. Both actually and metaphorically it delimits and defines the inner life of humans.

---

[5]Symbolization is a form of indirect representation that functionally disguises what is an unacceptable wish or drive while allowing partial gratification of this wish or drive or the internal retention of an important lost object. It is believed to be the most uniquely human trait involved in all mental activity, from primitive symbols for body parts and their functions to literary and artistic forms.

During the oedipal phase we learn what it means to be either a man or a woman. We define ourselves against the more evolved masculinity or femininity of our parents and desire to be the exclusively loved one of the opposite-sex parent. Thus, the same-sex parent becomes a rival. Only after a great deal of inner turmoil is the child willing to give up the struggle for emotional supremacy in favor of loving and being loved by both parents. Later, during adolescence, the same conflicts are worked through again, this time under the auspices of a more evolved ego. But it is the oedipal phase that provides the base from which we learn to love, work, and play. The families described in this book were, for the most part, unable to establish the matrix from which their children could evolve. Many took the helping hand offered during their children's therapy; some did not.

Most earlier phases are traversed in the service of discrete functions. During preoedipality, the emphasis is on the oral, anal, and phallic strivings linked to body zones. Frustration tolerance, perceptual discrimination, and intellectual synthesis all had to be laboriously integrated through the agency of caretaking others. The dangers of growing up were usually envisioned by the infant and toddler as being external ones. But the care and nurture of the important others in the child's world alleviated all dangers. Even if the child experienced the important others as being capable of abandonment, of ceasing to care, or of inflicting injuries, it could come to terms with this possibility by accepting its actual and fantasized environment. This acceptance entailed incorporating into itself proposed patterns, mobilizing age-adequate defenses, and modifying behavior. Even if the caretakers required that a child endure much more than could be safely tolerated, the plasticity of the infantile psyche is such that unempathic caretakers could be accommodated.

At the threshold of the oedipal phase, however, the situation shifts. The drives have advanced to a new plateau. Remembered and internalized images of important others can coordinate loving and aggressive currents with body zones and with people, so that wishes are less bound to concrete stimuli from the outer world, fastening on the wish to be the partner of the parent of the opposite sex. The Oedipus complex is a set of necessary, expectable experiences: incestuous desires, the feeling of murderous rivalry, and attendant dreadful threats. This sounds dangerous and ridiculous to the layman, yet every family finds it adorable when little daughters want to marry their daddies and little sons chivalrously declare that they wish to marry mother. Frequently overlooked, even in nurturing households, is that such infantile devotion carries with it inevitable disappointment, which must be dealt with. Little boys discover soon enough that they are not physically equipped to give mother pleasure. Little girls are unhappy that they do not yet have breasts or the ability to bear children. Both sexes experience metaphorical, and, on occasion, actual castration anxiety. By actual castration anxiety I mean reactions to such unthinking or uninformed adult remarks as "You'll go blind if you keep your hands in your pants", or "Your penis will fall off if you don't stop pulling on it," or "You'll get an infection down there if you keep sticking your finger in your vagina." Another way to warp a child's budding relationship with its own body is to offer food as a distraction when the child is sexually or aggressively aroused.

Freud (1925) hypothesized that children's interest in their genitals is stimulated biologically by an intensification of genital sensations. The child's observation of the anatomical difference between the sexes and the attendant castration complex were seen to have a fateful impact on both male and female development (see Freud, 1932, 1933). Castration anxiety in both sexes was seen as inevitable. This has until recently been one of the most firmly established sets of constructs in psychoanalysis. While the oedipal phase remains, however, the cornerstone of the developmental sequence, how castration anxiety is viewed has changed as a result of more recent child research. In this book I adhere to this newer insight about preoedipal castration anxiety. As the case histories will show, many of the children had not reached the oedipal phase, yet they were haunted by castration anxieties of great magnitude. That many of these children had good mental and physical endowment and loved their parents still did not permit them to attain the consolidating aspects of the oedipal phase. The impingement of earlier, incompletely traversed phases lingered and kept the children from taking the next developmental step.

The research of Roiphe and Galenson (1981) has shown that Freud was right but that what he described as castration anxiety takes place at a much earlier time than he thought. They found that

infants, usually between 15th and 19th months, acquire a distinct awareness of their genitals. Their genital awareness occurs with such regularity and exerts such pervasive effect on all areas of functioning that we have designated it the early genital phase. One of the most conspicuous manifestations of the early castration reaction, a reaction sharply different in boys from what it is in girls: the boys attempt to deny the anatomical differences; the girls acknowledge the differences and become depressed and angry. These differences in reaction have led us to postulate that it is during the early genital phase, during the second half of the second year of life, that the infant begins to take on a discernible sexual identity [p. 2].

This hypothesis allows us to view the case histories and the volatile emotional happenings around the children I am writing about from a new point of view. They by and large had only incompletely reached the oedipal phase. Some had not gotten there at all. Roiphe and Galenson outline the consequences of such a lag in emotional development. They observe that "the preoedipal castration reactions, in contrast to later phallic-oedipal phase castration reactions, not only reflect a threat to the infant's sense of body intactness, but simultaneously are experienced as a threat of object loss (p. 14).

In the light of this research, the explosive reactions of the children described in this book can be understood as the reactions of children who had not been able to reach the oedipal phase. Their desperation signified fear of loss of self and fear of loss of the important others in their lives, no matter how unempathically they had been treated. For most of them, renewed growth took place during treatment. The information about what happened to them afterward is scant, but I have included it where it was available. From such scant follow-ups I have arrived at the cautious conclusion that the majority of the children I worked with managed at least to develop to a point where they could function within society without overt deviation. Does this mean that they all reached the oedipal level? I doubt it. They do, however, seem to have acquired psychological skills they lacked before treatment; that is, development continued because certain types of emotional learning blocks were dissolved. Gedo (1988) has a clear vision of how such learning blocks might be formed. During the treatment of certain adults, he noticed that they seemed to repeat certain self-destructive, even dangerous sequences of volatile feelings. He describes how one patient always seemed to be seeking external props to support "an innate cycle of sensations: first, a crescendo of pleasurable excitement, then overstimulation with a need for relief, later rage and helplessness, followed by autoaggressive activity, and finally exhaustion" (p. 21).

In the case histories in this book, it is noticeable that many of the children followed this pattern. They had learned no self-soothing devices that were not explosive or provocative. This important adaptive psychological skill—to be able to tolerate and to even like being alone, playing quietly and contentedly, or understanding one's body signals without panic—is an adaptive function that can be integrated only when the environment is structured but kind, empathic but firm. Again, it becomes clear in the case histories that the parents of these children themselves did not possess these skills and therefore were unable to pass them on to their children.

It is difficult in treatment to assess correctly whether one is dealing with a bona fide developmental arrest or with the return of a regressive memory. In treating my young patients, I always assumed that they simply did not possess the psychological skills needed to behave any differently than they did. Their efforts at tension regulation and their tenuous attempts to experience themselves as autonomous persons were almost always curtailed either by their families or by their own inability to reduce tension to societally acceptable limits. Gedo (1988) says, "The majority of children who experience widespread developmental derailments in earliest childhood prove to be capable of resuming their psychological growth by keeping in isolation those aspects of their inner world affected by these primitive vicissitudes" (p. 58).

These are prophetic words indeed. In the treatments I conducted, all the children seemed to grasp eagerly at the opportunity to reconstitute themselves or, perhaps for the first time, to constitute a self that belonged to them rather than to their parents. This is not at all the same as a failed symbiosis. These children had many intact aspects that helped them to function. They did not cling to their parents nor did they have the need to negate their own individuality. This negation of or total absence of a separate self is typical of people who have gotten stuck in the symbiotic phase. It is an essential developmental step for every human being to traverse the symbiotic phase. The loving dependency of mother and child on each other has been discussed by Mahler and her co-workers (1975) and by Spitz (1965). Vestiges of this symbiotic kind of dependency and mutual emotional fueling are part and parcel of every loving relationship in later life. But it isn't only the emotional fuel one brings along from the symbiotic phase. It is also the time in which perception and cognition are formed and become the base for self observation and exploration of the world. At the same time, inner memories are built up which allow the child to reach out and to shape its own world, so to speak, when it is old enough to separate from mother or primary caretaker. This psychological separation had taken place in most of the children I describe. Nevertheless, their selves were not autonomous. Because they had been so unempathically treated, they had vast holes, so to speak, in their inner structures. They simply could not, without help, soothe themselves or adapt to various societal demands; they seemed often to act like little savages. It is noteworthy that cognitive information offered by parents and teachers had been warded off, especially in the areas of sexual and social interaction. When the same information was presented by me within the gentle holding pattern of a trusting interpersonal relationship, it was integrated and enhanced the developmental growth of the child. Though it had been difficult for many of these children to reach the oedipal level, for some, like Loretta, the first vestiges of the Oedipus complex in its positive form did arrive. Others were in a familial situation that precluded further growth for them even if some isolated ego functions were activated and became useful to them. I am thinking of Adam, who wanted to rescue his mother from her pathology but could not. After all, he was just a little boy. He wished desperately to be big and powerful and in his grandiose reaching for impossible goals, was defeated.

A WORD ABOUT THE VERY BEGINNING OF TREATMENT: THE INTERVIEW WITH PARENTS

I usually see the parents for one session, take a developmental history of the child from them, and explore the possibility of their entering therapy with a colleague. I am fairly insistent about this. Children cannot change their lives by themselves. No matter how much they manage to grow and change, they need their parents to endorse and complete these changes. But giving their children over to a professional is viewed as a failure by many parents. They feel guilty, angry, and hurt, betrayed by the very children who will now cost so much money and effort to "fix." The word "fix" comes up often in such interviews, as though a psychotherapy were in the same category as orthodonture or optometry. Whatever the parents think about psychotherapy, they are rarely, at the outset, positive. Clearly, they need some sort of therapy or counseling to sustain them in their difficult task of realigning some of their most basic beliefs and habits. To change a personal dynamic, or a family interaction, "just for that kid" is very hard. Equally difficult is the guilt occasioned by having produced a child who appears not to share one's values or to be stubborn to such a degree that family life has become impossibly turbulent. Therapists may choose to see the child and the family, or just the mother or father, on separate occasions or together. Sperling (1978) even analyzed mothers and children at the same time. I find that this task can become enormously complicated. Children in trouble need a person they can emotionally call their own, whom they do not have to share with their families. They must learn to trust all over again, perhaps even make up developmental milestones they missed in growing up.[6] In my opinion, this process takes place much more smoothly if the youngster in question does not have to worry that any of his or her secrets will be divulged or that a family member is better liked by the therapist than he or she is. Understandably, parents do not always see the connection between their own behaviors and that of the child. They feel they have done the best they can. And, indeed, they often have. But denial of the forces of their own unconscious and the influences of the past upon the present prevent these parents from seeing where they could have been, or could be, more helpful to their children. So they ask, "Why do I have to be in therapy when it is Johnny who is in trouble?" I always try to demonstrate that in times of stress they too need someone in whom to confide and with whom, perhaps, to investigate what has made them respond to their children in just the way they do. I am careful not to be accusatory or judgmental. If my suggestion falls on deaf ears, I bring the subject up again at the next monthly meeting, another device I use to inform the parents about their child's therapy.

In the very first session I let it be known that my interventions will be less effective, and that we will have to discontinue the child's

---

[6]The ages at which certain maturational and developmental tasks are completed are well documented. Spitz (1965), Mahler, Pine, and Bergman (1975) and Roiphe and Galenson (1981) are among the more important psychoanalytic theoreticians who have investigated the phases of early human development.

treatment far short of its goals, if the parents themselves do not undertake treatment. Of course, this suggestion frequently arouses suspicion and fear, no matter how tactfully presented. I also tell parents that I will reevaluate my interaction with their offspring in a month's time and that if they cannot make a determination about themselves by then, we will have to discuss their reluctance further. I do not let up on this suggestion and will discontinue the child's treatment if the parents do not eventually commit themselves to at least a minimum kind of intervention. But that is not all. I also tell them that I will never tell them anything that the child wants to keep secret and that if the child wishes it, I will not see them even for the monthly fact-finding sessions. That is a very hard nut to digest for the vast majority of parents. But fortunately most are also relieved that finally there is a promise of something being done about their unhappiness. They regain a little hope, and this energizes them sufficiently to want to help both their children and themselves.

I cannot stress enough how important it is to be tactful and empathic under such circumstances. When a family is forced to recognize that something has gone terribly wrong with a child, they blame themselves, even if they deny it. Some feel guilty for no reason other than that they have misunderstood their child. Others actually have mistreated the child in one fashion or another. And here there often is a fine line. What constitutes mistreatment? Even sexual abuse is not always verifiable because, ultimately, children need to defend their parents. Even a bad parent is better than no parent at all! So it is best for the therapist to try to stay as nonjudgmental as is possible. Nothing is gained by accusations, but an entire family might regain its equilibrium and strength if some positive feelings can once again be liberated.

I also request a minimum of two sessions per week for the child. Experience has taught me that once-a-week interventions become holding patterns and support whatever ego strengths are there but do not make possible the crucial changes in the inner structure of the young patient. If finances make it impossible for the family to follow my suggestions, I either adjust my fee or find a colleague or clinic that can accommodate this particular family.

As a result, I always see the youngsters twice a week, more often when their needs dictate it. I have indicated in the case studies when the interaction was more frequent.

═══

CHAPTER 2

But I Don't Want to Be Me
Children Who Don't Accept Their Gender and Its Functions

F amilies find it particularly frightening when a child openly declares that it has no wish to accept its anatomical gender. Sometimes the child says so openly; more often such denial does not become apparent until the child is in treatment. Either way, it is an upsetting occurrence to all concerned. But before one decides that one is in the presence of deviant development,[1] it is appropriate to ask, Why does this child find it necessary to act like this? More often than not there are experiential forces at work that force the child to

---

[1]Freud (1905) assumed that there is such a thing as biological bisexuality. He could not phase-specifically conceptualize the opposing male and female developmental tendencies in his patients; therefore he decided that they must be a biologic given. But recent research has shown that, for instance, hormonal influences are deeply relevant only prenatally (Money, 1987). A boy's wish for a baby, for example, or the woman's role in intercourse can no longer be accepted as a biologic given. Rather, it is an early identification with the mother that accounts for the boy's feminine wishes. For girls, the situation is now viewed differently also. Freud's idea that many feminine characteristics are due to original sexual inferiority or women's genital deficiency has simply not proved valid. He thought that the vagina was unknown territory until a penis awakened feelings in it during intercourse. My own clinical findings show that the classic view that the young female lacks vaginal awareness is a pathological rather than a normal development (Siegel, 1984, 1988).

stay in the so-called undifferentiated phase postulated by Fast (1984). She proposes a gender-differentiation process during which both sexes wish for, and think they possess, the attributes of the other. Infantile omnipotence allows the little girl to assume that she too will grow a penis, and the little boy assumes that he can bear babies. While this is a charming phase in young children, it is frowned upon in our society later on. Whether such disapproval is appropriate or not is not the question; to help a child sift out what is right for him or her is the issue.

Probably around the second half of the second year, delimitation of possibilities inherent in sexual differences is accepted, along with anatomical sex differences (Roiphe and Galenson, 1981). But even before then infants know what gender they belong to. Their core gender identity (Stoller, 1964) is made known to them by correct sex assignment at birth and by the way their parents respond to them. Stoller also cites a biologic "force": originating in fetal life and usually genetic in origin, this effect—so far as is known—springs from the neurophysiologic (central nervous system) organizing of the fetal brain (p. 11). Nature and nurture combine to inform the infant if it is male or female. Yet this is an undifferentiated, all-inclusive phase. Young children do not know what functions their maleness or femaleness encompasses. Because children in the beginning of their lives make up for their helplessness by imagining themselves to be all-powerful and because their cognitive functions are not yet fully developed, they simply believe that all avenues of gender-related expression are open to them. During this time in their lives, toddlers are volatile, sometimes given to temper tantrums and not yet able to mediate all their moods. They need their parents to help them be secure in their growing sexual, gender-related identities. When either the mother or the father is not available, and no constant caretaker is present, the child is left to its own devices and often finds it difficult to decide who and what it is. Some children become developmentally stuck in this phase and stay grandiose, though labile, in their behavior. When instinctual overstimulation occurs, there is invariably a hypersensitivity to all stimuli or an extreme turning away from all feelings. These behaviors have to do with an attempt to deal with preoedipal castration anxiety.

Child researchers and direct child observation (Mahler et al., 1975; Roiphe and Galenson, 1981; Lichtenberg, 1983) have shown that castration anxiety occurs not only in the way Freud (1905) first described. He was of the opinion that children's femininity or masculinity was biologically determined. He did not question whether or how boys and girls learn to associate their normal genital excitement with either femininity or masculinity. Freud's major observation was that at about two or three years of age children become very interested in their genitals and discover the difference between the sexes. They begin to relate genital differences to sexual differences, but their observation of sex differences is associated with anxiety about losing their genitals, or having the wrong kind, or being damaged in some way. Eventually they identify with the parent of the same sex, setting aside their anxieties and the jealousies of the earlier times. Boys adopt their father's values instead of trying to take mother away from him, because they are afraid that his superior strength will castrate them. Girls stop hoping to grow a penis, or they give up their grudge against their mother for not having supplied them with one and settle for the hope of eventually receiving a baby not from father, but from a man of their own. According to Freud, men and masculinity are aligned with activity, women and femininity with passivity. Sex and gender in this Freudian framework are closely linked, and one cannot exist without the other. The resolution of all these oedipal problems are seen to take place somewhere around four to five years.

But, recent child research has found that most of the reactions Freud ascribed to the oedipal phase take place earlier than he thought and grow out of an undifferentiated phase. Because castration reactions can take place so early in life, they are strong and include aspects that Freud did not conceptualize. For instance, when a boy must acknowledge his masculinity he must also give up certain aspects of a perhaps cherished "feminine" assumption that he too can grow babies. A girl during this same time will, in accepting her femaleness, have to give up the idea that one day she will be anatomically like Dad or like brother. But because acceptance of physiologic and psychologic reality takes place so much earlier than Freud thought, these early castration anxieties include fear of loss of one's bodily integrity and fear of loss of the love of the important people in one's life. By imagining the fear-induced reactions of a toddler one can understand the reactions of older children who are caught up in this phase owing to trauma and overstimulation.

In my practice and in the institution where I supervised treatments, I came across many children who showed symptoms relating to an inability either to differentiate their gender identity or to accept it.

LORETTA

The First Interview

When Loretta's parents called me, they were so distressed they could hardly make themselves understood. They passed the phone from one to the other and shouted at me. Finally, we managed to establish a time for a meeting. I was immediately made aware that even the agreed-upon time was not really good for them. It seemed that mother had a good many appointments of her own. Before I ever met her, she had called me several times to let me know that her hairdresser, her manicurist, her pedicurist, and her fitness teacher all thought that psychotherapy for her daughter was a dangerous and probably uselessly expensive kind of undertaking. I tried to calm her by acknowledging her distress, but what she wanted was a written guarantee that Loretta would be all right. What was Loretta's trouble? The school felt they could not promote her into the fourth grade and wanted to put her into a class for learning disabled and retarded children. As a matter of fact, a diagnosis of mental retardation had been made, but both parents felt this to be "an outrage."

When I finally met them, they had arrived in an expensive car, accompanied by both their children, Loretta and Claudia. It is hard to describe how different from each other these two children looked in my small waiting room. Four-year-old Claudia, younger than Loretta by five years, was an absolutely beautiful child with golden curls and a dazzling smile. She was dressed in an organdy pinafore and seemed entirely at home in strange surroundings. Next to her, Loretta, nine years old and small for her age, looked as though she had just come from a game of dressing up. She wore extremely short and tight clothes suitable for a teenager, had her hair teased up in an eye-catching display of tight black spikes, and was perspiring profusely. Her nails were painted blood red but were bitten to the quick. She and her father stood half in and half out of the door while her mother and younger daughter lounged comfortably in the chairs. Loretta looked amazingly like her father. If not for her emphatically female attire, one could have mistaken her for a boy.

The mother, Mrs. S, interpreted my nonverbal reaction quite correctly. Before we were seated in my office, she informed me that Loretta hated being a girl, that she wanted to do everything like a boy, and that she (the mother) was desperately trying to teach Loretta how to be a woman. She felt that Loretta's unease with being a girl was her husband's fault. He had wanted a boy and at Loretta's birth had masked his disappointment by treating her as though she were a boy. The two were described as extremely close.

Mr. S had opened an auto supply business after a career as stock car racer. Both parents were very proud of their earlier life. They had toured the country, taking baby Loretta with them even though she had colic. Her father could miraculously quiet the screaming infant when mother failed to do so. Mr. S told me with pleasure that Loretta knew all about every make of car, practically carried an inventory of his business in her head, and liked to work with him on his new hobby of restoring antique cars. He was convinced that she was of more than average intelligence and confessed that he would like to beat up the school psychologist who had diagnosed Loretta as having a learning disability. He also wanted me to know that his wife had become "sensitive" since the birth of their second child. Indeed, under her heavy makeup, Mrs. S appeared frail. Mrs. S remembered Loretta's developmental milestones well. Loretta walked when she was a year old, and at the same time she also became constipated. She was given suppositories for this condition and, on tour, the toddler's retentiveness was cause for much jocular concern from the stock car drivers. Both parents laughed uproariously when they remembered how little Loretta had writhed and grunted in an effort to defecate and how their colleagues had responded to this small spectacle. Both parents also described Loretta as a person who "always hid her feelings." As far back as they could remember, Loretta had always gone to her own room if she was upset or had to cry. Neither parent could recall ever seeing her cry about anything once she was out of diapers. Father was very pleased with this. He thought his little girl was "tough"; mother sighed over such stubbornness. Mother also supplied the information that Loretta was a picky eater who could throw up her food at will. Apparently she controlled her environment quite well with this stunt.

Just as they were about to leave, Mrs. S thought to tell me another piece of information she felt might be relevant, although she wasn't sure what the connection could be. Mrs. S had sustained several miscarriages and had hemorrhaged heavily in the house but claimed that Loretta had no idea what had gone on. She thought she had successfully hidden from Loretta that she was ill and in need of help during such times. Mr. S was annoyed with his wife's confiding in me. He said he felt like a brute when his wife talked of her many pregnancies but that their religion required them to abstain from birth control.

Course of Treatment

Although we had agreed on a schedule of twice-weekly sessions and had agreed on a fee, I was not allowed to see Loretta until three months later. Both parents in the meantime tried to dissuade the school officials from placing Loretta in a special class. A "deal" was made that Loretta could remain with her regular class if she came into treatment. Mr. and Mrs. S vigorously warded off suggestions that they talk to a professional about their disappointments. They thought they might talk to one of their former buddies from the stock car races who had now gone into politics and was reputed to know how to handle people. After so much resistance and denial by the parents, I wondered if it would be possible to approach Loretta at all. What could this little girl in the costume of a teenage siren possibly think of me and of the idea of psychotherapy? I had no doubt that her parents loved her. But how much of themselves had they pushed onto this child? How much of their own fantasies did Loretta personify for them? Had she ever been allowed to develop freely and without having to entertain the adults around her? She looked bizarre enough to be a laughing stock for other children; that much was already clear to me.

At the initial interview she had not once looked at me while standing in the doorway with her father. Was she merely afraid, or did she not realize that she was in a new situation? There had been no protest from either girl when both parents came into my office. They sat together in the waiting room "like two dolls," as Mrs. S commented. Was Loretta really retarded? If her father was telling the truth, that was hardly likely; yet her test scores were pitiful. A well-trained school psychologist had diagnosed her as retarded. Why should I not believe him? Unlike many other mental health professionals, however, I am of the opinion that mentally retarded persons can benefit from psychoanalytically or psychodynamically informed intervention as much as more intellectually endowed ones. Therefore, I was looking forward to forming my own opinion about Loretta.

At our first meeting, Loretta again appeared in her fashionable but inappropriate garb. She showed no curiosity about any of the toys in my room, none about the room itself or about me. She merely settled into a chair, displaying her best manners, folded her hands in her lap, and informed me that she was very, very disappointed that she had to come to see me. When I asked her why, she did not answer but stared into space with the dazed and blank look that some retarded people exhibit. I waited in as receptive a mode as possible for her to give a further sign of wanting to investigate her surroundings or of showing interest in anything. Her blankness continued. As a matter of fact, I felt it deepen as the little girl sat in the shadow of a deep armchair, just staring blankly into space. I asked her if she would like me to tell her a story. No response. Would she like to play with the toys? No response. I asked why she didn't want to talk to me. No response. Did I remind her of someone or something? No response. Would she like to listen to records? No response. I told her I could understand her reluctance to talk. We could be silent with each other. No response. I mirrored her posture. This is a technique used by dance therapists to express nonverbally, "It's all right. I don't mind if you want to be the way you are." This physical mirroring is offered in a totally open, nonjudgmental kind of way, similar to the open neutrality psychoanalysts use. Again, I received no response. But her well-bred, ladylike stance made me feel as empty and closed-off as Loretta.

After a while, my back felt stiff and uncomfortable, because this closed-in, tightly held body posture is totally unlike my own customary movement pattern. But it also informed me that Loretta must be feeling similarly uncomfortable, held in, and overcontrolled. I wondered if I could risk telling Loretta about my discomfort, linking it interpretively to hers. Ordinarily, I do not share with patients what I feel. But Loretta seemed so hopelessly locked into her stance that I thought I might acknowledge my own discomfort and, at the same time, show her a way out of this position. One needs to be careful that no projection takes place in such cases.[2] In dance therapy, offering a nonverbal model to people who cannot understand verbal interactions or who are too depressed to acknowledge them has proven useful. Because Loretta seemed so impassive, I thought I might try to approach her on this very basic level. After all, in the beginning of life all learning takes place through the body alone until memory traces are laid down and a functioning ego evolves.

Following this reasoning and an intuition about Loretta, I stood up, stretched, and said, "My whole body feels stiff. I will do some exercises to make myself feel better." A flicker of interest crossed Loretta's face. I showed her the ballet barr in an extension of my treatment room and proceeded with some stretching exercises. Loretta got up and watched with interest. I asked her if she wanted to try stretching also. She readily agreed. Suddenly she became very talkative. Her friend in school had taken ballet lessons. Did I have ballet music handy? If so, she was prepared to take ballet lessons because it would please her mother if she were to do such a "girly" thing. I would have preferred Loretta to dance by herself, to indulge in a little improvisation. But that would have been too threatening for her. She staunchly planted herself in the middle of the room and demanded a ballet lesson. I understood that this was a compromise for her. If she needed to see a strange lady do strange things with, let it be in the familiar context of interaction like dance lessons. I offered her a simple eight-count ballet combination. She remembered and executed it perfectly; she even seemed to enjoy it. I stepped up my demands and offered a 16-count combination. Again Loretta was able to remember and execute the steps perfectly. By now I was convinced that Loretta was not retarded. She did not merely imitate me; she not only was able to pay close attention but could remember the combinations immediately. To test out my observation, I gave 32 counts in the next set of steps. Again Loretta performed without hesitation. She denied having had any lessons before and said only that her friend had told her about it and shown her some beginning steps. As she was leaving, a

---

[2]Psychoanalysts see projection as an important defense mechanism in which pleasant or painful impulses or ideas are attributed to the external world rather than to oneself. It is also possible to assume unconsciously that what feels good to oneself will feel good to another person. Obviously, this need not be so. Projection in any form is primarily an unconscious process. Research has shown that it forms in the earliest phases of life (Mahler et al., 1975; Spitz, 1965).

hugely satisfied Loretta informed her mother that she would not mind taking dancing lessons at all!

I was pleased also but somewhat perturbed that Loretta had experienced such a large dose of gratification. Too much gratification can quickly become a source of resistance if the patient demands it continuously and thinks she is entitled to it. In addition, overgratification can curtail autonomous functioning by making the person dependent on the gratifier. And what about the idea that I was a dance teacher? While it is true that the patient has the right to make the therapist into anything at all that is needed and wanted in his or her life, such fantasizing takes place in an interactional, fantasied, transference situation. Was my dance-therapy-oriented approach correct, or was I overstepping my bounds and thereby creating an antitherapeutic setting? I certainly did not want that to happen to Loretta.

As it turned out, I did not have to worry about Loretta. My hunch that her early life experiences had held insufficient appropriate gratification proved to be correct. Her need to be looked at and to be approved of was such that the next time she came she brought along some records she wanted to dance to. She treated me to all sorts of gyrations and bounces and asked after each performance, "Did you love that?" Finally, she declared that she thought I loved her. She seemed quite satisfied both with her inept performances and with her own statements; no answer was required of me. Unlike many dance therapists, I did not dance with Loretta but tried to discuss with her what her dances made her feel like, if she had any thoughts about them, and if they were like something she had seen before. She usually gave me monosyllabic answers that did not lead us anywhere. I began to understand why others thought her retarded, because her answers were always totally concrete and her affect bland. I began to wonder if perhaps I had, after all, fallen prey to a countertransference[3] in which I had projected my own wishes onto Loretta. At the same time it was clear to me that Loretta had to make up for deficits in her development that could be met only on a bodily level. It seemed to me that her dancing was like a reaching for an ideal she could never attain.

During the next parent interview, both Mr. and Mrs. S told me

---

[3]In a countertransference, the analyst displaces onto the patient attitudes and feelings derived from earlier situations in his or her own life.

that they wanted to discontinue the treatment. Loretta could learn how to dance much more cheaply in a neighborhood studio. They were quite provoked with her because she had refused their offer to take ballet lessons and had insisted on coming to see me. They wanted Loretta to learn how to read and to behave like a normal girl, so what was she doing here, dancing? I tried to tell them a little about the interpersonal dynamic that takes place during sessions. Mr. S finally said, "She doesn't need a stranger to love her. We are her parents and we love her enough." I assured him that I had no wish to steal his daughter, and he seemed a bit reassured but declined to discuss the situation further. Mrs. S, on the other hand, seemed quite comfortable with me as an expensive dancing teacher. It was something she could talk about with her confidantes without feeling humiliated at the thought that her child needed psychological help.

Loretta now began to tell me that she really had no business coming to see me. It was too expensive and too hard on her parents. Her mother cried all the time, and she herself was bad, very bad because she still was getting bad marks in school. Although the contents of her speech were very infantile, we were at least communicating verbally. I now began to view her dances as a recapitulation of earlier overstimulation, an attempt to master the inner tensions occasioned by being laughed at and observed when she was constipated as an infant. Her dances had consisted of gyrations and a bent-kneed pushing down, which reminded me of someone trying to relieve herself on the toilet. She had also wanted me to love her for her efforts, much as a toddler might wish for praise when her bowel movements were successfully deposited in the toilet. Loretta's dance could have been an emotionally corrective experience for her because I did not laugh and overstimulate her and did not demand that she entertain me. Because I remained calm and did not demand anything from her, she had enough inner energy left to begin talking to me instead of acting out past experiences. I also wondered just how often she had needed suppositories. Was the early constipation perhaps a sign that she felt intruded upon and wanted to be left alone? If so, there could be a link between her holding back of emotions and running into her room to hide her feelings and that early, defensive physical retentiveness.

I had noticed during her dances that she occasionally touched her vagina and then glanced at me, obviously waiting for me to make a disparaging comment. I never said anything at all, other than to ask her what her dances meant to her. We both enjoyed her freedom to do as she pleased with the music and with her square little body. I also noticed that she often held her arms very stiffly but could use her pelvis like a rock and roll star. Eventually, I was to learn what this constellation of gestures and body stance symbolized. But at this point in the treatment, it was just an unexplained phenomenon I filed away as information. Although some of her behavior appeared to be overtly sexual, there was something naive and joyful about Loretta's dances. Therefore, I was quite satisfied with this phase, which I called "Look at me, Ma." Perhaps it was an evocation of the rapprochement phase (Mahler et al., 1975) in which the child looks for refueling and emotional fueling from mother. Loretta needed acceptance and enhancement of her badly bruised self.

During her performances I also had the sense of being in the presence of a toddler who needs to practice and then to separate from an all powerful other-than-self. Loretta danced with such abandon, was so impervious to discomfort, even pain, when she occasionally fell, that I thought of the infants that Mahler described as passing through the practicing subphase and as, a little later, reaching the rapprochement phase. As babies take possession of their own motor functions and explore their bodies and their surroundings, they become aware of their separateness and of their relative helplessness vis-à-vis the world without their admiring and helpful parents. I already knew from her parents' accounts that Loretta had been frequently "on display," so to speak, when they were on tour and that they and their colleagues had amused themselves by intruding on and laughing at Loretta's bodily functions. Thus, Loretta's struggle for individuation was fraught with difficulties from the start. In her struggles to become a separate person, she must have, on one hand, cherished her sense of being and doing for herself, but simultaneously must have felt invaded and on occasion overwhelmed. Her stubbornness was probably no more or less than an attempt to reinflate her sense of self, to approximate the lost illusion of being all-powerful. Thus, when she displayed herself to me now, it surely must have been out of a need for reinforcement and approval. Her developmental arrests were in the area of separation-individuation, not in the area of cognition, I then realized. This child had not been able to reach the oedipal phase at all. That she functioned as well as she did was to her credit.

Our nonverbal communication seemed to pave the way for what was to come. During one session she called me greatgrandpaw. This was so obvious a slip that I called her attention to it. We talked awhile about how strange it was that I, a lady, could seem just like great-grandpaw to her. Then Loretta remembered "when she was young." As is expectable when a transference interpretation has been correctly offered and accepted, Loretta recalled some significant events in her life. Her greatgrandfather had indeed lived with the family and had on occasion been entrusted with her care. Mother and father were still on the road and did not take her along because she had a urinary tract infection when she was three and a half years old. Greatgrandpaw ran after her with a chamberpot and made sure that she urinated. She had held her urine back because it hurt so much to let it out. She giggled and writhed and held her vagina when she told me that. In a seemingly unconnected story, she also told me that when she got her first bike, she painted it with flowers to make it smell good. I wondered out loud if it was really the bike that smelled bad and asked how greatgrandpaw knew that she had to "go." Loretta told me that when she was "young," she never said that she had to go to the toilet. That's why her mother got angry and left her. Greatgrandpaw knew anyway because she held on to her "dingus." I asked if she was sure that it was a "dingus" she held on to. I also asked her what, in her opinion, a dingus was. Oh, yes, it was a place that smelled bad and looked strange, Loretta assured me.

Then she drew a picture in which two sets of eyes and noses shared a tongue, or so she said (see Picture L1). One could also fold the thin strip of paper to hide the tongue. Then she told me a confused and confusing story. A nasty boy threw up a doll girl and then dragged her across the floor. Loretta seemed very pleased and relieved to have told me this story, as though it explained everything. I was pleased also because of the affective exchange between us, but at this point I could only understand Loretta's story in the most general way as a reflection of an infantile birth theory and as a symbolic acknowledgment of her gender-related difficulties. I also wondered silently if as transferential greatgrandpaw, I was felt to ask for urine, that is, did Loretta perform for me and tell me stories because she had felt me to be like the one

Picture L1

person in the world who had made her feel safe despite the discomfort attendant to the urinary tract infection and the psychological pain caused by the parents' absence? Loretta had begun to allow me to see her fantasy life, a huge step forward indeed. Instead of getting better, however, the situation at home and at school worsened. Loretta started to play cops and robbers at school and terrorized some children. She felt absolutely no guilt or shame but was gleeful about her exploits. This made sense to me. Loretta, after having once again found positive feelings for someone other than herself was now busy routing out those who had previously laughed at her. They represented everyone who had laughed at her and had not been able to empathize with her. Her aggressive games were, as well, both an attempt at mastery and revenge for the pain that had been inflicted on her.

She received with delight an interpretation along those lines but did not change her acting out. When children—whose conscience is not yet firmly in place, remember, they frequently continue to act out when an interpretation is made. They seem to have to remember in a very physical way, especially if they have to make up somehow for developmental lags. The tension of remembering builds in their bodies and has to be released. Even if they have acquired some frustration tolerance, remembering is felt by them as a regression is felt by adults because the children are not yet able to internalize cultural values. Their inner morality is still the archaic one of an eye for an eye, a tooth for a tooth. Loretta during this period acted like a toddler who wants to hit the wall on which she has bumped her head. In such cases an increase in sessions helps to structure aggression and the need to do something physical in order to release inner tensions. But parents who are not in treatment themselves are seldom willing to agree to such measures. If two sessions a week causes havoc, three or more sessions are even more dangerous, they feel. Predictably, Loretta's parents, claiming monetary difficulties, wanted to withdraw her from therapy again.

During the monthly interview, however, Loretta's mother thought of a very important reason why Loretta should stay in treatment. She again confirmed that "right from the beginning" the child had refused to believe she was a girl. At first, everyone thought it was cute when Loretta howled each time mother put a dress on her and smiled when she was allowed to wear jeans or shorts. Father especially was pleased to have a tomboy-daughter. He said that having one "princess"—mother—in the family was quite enough. He also "didn't know what to do" with Claudia, the angelic second child, who seemed to be mother's exclusive possession. Thus, while the father approved of Loretta and loved her, he also unconsciously gave her a message that she should be like him, a male. Femininity was a threat to him, especially his daughter's. Therefore, Loretta could not reach toward the oedipal constellation but had to remain locked in earlier phases in order to win his approval. In addition, Mother claimed that Loretta's early urinary tract infection had been caused by Loretta's refusal to "let go of her urine and wouldn't even go to the toilet for her father." It seemed that she herself had been too "squeamish" to toilet train her daughter. Now she felt powerless to help her daughter to become more feminine. That her daughter had to become more feminine was clear to her, but she could see that all her interventions, from buying fashionable clothes for Loretta to painting the child's fingernails and setting her hair, had been ineffective. Therefore, she persuaded father to allow Loretta to stay with the "dancing therapist", as Mr. S called me. He accepted the explanation that sometimes in treatment it is necessary to go symbolically all the way back to the place in development where the first difficulty occurred. He certainly wanted Loretta to grow up as a woman, he said. He, more than the mother, could empathize with Loretta's need for motor discharge of her many tensions.

For the time being, Loretta seemed overwhelmed by the conflicting storms of sensations and emotions she was experiencing. Her only relief and tranquility seemed to occur after her sessions. Mother jocularly asked if I could see Loretta every morning before she went to school since she was invariably "good" after having seen me.

In the sessions, Loretta no longer had a need to dance. She had discovered that she could hold my attention by telling me stories and reporting dreams. Just as a child learns to ask for whatever it needs instead of howling for it or having a temper tantrum, Loretta had successfully outgrown and desomatized bodily tensions.[4] At first, it was almost impossible to make head or tail out of what Loretta was telling me. She would report some story like the one in which a boy threw up a girl doll and then amuse herself by humming some sort of voiceless tune. She did not want to think that her stories meant anything; they were just stories, that was all. She was, however, willing to concede that maybe her humming and low-keyed singing could be a way of drowning out my voice. I asked if she felt "bossed around" when I talked to her. She perked up. Yes, that's how she felt. But how did I know that? We discussed the fact that I knew some things about her that her parents had told me and came to the conclusion that it would be better if I did not see the parents any more. Loretta thought she could tell me everything I wanted to know about her.

A very fruitful period now ensued. Loretta took up dancing again in that curiously sexual, hip-swinging way, but holding her arms stiffly by her side. She claimed not to have learned it anywhere. She also denied feeling warm, though she was obviously sweating. For myself, I was convinced that Loretta was once again symbolically telling me

---

[4]With progressive maturation, bodily responses to stimuli are replaced first by volitional acts, then by thought processes. This development is called desomatization (Schur, 1955).

something important, so important, in fact, that she could not find the right words just yet. She unfailingly chose rhythmic music, such as rumbas and sambas, for her dances, a curious choice, I thought, for a child who was living in the age of rock and roll. When I asked her why she preferred Latin rhythms, she told me with a look of disdain that they were right for the dances, which, indeed, they were.

Since they no longer had direct access to me, the parents' unease increased. They felt the need to monitor what Loretta and I were doing and telephoned me. Her marks in school were still terrible, but there were no more attacks on children in the form of cops and robbers games. I, of course, told Loretta that I had spoken to her parents on the phone and what the contents of our conversation had been. She stopped in the midst of her most convoluted rendition of a samba and for the first time settled down to telling me how she saw the reality of her life.

She had tried to beat up the other children because they had teased her about being dumb. Both her father and her greatgrandpaw had always taught her that "you must defend yourself against the bad guys, otherwise they will take advantage of you." She didn't feel dumb any more since she had me, but her new "smartness" was a secret between us. If her mother found out that she was really smart, she wouldn't be allowed to come for her dancing lessons any more. I told her that I thought she was acting like a truly good guy but that perhaps it was too much for her to do all that alone, that perhaps she needed someone like me to be on her side in the matter of therapy sessions and dealing with parents. Loretta had an interesting way of showing me that she understood. She picked up a record cover and flawlessly read from it. I thanked her for her confidence and said that I hoped that in school she would find another good guy like the two of us so that teachers could see her smartness too.

My hope was not immediately fulfilled. Report cards were, as usual, terrible. Father gave Loretta a "good hiding," but mother stood up for her, "merely" threatening to keep Loretta in her room all summer if she did not learn how to read better. Now the child was truly pressed to make a decision. Should she reveal that she really could read and lose her dancing therapist, or should she maintain the false front she had created? Once again her compromise with reality was both interesting and predictable. She chose to become very angry with me. Here, in the safety of her sessions, she blasted me for telling the truth and ruining everything for her.

She also reported her first dream: While she was standing in front of her house, a black 1928 Porter came by. It was driven by Paul McCartney, the famous Beatle, who was singing "Help, I want somebody." But he refused to wait until Loretta was old enough to marry him. By this time, Loretta knew and was willing to accept my insistence on deciphering meanings. She declared the black Porter to be her father's possession and thought that Paul McCartney must have something to do with me because Beatles' albums were in my room. "Well," I asked, "It seems you want either your dad or Paul McCartney to help you. But what about this marrying business? Whom do you want to marry?" With the most engaging smile, Loretta, the sexy pseudoteenager, said, "You, of course." She was quite serious about this and would brook no further investigation. "You always say we can do whatever I want here," she said, indicating that she understood the transferential aspects of her wish.

Loretta brought Origami paper with her to the next session and with the greatest dexterity began to fold small pockets and purses. They stood for girls because they had mouths. They only could eat vegetables in large quantities. I was to feed these little mouths. After several sessions of this, I asked if these girls were still hungry and why. The reasons, Loretta said, were obvious. If the girls ate enough, they might grow legs, like boys. In her opinion, it was much better to be a boy; then one could have fun. As a girl one had to wear these silly clothes and have one's hair set in the evening, maybe even have to sleep on curlers all night. No, it would be so much better to be a boy.

When I asked what she thought the difference between boys and girls might be, Loretta looked puzzled. According to her, the differences were only the outward one—different kinds of clothing and behavior. I told her that I had met some girls who wanted to be like boys because they were jealous of them. With this, Loretta was able to tell me why she had made so many "bags," as her Origami creations were now called. She wanted to find a way to make boys, because she had heard that boys were made in a very disgusting way. According to her, they were made in tubs with tubes infusing them with life and sometimes these tubes were broken in half. She closed her eyes tightly when she told me about this theory. Simultaneously, the odor of anxiety-sweat permeated the room. Loretta did not know how to say "I am anxious," or "I am afraid." Instead, her body odor signaled that she was anxious (Schilder, 1951; Schur, 1953; Siegel, 1988). Sweating when one is anxious not only helps to bind the wish to flee from danger, but also has the function of delineating the body periphery as it cools on the skin. In addition, the odor of such sweating has a characteristic, somewhat moldy quality quite different from the odor of a person who is exerting herself physically.

I began to realize that Loretta's somatic expressions indicated something besides misinformation and a highly developed fantasy world. As gently as I could, I told Loretta that it seemed to me the two of us had done a good job feeding the paper-bag girls. They couldn't be expected to grow legs, like boys. But they could have legs, and vaginas as well, like girls. At this, Loretta needed to rinse her mouth out. My words and the attendant response tasted like vomit to her. I made the link between her dream and her earlier story about the boy who threw up a doll girl. I asked if perhaps Loretta was mixing up who could have babies, boys or girls, and that maybe she thought babies might be born out of the mouth instead of out of the vaginal opening. Loretta was so relieved by this suggestion that she threw her arms around me and kissed me. She declared me to be the best person in the world, better even than greatgrandpaw, because I knew "how to do meanings." It seemed that, at least in this session, Loretta was willing to be a girl and did not have the need to forcibly eject her femaleness, as she had done in her dream.

After this session, I again received frantic phone calls from the parents. Loretta could not sleep, they reported. All she talked about was her dancing therapist. How dare I make their child dependent on me! They agreed, however, that except for this momentary reaction, Loretta was much improved. She had begun to make friends, and the teacher had told them that Loretta now was finishing her work in school and showed every indication of an ability to read although she still refused to do so out loud.

Loretta came in with another dream: The black Porter 1928 drove past her house again, this time without a driver. She jumped in and tried to drive it, but a cop stopped her and asked for her license. She said, "I'm just a kid. I don't have a license yet." I did not even have to ask Loretta what came to her mind about this dream. She eagerly told me that it was about her father, who wanted her to be his pal and who did strange things. She was afraid that some day he would ask her to do strange things too. For instance, she knew that he and her mother went to the stock car races and that is where her mother had gotten hurt. She could not specify how her mother had been hurt. Instead, she blew up a long balloon, twisted it, but seemed unable to decide what to do with it. Then she remembered that her father urinated standing up at a urinal in the corner of his shop, as did many of his pals. They thought Loretta was too little to understand or that she would not care about what she saw.

Following this memory, Loretta wanted to dance again. But instead of the rumbas and sambas, she wanted to sway to the Moldavian Suite; she looked soft and feminine for the first time. I asked her if she wished that her father and his friends had taken better care of her and not made her look at their genitals. Oh, she said, she didn't think it was their fault. They had never *made* her look. She had just wanted to. As a matter of fact, she thought she was a very nosy girl. She always looked at things that got her into trouble. Like the snake that bled to death on her living room floor. It sounded to me as though Loretta were talking about the normal oedipal disappointments and wishes, and I asked her if she was angry at dad for already being married to mother. Oh, no, she said. She didn't want to get married, ever. Getting married meant having no fun, like mother had no fun. Men have all the fun. I asked Loretta if her mother said that, and she answered yes, quite matter of factly. Not only her mother but *all* the women she knew thought that being a woman was really a hard lot. That's why she used to like it when her father treated her like a boy and let her do boy things; only her dingus was the wrong kind for that. I commented that people have the right kind of genital for them, but my words fell on deaf ears, or so I thought. Loretta ignored me, went to the toy corner, and picked up a plush snake. For the next few sessions, she wrestled with the snake, alternately cooing to it and making slicing gestures as though hacking it to pieces. Of course, I knew by this time that Loretta's nonverbal answers were the clues to look at, but there was no way I could decipher this particular play fantasy, except to relate it to the snake she imagined had bled to death on the living room floor.

In the meantime, Loretta was becoming a much more ordinary child, who wore appropriate clothing, played with other children, and giggled with girlfriends on the phone. It was at this time that both parents decided that Mrs. S should seek treatment. Loretta's improvement signaled to them that therapy was not all in vain, though they continued to find paying fees and bringing Loretta to sessions painful. This, incidentally, is a very unusual sequence of events. More often one finds families recoiling when children improve. The family dynamic changes of necessity when a child no longer acts in a way that the members of his family expect. Mrs. S found the new Loretta difficult to deal with also. She felt she was "losing her grip as a mother," a very apt expression, I thought.

Loretta had another of her explanatory dreams. Her dog bit a snake in half, and there was so much blood on the floor that it sickened her. She had to throw up. After she reported this dream, she started to push me around the room and finally pushed me into a chair and poured bubble soap on me. The soap was instead of blood, she explained. I asked her whom I was supposed to represent. "My mother," she said. "When she had the babies fall out of her, she always bled so much. And she was so mean. She never let me help her. They locked me in my room, and they thought I didn't know. But my mother cried, and I wanted to help her and she wouldn't let me. And then she said I shouldn't be like her. She said some day I would bleed too and have no fun, like her. I don't want to bleed once a month and have babies fall out of me and become pale like a ghost. Boys have it better that way."

We talked for a long time about how scary it is to have one's mother so ill. Loretta even wondered if after she was born her mother had also been pale as a ghost and if she herself had robbed her mother of blood. She also thought that her father did strange things to her mother that had to do with babies. Even though she was locked in her room, she had sometimes succeeded in sneaking to their bedroom door and had seen "daddy hacking at mother with his snake, or maybe it wasn't a snake. Maybe it was a dingus. But that is disgusting. Why should mommy laugh if a dingus pees into her?." Loretta gravely listened to my clarifications of her primal scene experiences. I gathered there must have been quite a few.

A surprisingly short time after this work, mother and daughter were able to reestablish a loving relationship once more. "She didn't mean to be mean. She just thought I was too dumb to know," Loretta put it succinctly. She actively courted her mother, tried to be with her and to help her with the household chores. While this behavior looked charming and was very satisfying to both partners in the dyad, I saw it as an indication that Loretta had not yet given up her wish to be a boy. Rather, it seemed that she wanted to take her father's place with her mother. Usurping of the male role was convenient for another reason also. If Loretta could in fantasy marry mother, then Claudia, the envied sister, could be Loretta's own child; Loretta herself could hold on to the fantasy that she had a penis.

But Loretta's affect was such that I soon began to realize that I had overestimated what was going on. She was in reality still subject to many violent rages, stubborn to the extreme, and temporarily not at all accessible to interpretation. These stormy feelings alerted me to the fact that Loretta was engaged in an earlier phase than I had at first suspected. She was not in the negative oedipal phase but in the undifferentiated phase (Fast, 1984), in which both boys and girls assume that they have the attributes of both sexes. That she was in this earlier phase also accounted for the intensity of her feelings, because during the undifferentiated phase, infantile omnipotence is still intact and anything that threatens it is violently opposed. Loretta's new attachment to her mother, then, could, on one hand, be seen as a warding off of preoedipal castration anxiety (Roiphe and Galenson, 1981); on the other hand, it provided her with another chance to identify with and to integrate her mother's femininity. Her courting of mother had yet another meaning: to protect mother from more miscarriages and possibly bleeding to death. Loretta told me about these fears in great detail and seemed calmer when we could together talk about how frightening it was to see mother so pale.

We had been together for two years by now. Eleven-year-old Loretta began to show signs of puberty. She tried not to pay attention to her "chest" and the "fuzz" under her arms and on her pubis. Mother, in her own way, was frightened also. She was actually hoping that Loretta would start to menstruate early because then "Loretta would be forced to know she is a girl." But Loretta feared what was to come. Maybe she would really have to take care of mother and Claudia when she "became a girl." Eventually she dreamed that a hated neighbor had a cesspool that overflowed and caved in. The father was left with only half a neck. Loretta was able to associate that she wished her father were less "bossy" and that she remembered that he and his men friends seemed to have penises of varying sizes, sometimes big, sometimes small. Maybe that was why he had only half a neck in the dream. She thought the cesspool was a good picture of how she sometimes felt—smelly and possessing a cave. She laughed at the thought that her vaginal opening could be as big or as smelly as a cesspool. No, she said. It was quite a nice place; she could touch it now. Did I remember how she used to dance with stiff arms? That was so she wouldn't touch her vagina. Mother had forbidden it, and she wanted me to see how "good" she was. The dancing was what her mother and father did on Saturday nights. When she was "young" dancing like that had made her feel good between her legs, especially when I didn't forbid it. Little by little, Loretta found words to describe the many traumatic events in her life. Concomitant with the distancing from her conflictual past, she was able to identify with her mother's femaleness. Mrs. S had in the meantime learned a lot about herself in her own therapy and was more able to respond to her daughter as a mother. Nevertheless, many problems remained.

Dealing with the overstimulating behavior Loretta had experienced at her father's shop was more difficult. She was both fascinated with and repelled by the memory of having seen grown men urinate in her presence. There might have been masturbatory incidents as well. For a long time Loretta talked about how penises are of varying sizes, and she could not accept information about penile erections. She seemed to confuse erection and detumescence with the bleeding snake she had once used as a symbol for her mother in the throes of miscarrying. It took a very long time before she could verbalize her assumption that her mother had had a penis that was cut off when "babies fell out of her." My impression was that the sights, sounds, and smells in her father's shop in many ways reinforced Loretta's latent memories of being an infant on the road whose body functions were open to the scrutiny of many. Those experiences must have frightened the child, preventing her from forming a reliable body image.[5] At that time, she had no steady home and lived only in her parents' motel rooms. I was certain that a connection and confusion existed among all these phases in Loretta's life, packed as they were with frightening,

---

[5]The body image is the conscious and unconscious representation of one's body. It is built up piecemeal through visual and tactile exploration when the baby is young, and it continues to be modified throughout life by the interaction with inner and outer, often interpersonal, stimuli. Sensations from inner organs and the skeletomuscular system, as well as from the skin, add to the construct. However, depending on one's conflicts, the body image may be realistic or unrealistic.

exhibitionistic, intrusive behavior of the adults around her from which her frail mother had been unable to protect her.

Despite all these difficulties, Loretta made steady progress. She had reestablished trust in her mother and needed me less and less as a buffer between her felt experiences and the world. She seemed quite confident now that anything she felt or did could be explained. She often said that it felt nice to her that nothing was ever "just like that." The concept of meaning-giving through interpretation made a lot of sense to her. Her intelligence blossomed as the pieces to the puzzle of her young life came together. In identification with me, she decided to interpret the picture she had drawn so many months ago: "It is both a man and a lady," she told me. "When you fold it up, you can't see the tongue. It's a crack, like a lady has. When you open it up, then you can see the tongue like the dingus I used to think I had" (Picture L2).

In school, things seemed to have become normal. No one thought of Loretta as retarded any more. Her interactions with her peers remained somewhat shaky, but Loretta had now acquired a new and steady best friend, Mary, a girl her own age who was a dwarf. Loretta took it upon herself to champion this child. It was as though in the defense of her friend Mary she could show herself tough, as her father wanted her to be, and tender, as her mother had learned to be. The sessions became less affect laden. Loretta talked of school and was openly affectionate toward me. She also thought that maybe it was time for her to leave. With a twinkle in her eye, she told me that she had known all along that I wasn't a dancing teacher but a therapist. She dreamed that we bought a house together that had extensions in the front and in the back. It was no longer necessary to ask Loretta for

Picture L2

"meanings." She declared that the extension in front meant "bosoms." After all, she had just bought her first bra. She was not so sure about the back extension but thought that it could be "a turned around vagina with a baby coming out of it." In another farewell dream she saw me finding a new friend. This made her sad, but she hoped I would find a friend like Mary. She also wanted me to know that she had thought of another meaning for the extensions. Maybe her dream meant the kind of dancing we did at the very beginning of our interaction together when I showed her ballet extensions on the barr.

Discussion

When Loretta left therapy, she had achieved a reliable body image and a much firmer sexual identity. She was able to identify herself as a girl with a vagina and growing breasts. She was now able to touch her genitals and to represent them symbolically in a drawing. In other words, Loretta had left behind the undifferentiated phase and the primitive emotions associated with it. She no longer needed to act her inner tensions but could verbalize them. With her entry into a higher developmental level, her intelligence was liberated. Clearly, she had been a sensitive infant who felt intruded upon and misunderstood when her body functions were viewed and commented upon by many people. Her mother's inability to protect her made it impossible for Loretta to identify with her. Father's overstimulating and seductive, rough behavior further forced Loretta into a shell she really did not want to wear. But her mother was so fragile and her father appeared so strong: Whom could she identify with in order to grow up?

Her unconscious solution, to stay put on the assumption that she could be both male and female, was an ingenious one because it allowed her to stay in loving contact with both parents. She admired her mother's loveliness and wanted to protect her. But she also loved her father, even though he seemed to have no regard for her girlness and had even resented it. Loretta's attachment to her father was not an oedipal love. Rather, it was a defensive adaptation. To please him, she had to be like him. But at the same time she knew that he was somehow connected with, and even responsible for, her mother's repeated miscarriages. To deny this painful truth, she "forgot" not only the many scenes of mother's bleeding and pain but also the frightening sight of men handling their genitals.

In her games she was able to express what had been suppressed. Not only her mother's image was represented as a bleeding snake. In her nonverbal wrestling with the plush snake she had also tried to tell me of seeing men's penises in both erect and flaccid states. To acknowledge so much traumatization verbally was at first quite impossible for Loretta; she needed to see her parents as perfect. But with her unconscious efforts to keep the image of her parents as loving and kind intact, Loretta gave up knowing anything. She seemed retarded, a state of affairs her father fortunately never accepted. Despite his gruff negation of his daughter's femininity, he was very fond of her and when she was a baby had been able to sooth her when mother was unable to do so.

At the beginning of treatment, Loretta was sometimes noisy and agitated, like a much younger child. When prompted by her parents to act her age, she became frozen and withdrawn. She was on the way to becoming school phobic and suffered from learning disabilities. In numerous circumstances, she did exactly the opposite of what was expected of her. She was at first quite unable to express verbally what she wanted to convey and revealed her fantasy about snakes bleeding to death as though she were borderline psychotic. Being allowed first to dance, imitating her parents in dances that represented them both, Loretta released the enormous tensions engendered by all that had happened to her, so that at long last she was able to accept herself as a girl. When she left therapy, she was still enraptured with the her dwarfish girlfriend. Although she did not say so, I am of the opinion that in this dyad Loretta practiced being a mother and a protector, thus finally identifying with the mothering functions of both her mother and her therapist. Some aspects of the oedipal stage had been ushered in during therapy. Loretta now felt genuine concern about her relationship with her father and her wish to be a woman. To a certain extent, she thus made up for the doll play she had never engaged in when she was younger. Playing as a way of mastering living skills by imitation and through identification is a very important developmental step (Winnicott, 1971; Siegel, 1986). The release of tension and gain in pleasure are also not to be underestimated.

A most important aspect of Loretta's history is that her parents loved her enough to overcome their aversion to therapy and their prejudices about children's rights. They seemed at first to have overlooked the fact that children see and hear, even feel very acutely what goes on around them. Her father went so far as to ignore that his daughter was a girl. He wanted a son and was unable at first to give up this wish. But he did love his little girl, in his own way. His acceptance of Loretta's essential femaleness was a factor in bringing the treatment to a relatively successful end. He, more than his wife, had trouble understanding the unconscious determinants and developmental aspects of Loretta's difficulties. It was hard for him to see Loretta blossoming under the care of someone other than himself or his wife. Nevertheless, in the final analysis, Loretta's well-being was the most important factor to both parents.

The techniques used to help Loretta free herself were nonverbal and verbal mirroring, music, drawing, story telling and interpretation. The specific, identifiable sources of her overstimulation were the sight of men masturbating, the sight of her mother's miscarriages, repeated enemas, and the extreme negativism of her father toward her anatomical sex.

Recently I heard from a teacher in Loretta's school district that she now owns a beauty salon and has been married for two years. Her salon is reputed to be "stylish." It pleases me to think that Loretta has been able to internalize what she learned as a child in her therapy, that she is able to help other women to be beautiful as she experienced her mother to be.

Loretta's problems were clearly traceable to traumatic experiences. She had been exposed to sexual stimuli she could not understand but that aroused her and made her tense. Yet she was developmentally somewhat further ahead than Gino, who also came to me because he had trouble in school. His repertoire of defensive adaptation included negation of the difference between the sexes also. But the overstimulation in his case consisted of punitive behavior by his parents that sometimes was extremely harsh.

GINO

The First Interview.

Gino was the son of recent immigrants from Latin America. He was referred by a school psychologist because of "elective mutism." He refused to speak in school and had recently fallen silent at home as well. He had taught himself to write beyond his grade level so he could answer with a note if he was spoken to. Otherwise he performed poorly in school and did not follow instructions. Although the school administration had immediately alerted the parents to his strange behavior, he was not brought to therapy until he wet his pants in school about a year after therapy had been advised. Both mother and father worked in a restaurant that they denied owning. During the initial interview, speaking in heavily accented English, they told me of huge debts and gave me to understand that the therapy would be a heavy burden on them both financially and in terms of time.

The mother could not recall specifics about Gino's developmental milestones but assured me that "everything went all right" until Gino had to go to school. She noticed then that he began to hit his head and to call himself "cuckoohead". Nevertheless, she was sure that he was the smartest of her three children. The oldest son, already a teenager, was mainly interested in baseball and helped in the restaurant. A baby daughter was not expected to be smart. The single significant event in Gino's life that the mother could recall took place when he was four years old. The family was visiting in their country of origin and took a night train to meet relatives in a distant city. The mother and Gino shared a bunk on the train when he suddenly woke up, screamed, and pointed to the wall. Mother thought he had a religious vision because he babbled about a beautiful woman; she thought he meant the Madonna.

In general, she described Gino as a good, obedient child whose recent behavior was inexplicable. The father wanted me to "fix" the child and bargained about the fee. Neither parent seemed to have noticed Gino's profound confusion about the role and function of his gender, which his classroom teacher had noticed in her anecdotal report.

Course of Treatment

Gino was a pale, waiflike child with huge eyes in a round, blank face. He looked younger than his eight years, perhaps because he was dressed in old-fashioned short trousers. Much to my surprise, he had no trouble whatsoever in talking to me. He immediately spoke to me, although in a whisper and in a very disorganized way. He wanted to play cards. While doing so, he informed me casually that his father was as strong as God and that he hated his brother and wanted to hit him. He could not tell which boy, he or his teenage brother, was the larger person. He suddenly hit himself hard, striking his forehead and temples with his fist, all with a totally blank expression on his face. Completely surprised by the suddenness of the attack, I took his hand in mine and asked him why he wanted to hurt himself. He asked with much concern, "Is there blood?" I told him there was not, but he wailed, "Now you'll kill me. They kill me. I make all these booboos. I shouldn't go nowhere. I shouldn't have come here. I shouldn't have to see you!" Interestingly, he managed to keep his wails very low so that only I could hear him.

These seemingly disjointed outbursts were to stay with us for a good while. Gino struggled to accept his father's values and his father's image; that much was clear. But why was that struggle so hard? Gino appeared so disorganized that at first I thought the diagnosis of elective mutism a benign error; such fragmentation is seldom seen in a child who is not psychotic. Obviously, being like father was too much for Gino. He could play cards like father, but how could he be godlike? Later I was to learn that wanting to hit the brother, Sylvestro, was also a splinter of identification with father, who regularly administered corporal punishment to both sons, sometimes with a belt.

Gino's first outburst was repeated several times during subsequent sessions. Such outbursts seemed to be Gino's substitute for an answer to my questions. Eventually, Gino was able to show me what he really meant. Using the mother and father dolls in my office, he acted out how his parents dealt with him. When Gino misbehaved or failed to speak, mother would slap her own forehead and weep about her ill fortune in having a son like Gino, who had to go for therapy. I explained to him that he did not have to act like mother or like father. He did not have to hit his forehead or punish himself. He could act like Gino. He was delighted when I understood "what it was all about." This was his father's phrase, which Gino whispered to me. I always answered in a whisper, and this delighted him even more. He took my words to be permission to start experimenting with who "Gino" was and at least during the sessions gave up enacting raw introjects[6] of aspects of parental behavior.

---

[6]In this context, the word introject is used to mean the assimilation of certain aspects of the parents without proper differentiation of the self, that is, when the boundaries between self and other are indistinct. For people like Gino this means that there is confusion about one's identity and separateness.

Along with his shifting and confusing identifications with parents, Gino was puzzled about time and about sizes. He could read a clock but was unable to remember sequences of events, such as did he come to sessions first or go to school first? He could not identify round or square puzzle pieces and misperceived the size of people. I was beginning to suspect that an organic syndrome might be present when another aspect of Gino's unevolved personality came to the fore. He often asked me if I would hit him. When I declined, he would knock his forehead with his fist and whisper with an engaging grin, "I am not my father! I am not my mother!" Having thus reassured himself, he would blow up balloons and try to stretch them to their limit. He yelled with glee when they finally burst. These loud vocalizations nearly disrupted the therapy prematurely because during one session mother heard Gino shout and reported to father that Gino was "fixed." I understood Gino's behavior as an attempt to deal with early castration anxiety and to find his selfhood regardless of the potential threat contained in individuation.

Three meetings were necessary to convince the parents that Gino was far from "fixed." Reminders that he had not yet uttered one word either in school or at home initially fell on deaf ears. Both parents were very angry that Gino seemed to prefer me. They feared that his attachment to me would disrupt family life. I told them I could understand their hurt and that his attachment to me could seem like disloyalty to them. They were able to see that Gino was still a confused little boy who had to grow up further before he could function like other children. Reluctantly, they agreed to let him stay but informed me once again that they really did not own the restaurant (again pleading financial hardship). I responded that the mortgage holder probably wanted a lot of interest. Both parents relaxed at this point. The father shook my hand and declared me to have a "business head," that I was the person to whom he could entrust his son. I took this new opportunity to recommend that they speak to someone about their problems. Although they were upset again, they agreed to speak to their parish priest. Their doing so turned out to be a great boon to the therapy because the priest helped me to convince the father to refrain from beating Gino and his other children.

In sessions after this interchange with his parents, at which he was not present, Gino, magically, spoke to me in a normal voice. I had, of course, told him about the meeting before it took place. I could not ascertain whether anything had been said to him but hypothesized that in his symbiotic attachment to his parents Gino had felt their more positive attitude toward me and therefore felt safer in talking to me. But silence still reigned everywhere else.

The balloon play continued. Long, thin balloons were now put to bed and were given the name of his baby sister, Patricia. Gino was gentle with the balloon baby for several sessions, then viciously attacked it with a pillow. When the balloon broke, he started to shiver and shake and turned pale. "Now you love me no more," he mourned. I answered, "You are shaking. Sometimes children feel very cold when they think nobody loves them after they have done something angry." This time Gino did not have to pantomime. He told me that his grandmother hit him and the baby when mother was at work. Then he would take pots and pans and make a lot of noise. After this, he would crawl into the cabinet under the sink until mother came home. She would pull his hair but also stroke his face and kiss him if he cried. He did not know whether mother loved him or not, but he did know that sometimes she was nice. "Like on the train, you know," he reminisced. "I slept with her. I still like to play train and sleeping with her." Also, mother had tried to show him how to hold his "weeny" in his hand to urinate, but grandmother said that was dirty and big brother Sylvestro laughed at him and called him a girl. Father also said he was a girl when he tried to crawl in bed with mother at night when he was frightened. Was being a girl bad? Gino was confused about that too. Everybody seemed to love baby girl Patricia. So why was it bad for him, Gino, to be a girl?

It became clear that Gino could not leave behind the undifferentiated phase (Fast, 1984). Strong preoedipal castration anxiety threatened him with the possible loss of important others like his parents and even the dominating grandmother. He feared for the integrity of his body. After all, the all-powerful father could "kill" him any time and, in Gino's view, started the murder every time he beat his children. The frightened child was prevented from learning about the functions of his maleness and what was expected of a boy. The adults around him all were so strong and uncontrolled that it was too frightening to be like any of them, except perhaps mother, but she was so exciting too! In later sessions, Gino confessed that he was not sure if he liked having a "weeny." Since telling me his wish to be a girl, he had started to wet his bed. Now "they" wouldn't let him drink any water. And he was so thirsty all the time! I asked him if perhaps it wasn't so much that he wanted to be a girl but, rather, that being a baby seemed like fun since everyone in his family liked baby Patricia so much. Gino thought that was a terrific idea. Could boys be babies too? He was astonished to hear that everyone has to start as a baby and was thoroughly enchanted by the idea that some day he could be a father. But for Gino, thinking and somatic reactions were still very close together. He began to defecate in his pants, much to the volatile disappointment of both parents, who once again threatened to remove him from therapy. But this time I had two allies, the parish priest, who had undertaken to have weekly chats with the parents, and the classroom teacher, who had noted improvement in Gino's schoolwork, if not in his verbal communications. The crisis was averted.

Gino now took possession of a toy cup in my room, wrote his name on it with a magic marker, and proceeded to drink water, mischievously inviting me to stop him. And, yes, he was now quite sure he would like to be my baby. I assured him that I liked baby boys and their "weenies." This had an interesting effect on him. He began to write long lines of numerals and constructed calendars, which were kept in a special place on my desk. If I touched them, he snarled and called me "a swine." When I asked what he meant by that, he informed me that it was my fault he was a swine who made in his pants and talked dirty about babies. Big brother Sylvestro said so. Grandmother said little boys had no business knowing they could become fathers. I told him that I had to disagree with grandmother. Little boys grow into big boys and later into big men if they learned what big boys and big men can do. Gino thoughtfully listened and answered by assuring me that he could go to the toilet and wipe himself.

Our interactions by now were no longer disjointed but had a sequential flow of questions and answers. Gino understood quite well that it was inappropriate for him to act like a baby, but he could not give up this behavior until I built the verbal bridge to his behavior. He continued to labor over his number games in an attempt, I thought, to organize his heretofore disorganized universe. He covered whole sheets with various simple additions and subtractions revolving around $3 + 5$ and $1 + 7$. He also brought his arithmetic work sheets from school to the sessions. Although his number games had a ritualistic aspect, they appeared to serve the very important function of organizing periodically fragmented thought processes. I saw them as outward reflections of a growing inner structure. Gino's time and space perceptions were becoming more fully developed but were still shaky at times. While laboring over his number games, Gino discussed whether "ladies have weenies when they have babies." He thought that maybe boys could have babies, too, when they made "big sausages" in the toilet. What he meant was, through what opening are babies born? Gino became very sad when he realized that even his big BMs would never transform into babies "because BMs come out in back," as he said.

Along with his number games he now began to bring in dinosaur books and sported a tee shirt with the logo of his favorite ball team. According to him "all the guys in school like sports and dinosaurs." He was talking to the guys in school but not to grandmother. He also wanted me to know that he preferred numbers 1 + 7 because they were straight and didn't like 5 + 3 because they were round. Asked what was so repellent about 5 + 3, he said, "You know, like big stomachs with babies in them." His mother had given him a book with pictures of how babies are born when he asked her about it. She was so delighted with his speaking at all that she "didn't think he talked dirty." The numbers 1 and 7 were nice because they were straight. When I interpreted that straight perhaps could mean "an erection," he blushed and smiled happily.

Further investigation of Gino's many remaining conflicts were curtailed when he was abruptly removed from treatment after his major symptoms, elective mutism and sexual identity confusion with concomitant misperceptions of time and space, disappeared. Gino's confusions were resolved when he had a chance in therapy to establish his identity as a male and learned what a boy could and could not do.

Discussion

The disorganized and self-destructive behavior Gino showed at the beginning of treatment was a reflection of a profound lack of inner structure. He assimilated the violent, even brutal, behavior of his father and grandmother as the norm. He dared not question if they were right. For him, father was godlike. Given such unempathic surroundings, it was not surprising that he developed only piecemeal, so to speak. His intelligence never deserted him but went into hiding when he was overwhelmed by a rage that had to be suppressed at all cost. Although he, like Loretta, appeared at times to be psychotic, he was not. There was such an uneven development that fear of loss of self and important others was predominant. Denial of his sexual identity was pronounced. Gino lived in constant fear of losing what little sexual identity he had. He experienced real and imagined threats to his bodily integrity, which never allowed him to put aside early castration fears.

Father was quick to hit all his children either with his fists or with a belt. The parish priest reported that father was very surprised when told that he was doing something wrong in beating his children. He had been raised that way and thought of himself as an excellent father. His own mother, who helped in his household, was of the same opinion and warned him that Gino would turn homosexual if he did not chastise him sufficiently. Yet this man did love his sons. Strangely, he did not seem to have lost control when administering the beatings, and therefore his extreme measures seemed to Gino to be the incomprehensible doings of a God whose whims had to be obeyed. But Gino's own nature could not identify with such harsh events. He would have liked to be gentler, more like his mother, but he knew that this was an avenue not open to him. Finally, he settled on the compromise of not growing up, of wishing to be a baby girl.

Yet he was not at all psychotic. He was able to form a fairly reliable transference relationship with me and, in his silent way, liked his teacher and schoolmates. I concluded that the early mothering he had received must have been adequate, being interrupted only when he was overstimulated and frightened by sleeping in the same bunk with his mother. Although I am not certain, it seems to me there must have been other times when he crept into his mother's bed and was warmly received there, since he talked about trying to do so unsuccessfully. During treatment, Gino's life situation certainly changed. His mother was able to respond lovingly to him when he gave up his defensive silence. Father managed to curtail his punitive behavior, though neither parent appreciated just how desperate Gino had been. The only special technique I used in Gino's treatment was to rely heavily on the parish priest to influence the parents. He was not at all psychodynamically inclined but liked using his influence in a benevolent kind of way.

Gino was unable to form a firm gender identity because he had been unable to traverse the undifferentiated phase, with its heightened form of castration anxiety. His parents were unable to support his age-appropriate striving for mastery and independence. They thought it was their duty as parents to use threats and corporal punishment. Even the grandmother was of that opinion; and, until the end of our interaction, Gino punished her either by making a lot of noise or by not talking to her even when he had given up his mutism. He did not dare to punish his father but withdrew into silence before this man, who seemed invincible to him. In treatment, he blossomed when he was allowed to give vent to his frustrations but also to play his number games and to voice his fantasies. Because of the impossibility of being like father, Gino was driven into an aggressive ambivalence toward his mother. He became more closely attached to her and identified with her and his baby sister. But despite the harshness of his family life, both parents were involved with their son and wished for his well-being. Gino, despite not being able to finish his therapy, stood a good chance for a fairly healthy development. Although he was certainly caught in the separation-individuation struggle, some healthy fluidity in his family dynamic seemed to herald the oedipal phase, as when his mother forewent her rigid rules and focus on her own inner needs and instead appreciated his psychological gains. I have often wondered if Ted, whose story follows, fared as well.

TED

The First Interview

Ted was literally dragged to therapy because his angry parents felt they could no longer cope with him. Twelve years old, very small for his age, and shy, he regularly wet his bed and refused to do his chores. Recently he had begun to neglect his schoolwork as well. During the initial intake session both parents were very upset and wanted to talk more about each other than about Ted. Mr. W was an extremely successful businessman who had married his wife when both were relatively low-level office workers. After marrying, Mrs. W had become a homemaker and was happy in that role for many years. She had two daughters, Linda and Lisa, whom she adored. When Mr. W "made it big," they decided to have more children. Both parents broke out in an anxiety sweat when Mrs. W confessed that this had been a bad decision.

Ted, born 10 years after Lisa, was a difficult baby from the start. Mother put up with his constant crying and whining only because the two older girls helped to soothe him; she seemed to think a whining infant represented a burden one could and should farm out. "Ted was always in somebody's arms until he could walk at two and a half years of age," mother reported. However, Ted was also an alert baby who "didn't miss a trick." He spoke early. When he was three, a brother, Collin, was born. Collin was retarded. For a while things went well. Ted liked the baby, played with him a lot, and even cheered up the family in their mourning for the atypical child's future. Ted seemed to have turned overnight "from a fretful monster into a mother's helper." The older girls, embarrassed by Collin's disability, began to pour even more attention on Ted and showered him with praise. According to mother, "Suddenly Ted was six years old and still wetting the bed. The whole house stinks of his mattress, but we just won't buy another one until he stops. He doesn't care if he has to wash his own linens. He likes being a pig." Tofranil was prescribed by the family physician, to no avail. Bell-ringing devices to wake Ted up did not help either.

Mr. W was of the opinion that Ted's enuresis was "all spite work." He never entertained his business associates in his home any more as he used to "before it stank like a garbage can." He had taken to coming home late, so that Mrs. W seldom saw him except on Sundays, when the entire family went to church together. Mr. W felt that "as long as they prayed together, they would stay together." This philosophy helped Mrs. W and the daughters to believe that the family was essentially intact. Linda and Lisa were sure that their father had a mistress and openly discussed this possibility with mother, who agreed. She blamed her husband's infidelity on his disappointment with his sons. Mr. W denied having any adulterous thoughts and rolled his eyes to heaven when the accusations were brought forth in bitter tones during our first session. Family therapy had been begun but terminated after three months. Both parents expected Ted's therapy to be unsuccessful as well but did not want to "feel guilty for not trying everything." They thought Ted was a "sissy and wouldn't amount to much."

Course of Treatment

When I met Ted, I discovered that I had not heard of all his symptoms by far. He cried silently all the time and reported that he could not control his tears. They "flowed out of his eyes" even in school, where the other kids made fun of him and never picked him for team sports. In addition, he had a tic in his right leg, which bobbed up and down uncontrollably while he spoke. He also smelled of urine, although he was nicely dressed. Actually, he was a handsome boy with a freckled face, large green eyes, and a mop of auburn curls. But because he habitually kept his face averted, it was hard to experience him as present at all.

His view of the situation was quite different from that of his parents. He felt exploited and put upon because his mother and his sisters asked him to run errands on his bike and take the garbage out. Huge fights ensued about these issues. Linda had learned judo and regularly threw Ted across the floor when he did not obey her. His mother did nothing to protect him from the "ugly Amazon." Ted could hardly sit still while telling me about this and tried frantically to control the tic with his hands, apologizing for this "infraction of rules." I told him that I thought he had a very good command of the language, whereupon he was immediately able to release some of his tensions. He poured out a complicated tale of running into an iron fence with a tricycle when he was a toddler. He lifted his hair from his forehead to show me a fairly long scar that had resulted from that accident. He then exhibited other injuries to his body integrity; a tracheotomy at age six, of which he remembered every medical detail and especially being frightened in a dark room; a dog bite somewhat later; and several falls that resulted in broken bones. He reported his many accidents without affect but in great detail as though they had happened to someone else. When I commented that it must have been difficult for him to sustain so many injuries, he answered, "Yes. It would be better if I were a girl. They have all the advantages." But he did have one "helper." His father taught him to sing "I've Been Working on the Railroad" to help him through pain after the medical interventions, but his sisters laughed at his rendition and at his high, breathy voice after the tracheotomy.

A school assignment to write about Apollo enraged him. He

preferred Zeus. He did not want to write about a god who loved women. Ted became confused when I pointed out that Zeus can be seen as the father of the mythical gods. He blurted out that he didn't love his father and didn't want to be like him. The person he secretly admired but feared was Linda, who could pick him up bodily and force him to do things. He wished for that sort of strength for himself. He saw no difficulty in being a boy who wanted to be like a girl and insisted "it's all the same." After several sessions during which he insisted that boys and girls are the same, because his mother and father always said so about chores, he finally asked if what he had heard in school was true; that "girls look different, you know where." It turned out that he had no word for penis or vagina and seemed vastly relieved to be given accurate information. Nevertheless, he began to play with some scabs, peeled them off, and then asked if the freely flowing blood was like his sisters' "monthlies." Again, he seemed relieved when given appropriate information. Nevertheless, he denied ever having seen any physical evidence of his sisters' menses.

Somewhat later, a pale, crying Ted arrived, driven by a wild-eyed mother, who insisted on intruding in the session to tell me that Ted, using a steady stream of obscenity, had started to wet the bed again. This was the first time I heard that Ted had been dry at all. Finally, after managing to calm the mother and to escort her into the waiting room, I turned to Ted. He told me of a boy who had made fun of Collin. Linda came out of the house and offered to "mess up the street with him." Then she threw Ted down the cellar steps. Why? Ted himself was the boy who had pestered Collin, who wanted to play ball. Again Ted said he wanted to be like Linda. "She's much too powerful; it's not fair, and she is not fair. I want to get even with them all, but especially with her," he said. He felt ashamed that he had been unable to defend himself and was furious with his mother for her inability to protect him.

In subsequent sessions we discussed the fact that Linda was indeed much stronger than he and how that made him feel less like a boy. But, again, the fantasy emerged that he was not a boy at all but only someone resembling a boy. He was not quite sure what sort of person he was trying to describe but eventually managed to defend himself internally against the overwhelmingly castrative Linda. Instead of identifying with her as the dominant aggressor and wishing to be like her,[7] he looked for a weakness in her. He recognized that "she was not an Amazon at all; she complained that her muscles hurt her when she worked out. Ted was very pleased with his discovery, for Linda's aching muscles made her seem more human. Ted decided that he could be more "like he used to be." Apparently this meant how he was when Collin was first born, a time when the family's, and Linda's, favors were bestowed on him. During that period, he had been able to give free range to his creativity and ability to nurture others. Possibly this had to do with an identification with his mother and his sisters, whose favorite plaything he had been until Collin's birth. Father as a role model was conspicuously absent even then.

With Linda, the Amazon, safely relegated to the deepest recesses of his mind, Ted found ways to tell me about yet other traumas that had impinged on his development. He did so in a playful way, as though to diminish the importance of these events. He brought in old socks and converted them into puppets by stuffing them and giving them painted faces. He had done this sort of thing with Collin, he explained. He used the puppets to act out what he could not talk about. For instance, his grandfather, in an effort "to toughen him up" and to "rescue him from all those women," had disguised himself with a stocking over his head and jumped out when the unsuspecting child turned a corner. Neither parent could understand why the child complained. Grandfather was only playing, they said. Another sadistic game was approved of by both parents before Collin was born. Grandfather pushed the little boy down over and over again until he could not get up any more; this was supposed to make a fighter out of him. One can only speculate that with such a father, Mr. W had identified with the aggressor as well and had never evolved a mode of being in the world that precluded mistreating children. I also began to wonder what must have happened to Linda to make such an aggressive person out of her. Clearly, aggression was accepted, even fostered, in this family.

After enacting the scenes of being assaulted by his grandfather, Ted stopped crying at inopportune times and was able to tell me what

---

[7]Identification with the aggressor is an important defense mechanism, first described by Anna Freud in 1946. By impersonating the aggressor, assuming his attributes, or imitating the aggressive act, the child transforms himself from the person threatened into the person who makes the threat.

he remembered. The activity with the puppets had apparently helped him to draw off enough tensions so that he could desomatize what had happened to him and was able to start the trial activity of talking instead. While talking, he relived with extraordinary intensity the threat to his body boundaries. Again, he seemed to regress to the point where he was no longer sure that he was a boy. He liked to pick on his many scabs and watch the blood flow down his leg or his arm. But this time, he sucked it up, licking himself fervently, declaring that he needed to drink his own blood "to cleanse myself because I hate milk." He also insisted that if his sisters could bleed, so could he. He responded to renewed realistic information with puzzlement, then talked of wanting to be a bloodsucking vampire like a baby. These psychotic-sounding statements turned out to be condensations of events nobody had explained to Ted. It was Collin who, according to Ted, had sucked blood out of mother. He did not believe that nursing an infant was a normal event; his mother had turned pale and fainted because "she gave Collin too much blood."

It is not hard to understand that for Ted the birth of Collin was indeed a fall from grace. The undisputed favorite of the important women in his life, who had coddled and spoiled him, he was now left to his own devices. He knew that Collin had pushed the family into mourning and despair, and he tried his best to help. But in his unconscious he did not accept that this unwanted rival was afflicted. Collin became a vampire who took mother's and the family's blood. Ted was at first unable to absorb interpretations about the working of his fantasies. Instead, we explored the existence and function of various body fluids: blood, urine, milk, semen. I suggested that perhaps when Ted sucked his own blood, he was trying to nurse himself. He thought about this for some time and then confessed with great reluctance that "some stuff" now came out of his penis at night. This frightened him because he thought he was turning into a "nursing cow." He preferred the red color of blood. Semen looked like milk, which he hated. He was relieved to hear that nocturnal emissions are a normal event but did not go on to remember other events until I mentioned as offhandedly as I could that sometimes boys have a fantasy that their penis can do what a woman's breast does. He thought this was a very funny idea but one that made sense. "I have too many women around," he announced with a bright smile, going on without interruption to recall intravenous blood and plasma transfusions during his hospital stays and how these had frightened him. While in the hospital, he had wondered how blood for transfusions was acquired and decided that there must be a host of vampires employed who "spat out the blood into vials." He also recalled that his mother had given him correct sex information but that he had not believed her. Our work together seemed to enable him to disentangle mistaken perceptions and condensations of certain bodily processes. He now understood that women nurse babies with their breasts and have menses when not pregnant and that men produce semen but not milk. He remained unclear about whether he still wet his bed or not, indicating to me that urine and semen were still seen as one and the same fluid.

During the following months, Ted spent almost all of his time in session wrestling with the plush snake, inflicting on this toy every insult that had ever befallen him. He seemed unperturbed by my presence but did not want to talk to me. He instructed me that watching him was enough, that what I said was too frightening and nagging. He wanted to work out things his own way, as long as I promised not to tell anyone that he wrestled with a toy snake. I appeared transferentially to have become a good enough mother who allowed her child to have space to play in, but also a phallic, controlling mother whose aggression he had to control.

During this time, Ted's grandfather died. Ted declared, "It served him right." He went on with his wrestling games. Revengeful feelings for the many narcissistic injuries his grandfather had inflicted did not abate during the entire treatment. Instead, they fueled sadism and heightened aggression. But this also served to divert and to displace these feelings from Ted's nuclear family to grandfather. As long as he stayed angry with this unhappy old man, he could continue to relate with some semblance of civility to his equally unhappy mother and sisters.

Family dissension seemed to escalate after grandfather's death. Mother had a dream that Ted wanted to discuss with me. She dreamed that the whole family was stuck in a car on some train track and was killed by a train. She awoke screaming and quickly gathered her brood about her to make certain they were alive. But Ted was skeptical. "I think she really wants us dead, especially me and Collin," he said. He was sad for the first time after this disclosure. He cheered up, however, at the thought—a new one for him—that one day he could have a loving wife and a loving family when he himself married.

Then Ted had a dream, the first one after 18 months of treatment. He was on a train with his family, who was being threatened by a gangster. He had a gun and saved them. We discussed at length that in the dream he could do what his mother could not do in her dream: he rescued the family even though they so often misunderstood and mistreated him. A certain portion of Ted's sadism and ambivalence seemed to be conquered after this although he avoided conscious awareness that having a gun might mean having a penis. The snake wrestling stopped, however. His bed was reliably dry, even though family conflicts were more pronounced than ever. Mother and father fought constantly when father was home; father stayed away for days on end. Ted watched the fights with resignation and made sure to stay out of both parents' way. Once again he distrusted adults, including me. Strangely, his school performance became acceptable again. He also was able to play some football. Some separation and individuation had taken place, though much too quickly for Ted's fragile object representations. I speculated silently on the familiar quality of his strengths, a quality that seemed reminiscent of the way he had reacted to the birth of Collin. In both instances, he reached beyond his age to adapt to and defend against an impoverishing environment.

Soon he reported some decidedly sadistic actions against his brother and sisters. He wanted to get even. His mother called to complain that he was becoming a hoodlum who hung out with the wrong crowd. Ted calmly corroborated her claim. He now carried a knife for protection against a boy named Dennis, who was always in trouble but managed to get out of it. In a dream, he and Dennis looked at a minibike engine and found it to be good. Convulsed with laughter, Ted thought the minibike engine might represent his penis.

Shortly thereafter, the family removed Ted from therapy, convinced, despite the absence of symptoms, that it had failed. The reason: Ted had become a formidably rambunctious teenager. Although I shared their concern about his unduly rough behavior, I also saw it as a partial resolution of his formerly pronounced sexual identity confusion and fear of loss of self and of objects.

Discussion

That Ted managed to get by as well as he did often amazed me. His innate intelligence and his ability to adapt to, and even to a certain extent to metabolize, his many traumas, were signs of a strong ego. His mother's and his sisters' holding him and catering to him during his infancy not only served their needs but met his as well. Otherwise he could not have psychologically survived the many assaults on his person. The extreme negativism and lack of empathy his parents displayed toward him were regarded by him as so many obstacles to be overcome, often with tragic results. He frequently hurt himself as though to test that his world was really how the world was supposed to be. He resorted to psychoticlike fantasies to comfort himself and to explain phenomena that were otherwise not understandable, such as his mother's fainting while nursing his brother.

Sometimes, his own fantasies seemed so real to him that he could no longer learn. He was stuffed to overflowing with venom engendered by the sadistic games his grandfather and his sister played with him. He did not even complain about the many accidents he had and thought that physical pain was simply something one merely needed to get used to. He held on to his pathetic little song, "I've Been Working on the Railroad," as the single positive "helper" he had ever received from his father. Small wonder that he thought it would be preferable to be a girl! Unfortunately, he never permitted an investigation of the self-punitive aspect of being accident prone. Nevertheless, toward the end of treatment, he no longer was covered with scabs and bruises. At least he had learned to value his person sufficiently to avoid the many cuts and scratches he used to acquire mysteriously.

His sexual-identity confusion was, in my opinion, a developmental lag caused by the castrative behavior of both his grandfather and his sister Linda. Neither of them seemed to have any respect for his bodily integrity, which he could not actively defend. He had to resort at first to identifying with Linda, the aggressor, the Amazon. The pleasure in his maleness evinced in the last dream represented only a tenuous gain. That he had to carry a knife to protect himself against real or imagined danger and allied with an antisocial group showed me that he had assimilated his family's value system, although not in the form they consciously envisioned it. Clearly, there was a danger that he would act on aggressive internalizations in the future; we had been unable in therapy to deal effectively with all his revengeful feelings. Although he had made gains and appeared to like me, he was at the end still distrustful of me. His treatment did not go far enough to alleviate all danger of acting out his original traumas in the form of antisocial behavior.

I had to be content that Ted was able to give up bed wetting, a tic, and uncontrolled crying; above all, he was able to firm up his sexual identity. The overstimulation in his case had been almost exclusively of a negative and abusive kind. An unusual feature of the treatment was Ted's use of puppets, which he made himself. Unable to verbalize what troubled him at that time, by adroitly presenting plays about being assaulted in many ways, he showed me just what had happened.

Had Ted reached the oedipal level? I doubt it, though he seemed to have garnered more libidinal supplies in therapy than I realized. His negativism toward women never left him while he was still in treatment. I could empathize with his dislike of the Amazon sister and with his disappointment in his mother's many empathic failures. Although he had achieved a strong male identity, I was not sure how he would use his male functions. At a recent convention, however, I met the school psychologist who had originally referred him to me. It appears that Ted, much to the chagrin of his family, has chosen a career in law enforcement. I am hard pressed to assess if this choice constitutes a true mastery of his many traumas or if he is merely trying to "boss" others around as he was bossed.

SUMMARY

The three children whose cases are presented here were all in danger of permanently settling into a state of confusion about their sexual identity. Although Loretta knew she was a girl, she had no understanding about what being a girl might mean; the same can be said about Gino's and Ted's gender identity. They knew they were boys but were not at all certain that being a boy was desirable, possible, or useful to them. Their learning blocks cleared up first, and other symptoms followed suit. As their body boundaries became firm and the possibility of coping with the instinctual overstimulation that had been visited on them, they were able to let go of defensive infantile omnipotence and accept their gender.

═══

CHAPTER 3

I'm Really Really Scared and I Feel So Bad
Children Who Have Been Exposed to Adult Sex Play

I t has long been thought that it is detrimental for children to see what adults do when they make love. Psychoanalysts have pro- duced a lengthy list of cases in which viewing the so-called primal scene[1] had a bad effect on development. Freud (1908) enlarged on his earlier (1905) view that children always misinterpret the sexual act as an attack or murder. He thought that there were several reasons for this misinterpretation: (a) the child might have seen a real battle of the sexes in vigorous foreplay; (b) some mothers may actually resist intercourse; (c) there might be fighting and quarreling between the parents during the day, and the child now thinks he or she is witnessing another quarrel; or (d) the child might see blood on the sheets or on the mother's underwear. These observations and formu-

---

[1]Freud (1908, 1917, 1939) had a particularly gloomy outlook on what the effect of viewing adults in intercourse on a child could be. He was convinced that it was always misinterpreted by the child as a sadistic attack and would decisively shape the child's own sexuality and sexual fantasies. Even if the primal scene is not seen, the child will develop fantasies anyway; and these will be determined by hereditary, phylogenetic influences that operate intrapsychically the same way as the actual experience of seeing coitus. In other words, nobody escapes!

lations have been found to be the cause of many a child's emotional difficulties.

It is also true, however, that one cannot always generalize so broadly, despite the fact that psychoanalysts have been able to demonstrate the roots of much psychopathology in the experience of being present at parents' sexual intercourse. That children are over-stimulated by such an event, especially if it occurs repeatedly, cannot be denied. The developmental phase in which a child was exposed, and how the particular conflicts related to this phase have affected the child's perceptions, are, however, of crucial importance. Coren and Saldinger (1967) have demonstrated the genesis of visual hallucinosis in connection with primal scene exposure.

When children imagine they see something that is not there, they are often accused of lying until the frequency of their insistence that they see something like a snake or a monster alerts their caretakers that something is amiss. This phenomenon is quite different from story telling and fantasy games young children play. Extreme fear and high anxiety are often attached to these visual hallucinations. There is also usually a harmless incident that precipitates the first occurrence of this symptom. The unrelated incident is used to symbolize the feared and frightening trauma, such as primal scene exposure. It is easier for the child to imagine that there is a monster in the parents' bedroom than to think that they are murdering each other. To try to demonstrate the absence of a monster in such cases is quite fruitless. The child might outwardly agree but inwardly will hold on to his own ideas and sink deeper into disorientation until his trauma is understood and interpreted.

Children who are very young, perhaps in the oral phase, may develop night terrors. Weil (1989) reported the occurrence of night terrors in 69% of 180 children who had suffered exposure to their parents intercourse. Also common are hysterical twilight states in which children appear to be in a daze and disassociated from what is going on. Actually, they are trying not to remember what has been so frightening and anxiety provoking. In addition, they may have forbidden wishes toward one or both parents that need to be repressed but are trying to surface. Anna Freud (1946) linked certain feeding disturbances to the phallic phase but cautioned that a host of other influences also must be taken into consideration.

Anthropologists have reported other reactions in different societies. For instance, Róheim (1958) reported that Australian aborigines do not seem to suffer from exposure to parental intercourse. Mead (1928) similarly reported that in Samoa sexual behavior was very free and open and observation of it did not adversely influence children. But these findings were obtained from studies of societies where privacy was unknown, clothing was little used, and body functions were completely open. Moreover, such data were gathered from observation of overt behavior. Anthropologists interpret only the material that is on the surface and therefore cannot really gain the psychological insights needed to correlate their findings with those of psychoanalysis.

I cite these reports because, in working with children who were exposed to their parents' sexual behavior, I have often been told that I must be wrong, that such natural functions could not possibly harm a child. Other parents felt that if it was so shocking for children to see such things, why did they keep looking. These parents often did not want to change their behavior, either because they did not wish to be inhibited in their sexual expression or because they wanted to ward off guilt.

Some of the children were told "to get lost" when they caught their parents in sexual activity; others were ignored or even invited to watch. None reported an empathic response from their parents or even that they were given information about what was happening.

They were left to fend for themselves with the excitation, fear, and anxiety engendered by their parents' inexplicable behavior. Often, their terror on seeing something so "weird" was amplified by the parents' angry or guilt-ridden responses. The children's states of excitation were often so high that native intelligence seemed to have abandoned them. Regressive behavior ruled the day and would not give way to instruction or entreaty. Hyperactivity, inability to learn despite good intellectual endowment; something the parents' called "silly behavior," with a lot of giggling and grimacing; bodily contortions; complaints about not having any friends; telling tall tales; or being stuck in a fantasy world that nobody else could understand – all these plagued the children whose cases I am about to present.

These children were always aware that something in their parents' behavior was inappropriate. They found varying ways to defend their own sexual excitation and developed more or less satisfying coping mechanisms. They had in common at the beginning of treatment the assumption that they must be very bad children because they always felt so scared and bad. These two words, scared and bad, seemed to be linked for the youngsters I treated. To them, a happy child could not possibly be a bad child.

ADAM

The First Interview

Adam's mother contacted me at the suggestion of the school psychologist. Despite better than average intelligence, Adam had little frustration tolerance, beat up other children, and was afraid to stay by himself even for a second. Special education classes had at first helped him to "behave," but now Adam was "worse than he had ever been." His teacher felt he should no longer attend the mainstream classes he had been assigned to. She cited as a major complaint that although he enjoyed taking books out of the library, he was apparently phobic of putting books back on the shelf and spent the time in the library to get into fights with the other children. Mrs. A sounded vague about her son's difficulties but managed to tell me that she had no confidence in psychotherapy, that her religious faith would see her through. Nonetheless, an appointment was made with both parents and promptly broken.

Adam's grandmother came instead and informed me that she was now caring for Adam and also would pay for therapy. Questioned about this unusual arrangement, she spoke of her own guilt about the inadequate way she had raised her own daughter, Adam's mother. Rather than telling me about Adam, the grandmother told me of her daughter's rebellious adolescence and her marriage at 17 to Adam's father, a soldier who was about to be shipped overseas. Adam was born in an army hospital. He was a poor eater and vomited often, but no physical cause could be found. Despite his constant vomiting, he thrived, passing all his physical milestones early. Grandmother was particularly pleased that Adam had spoken at eight months, but she was distressed that now, at 7 years old, he retained a childish lisp. He still was not toilet trained.

Encopresis was a problem nobody could cope with. Adam defecated in his pants whenever he felt like it and then hid his clothes. Grandmother beseeched me to help this "poor unfortunate." From babyhood, Adam was said to have disliked body contact of any sort from his parents, making himself stiff whenever they tried to hug him. Torrents of tears almost stopped her from telling me that Adam's condition had worsened since the birth of his brother, Eddy. Eddy was two years younger than Adam, a model child who could do no wrong. Grandmother reported that her daughter had become cruel to Adam as soon as she became pregnant with Eddy; she had pushed her older son aside when he wanted to hug her and kept him confined in his room. Later, when grandmother objected to this behavior, a gate was installed that allowed Adam to see what was going on but kept him from contact with his brother or mother. When his father came home in the evening, Adam was allowed to come out. Father could physically control him. Apparently Adam was very destructive. He broke things, made sinks and toilets overflow, and beat up Eddy whenever mother's back was turned. Grandmother thought her daughter should understand Adam. After all, mother had been a difficult child and a hard-to-control teenager herself. Mr. A had chosen the army as his career but was fortunate to be stationed near his family's home. When he came home in the evenings, he amused himself by playing with Adam and drilling him like the recruits in his platoon. Adam liked these games very much, but grandmother objected to them strongly, feeling they were too hard on Adam. She feared that this strict discipline would make Adam even more destructive.

I asked to see Adam's parents before starting treatment, but grandmother did not think they would come in. She was quite right. Mrs. A called to tell me that she was willing to send me a note giving me permission to start treatment of her son. I told her I really could not begin treatment until I had met her and her husband. After many phone calls, she eventually agreed to an interview because Adam's teacher threatened to have the child committed to a psychiatric hospital. Mrs. A seemed unaware that the teacher could do nothing without her approval. She even appeared somewhat relieved that someone besides herself saw her son as incorrigible.

When Mr. and Mrs. A finally arrived, with both their sons in tow, they told me that they wanted me to see them all together so I could get an idea of how difficult Adam was. Adam disappointed them. He played quietly in a corner with some toys, after first politely shaking my hand and telling me that he was looking forward to working with me. Mrs. A flew into a rage at this deceit and had to be quieted by her husband. She then told me basically the same things grandmother had told me but added that her mother's help was essential, that she was unable to manage her family without help. The A's were an extraordinarily handsome couple, very quiet in their ways and well spoken. Mr. A appeared gallantly protective of his wife and fond of the boys. Eddy spent the entire interview under his mother's chair. His parents did not comment on his behavior at all; they just stressed that he was a good boy as opposed to the "hard child," Adam. They vigorously resisted suggestions for counseling. Mrs. A again told me that her religious faith would help her, Mr. A felt that he had no time for counseling, and they both hoped that I would be able to quiet Adam down. In the meantime, both boys had been as quiet as mice, a fact Mr. and Mrs. A chose to ignore. When I mentioned it, it became clear that one of the overriding dynamics in this family was to keep mother satisfied. When her expectations were not fulfilled, Mrs. A became agitated again, as though Adam's exemplary behavior were in some way a threat to her. He had not been "bad," as expected.

Despite such an unpromising beginning, we managed to set up a treatment schedule. Grandmother would bring the boy, father would pick him up, and we would see if the parents could manage to come for the monthly interview.

Course of Treatment

When Adam and I finally met, he eyed me with a great deal of suspicion. He could not imagine someone who was totally on his side. He recited a litany of his wrongdoings and seemed surprised that I was unperturbed by them. I told him, "We will try to find out why all these things happened to you." He thought that over for a while and then decided that we would play "army," by which he meant that I had to stand at attention and follow commands he gave. I commented that he was playing like Daddy. A big grin was my reward. He found some of my records and picked out a military march. We now marched and presented a whole parade to an imaginary audience. Adam was so overcome by "how nice it was" that he decided to make up a dance. It was called "Happy Mr. Caneman." He took a cane and a top hat from the shelf and proceeded to do a fair imitation of Fred Astaire. As a special present, he drew a picture for me. It showed a faceless man who, said Adam, was making his BM on the floor (see Picture A1).

I was very encouraged by this beginning. Adam had shown me that he wanted to control me as his father controlled him, with "fun games," but that we could join together in such activities and be friends. Further, he had let me see both his creative side in the Mr. Caneman dance and his pathology in the picture he drew. He also let me see his reading skills by selecting suitable records from their jackets. I did not comment on or interpret anything that happened. Not saying too much in the beginning of therapy is generally a good rule because the patient of whatever age needs to feel confident and trusting before starting to explore unconscious motives. With a frightened, angry child like Adam it was even more important to let him become accustomed to the therapist and to the situation. Clearly, he had already learned how to manipulate his environment, as his behavior during the family visit demonstrated.

Picture A1   Faceless man who is making BM.

I was struck by his response to music. He had picked up rhythms smoothly and managed a fair imitation of Fred Astaire. Such imitative behavior is the first step toward identification of a solid kind. It made me wonder if his imitation of his soldier father was of the same variety. One thing was certain: I had not seen a trace of his major symptom, the hyperkinesis, at all; nor was I ever to see it throughout the treatment. As long as Adam had an avenue for expressing his many fantasies and observations, he was reachable and could quite easily be persuaded to "behave."

The minute he felt any pressure to conform, however, he was unable to contain himself, or so his teachers told me. As a matter of fact, no sooner had we begun the treatment when his teacher began to call. It seemed that Adam was entertaining his classmates with a new fantasy. He told everyone that his mother was a witch who on occasion danced naked in the moonlight. When the other children either laughed at him or called him a liar, he showed them her dance and told them of herbs and mushrooms she used for medicinal and other purposes. The teacher wanted me to stop Adam from telling such outrageous lies and was unable to concede that sometimes children tell tall tales. In her opinion, such storytelling was to be confined to the hours she set aside for such activities. I negotiated this request with Adam, who was quite willing to try. Unfortunately, he ran into another roadblock. He was not allowed to tell "the truth" about his mother even at storytelling time.

By this time, my interest was piqued, and I requested an interview with mother. She declined but was willing to speak with me about her religious beliefs. She did not approve of either her parents' or her husband's religions, but she did believe in witchcraft and white magic and even belonged to a coven. This time, she felt it was important to go to bat for Adam. She thought she needed to defend not only Adam but her way of viewing the world. At my prompting, she informed the teacher of her religious orientation. Adam was in seventh heaven. His mother had never been to school before, not even to sign his individual educational plans (IEP). He felt he was a hero and was reinforced in this belief by the teacher, who cleverly used the situation to teach a unit on folk belief and magic.

Meanwhile, the focus of my meetings with Adam shifted. He was no longer interested in playing, drawing, and dancing. He wanted me to know how he felt and what he experienced. He had learned from the incident that I was not out to destroy his perceptions and that I could perhaps be trusted. But this new trust did not show itself in gentler or more obedient behavior. Quite the contrary. He began to drag me roughly to the bathroom and tried to lock me in. Then, he would open the door again, throw some toys in, and say, "Play and leave me alone." I could hear him anxiously breathing and hopping up and down with excitement. "May I come out?" I called. "When Daddy comes home" was the answer. Each time this game was played, I interpreted the role reversal, commenting how lonely and upset children feel when their mother tells them to stay away. That seemed to calm Adam, though he frequently wet his pants and pulled on his crotch before he let me out of confinement. When I asked him if perhaps he had wet his pants because he couldn't get to the toilet on time, he answered that, no, he had spilled water on himself while drinking and now had to stretch his pee-er to quiet it down. I wondered out loud why his pee-er needed quieting, and he informed me that that was how he always felt, that his pee-er would stick straight up when he didn't want it to. He wanted it to stay down because it annoyed his mother so much when it was erect. He seemed vastly relieved when I told him that all boys like to touch their penises and that sometimes it feels so good, they just can't stop touching, especially when they need good feelings after being frightened. By this time, Adam had evolved a symbolic language through which he let me know how he felt. He danced Mr. Caneman for me when he was joyful. This time, he added a dash to the bathroom to urinate. Then he was unable to flush. Clearly, he expected punishment for this "transgression." I asked him if perhaps he had left his urine for me as a gift. Of course, one wouldn't want to flush away a gift! At that, he both flushed and danced Mr. Caneman before trotting off with a hugely satisfied grin on his face.

In the meantime mother and grandmother were less than pleased with the treatment. What kind of a therapist lets a kid pee in his pants during sessions? they wondered. Mother and daughter united, for once, to call me to task. They felt that I was dodging the issue when I once again suggested counseling or therapy for the family. They declined, and I used the next few monthly interviews to talk about the fact that children (and adults!) in treatment sometimes get worse before they can remember or talk about what really bothers them. They simply could not cope with the idea that a regression[2] can be a sign that things are going forward. I also requested that Adam be allowed to play outside and to leave his room at will. Father was for the idea; mother was not. We finally agreed that Adam would be permitted to spend a portion of each afternoon with his grandmother, who would take him for walks or play with him. Both parents feared he would beat up the neighborhood children if he were allowed to be by himself. In the meantime, he got a "good" in conduct on his report card, but this achievement did not impress Mr. and Mrs. A. They felt that Adam behaved himself in school only because there he was supervised every minute. And should he regress, then they were not interested in keeping him in treatment. On the other hand, they were afraid to withdraw him for fear that they would not be able to manage him. Both parents voiced feelings of jealousy toward grandmother's ability to handle Adam and were concerned lest he become too attached to his therapist. They did not like the singing and dancing during sessions that he told them about; they feared it would turn him into a sissy.

Adam meanwhile was winding his tortuous way through many fantasies. Sometimes he wanted to be like his teacher. Then he was sunny and affectionate, leaning against me and showing me that his teacher was loving toward him despite occasional harshness. He also loved it when I mirrored him (Siegel, 1983).[3] Invariably, this put him in a good mood.

He did not find it necessary to lock me in the bathroom very often

---

[2]A regression is a retreat to an earlier phase in life. It occurs when a maturational step presents an individual with conflicts he is unable to master. This retreat often has to do with some areas of weakness, or fixation, in the earlier period when there was stress in interpersonal relationships. Signs of such regression, or fixation, are thumb sucking after it has been abandoned, or falling back on anal masturbation after the genitals have been discovered to be the source of pleasure. In adults, the danger signals have to do with a return to infantile forms of sexuality, or there may be a reversion to earlier forms of functioning.

[3]Mirroring is used in a dance-movement therapy context here. The therapist reflects her patient's essence back to him bodily, using as many of his movements as she can accommodate without distortion. This technique often reestablishes a sense of self in people who either have not acquired a self-image or whose self-image has been destroyed. It equates with, but is not the same as, the loving mirror in a mother's eye.

any more, and when he did, had a new game. We were hidden from each other's sight when he played this game. While I was in the bathroom behind the closed door, he would stick a balloon through a crack under the door and blow it up. I could not at first make anything of this behavior despite its highly suggestive symbolism. We were facing a new roadblock at the time. Adam had been told not to talk about his family and, determined to be a good boy who earned everyone's approval, he no longer told anyone anything about his parents' doings. Instead, he identified with his parents' complaints about him and sorrowfully informed me that he "had too much energy. I have to ease up and not be so much trouble." Talking about anticipated—and hoped for—improvement was the only positive activity Adam indulged in. In school, his hyperkinesis rose to such heights that the teacher suggested medication, and outside of school he refused to stay behind his gate, in grandmother's fenced yard, or even in the house.

During sessions, he sang a lot of songs about a "shitdrinker" who lived under his sink and who had to build brick walls in order to contain the effluvium of many houses. Teacher once again was appalled, but soon we heard that the grandfather had gone into business constructing and manufacturing cesspools. I questioned Adam, who, in all innocence, confided that his parents laughed at his grandfather for being in this business and called the older man a shitdrinker. Once again, Adam's "schizophrenic symptom" had become understandable on a cognitive level. His urge to escape confinement also revealed itself as a need to be like grandfather, to look at many houses and to solicit business. Once this need had been uncovered in session by playing "Grandfather and the New Business," we could also talk about Adam's encopresis, which had not abated. I asked him if perhaps he wanted to be in the same business as his grandfather because he thought that would help him to keep his pants clean. He agreed that this might be so but first drew a picture of a shitdrinker as a powerful creature who, as Adam said, could destroy the world. This creature could manufacture bombs that exploded in midair and poisoned the surroundings. It was so powerful that it could pick up the whole world in its hands, hold it over its head, and smash the world to pieces.

We then talked a lot about how difficult it was to be a boy who was always doing things wrong, it seemed, a boy who had so little power that he could not always keep his BMs from slipping into his pants. Oh, no, Adam said. He didn't do that because he was powerless, Quite the contrary—he did it because those weren't only BMs. Those were bullets and bombs as powerful as the shitdrinker's, and he could get mother and grandmother really "dancing to his tune" when he used those bullets and bombs. And, yes, he was willing to draw me a picture of this creature (Picture A2). I admired the strength and power of this "monstrously strong" fantasy companion and likened him to Superman. "Oh, no," Adam said, "Shitdrinker is more powerful than Superman because he can make good stuff out of bad." Just as mother did when she danced naked for the moon. Adam was crestfallen as he left that day because he had once again talked about his parents when he was not supposed to.

But in subsequent sessions he could not help but return to what made him so excited. He placed me in a chair and told me to sit quietly while he showed me a new dance. He put on a record of Mother Goose songs, picked the rhythms up quite correctly, and then threw himself on the floor, writhing and panting. He asked me to come over to him

Picture A2   Shit drinker.

and give him balloons. When I did so, asking why, he was moaning, he answered, "Oh, you're killing me." From then on, he sought body contact each session, leaning against me but trembling, whether in fear or in excitation, I could not ascertain. Strangely, when after a while his trembling would subside as he sat on my lap or leaned against me while we talked or read a story, he called those times "fighting." Finally, he felt free enough to confide that mother and father "wrestled on the floor and mother is always the champion. She sits on top. But she still can't do everything herself, even if she is so strong. Robbers come in and I have to throw them in the duck pond. When dad isn't home and the other man comes to wrestle with mommy, then I have to call shitdrinker." Adam had broken into a cold sweat when he told me about what he had seen. But after this immense confession, he felt better, was calm for the first time in months, and once again danced Mr. Caneman. I used subsequent sessions to talk about the possibility that mom and dad were actually loving each other when they wrestled. Adam didn't think so: If wrestling meant loving each other, why didn't mom wrestle with him? She always told him she loved him when she put him behind the gate, but she only wrestled with dad and the other man. He then drew a rocket (Picture A3) that, he said, was to fill up a hole. I told him that I thought maybe he understood what I had told him but that it hurt a lot not to be mom's favorite and not to be able to wrestle with her like grown men did. He quite agreed.

I was unable to persuade the parents to come to their next interview. Adam was doing nicely in school; there was talk about mainstreaming him; he no longer ran away, nobody thought of him as hyperkinetic any more, so why did they have to see me? I asked if there were no complaints at all. Oh, yes, he still sometimes soiled his pants, and for that problem they might be persuaded to come in. During the session with these very anxious and disturbed parents, I tried to counsel restraint of their own sexual behavior in front of the children. They both thought me terribly old fashioned. They wanted their children to know the facts of life but were incensed when I told them that Adam had already received some knowledge about sexuality from me. They felt that I had overstepped my bounds and was interfering with their parental functions.

In the two months that followed, the parents sent word that they were thinking of removing Adam from therapy but wanted to give him time to say goodbye to me. Adam spent these last weeks

Picture A3 The rocket that fills up holes.

complaining that his brain hurt and developed a game in which he diapered some plush animals and then beat them up unmercifully, calling them "bastard." He denied that either he or his brother had been treated that way. He began every session by cleaning the sink with many groans and body language expressing much strain. He said he cleaned like grandmother. Once again, grandmother became the mediator. She called to say that Adam cried a lot at home, purposely stopped up their kitchen sink so that the water overflowed, and let his little brother Eddy out of the locked backyard. She understood that he was showing his dismay and anger about having to leave me but felt powerless to intervene on his behalf. As a farewell present, Adam gave me a self-portrait (Picture A4) so that I would never, ever forget him.

Discussion

Adam sounds as though he were a psychotic child, but he was not. Continual exposure to his mother's nude body, as well as exposure to

Picture A4 Self-portrait when leaving therapy.

her sexual behavior with at least two men, traumatized Adam. To make matters worse, the motor restraint imposed on him obviated physical tension release, for example, running and jumping, as a possibility for coping with his enormous excitation.

Cross-cultural studies (Ford and Beach, 1951) and Kinsey's (Kinsey, Pomeroy, and Martin, 1948) investigations of 4000 children have shown that Freud was right: Children do experience somatic sexual manifestations in childhood but have no way to reach a climax. Their sexual pleasures consist of looking and exhibiting, touching and mouthing. Adam, however, was not even permitted these pleasures. For him looking on became an unbearable excitation, which he unconsciously sought to bind with fantasies and through his hyperkinetic behavior and symbolic play. Since he was basically an intelligent and affectionate child, he did overcome his hyperkinetic tendencies while under my care. However, his sense of reality and reality testing were severely attacked by his parents' unusually exhibitionistic behavior. Even his teacher would not believe him when in actuality he was telling the truth.

In addition, his mother was hugely overburdened by the demands of two physically healthy children and could not cope with their motoric and other needs. Adam, in an attempt to grow up anyway, identified with his grandfather, even though his parents laughed at the business this man had chosen. Adam created a being who could become strong and powerful by ingesting the waste material of others. I have often thought that the creature symbolized his own role in that unhappy family: his mother needed him to see and accept her in roles unacceptable to the rest of her family. Adam was fascinated by, and simultaneously repelled by, his mother's role as witch. In addition, when he saw her taking her sexual pleasure with men, he became convinced of his own powerlessness and resorted to infantile ways of releasing tension while trying to control his mother with his encopresis. Anthony (1957), in a study involving 76 children who were encopretic, found that "where sphincter control remains defective or dependent on the mother's activity, the child's personality will appear unorganized and amorphous and his behavior uncontrolled and uncontrollable" (p. 155). This lack of integration certainly was true of Adam. Anna Freud (1963) showed that, in addition, intense disappointment with mother will lead to loss of bowel and bladder control and interfere with development to higher levels of autonomy. Adam, though, was an unusually creative child. He could sing and dance, draw, and tell stories. All these modalities of expression helped him, for a while, to stave off the overwhelming stimuli he was subjected to and the intense disappointment he suffered. In his fantasy he was strong and could create as much havoc as was created in him.

Special techniques used with him were dancing, singing, drawing, and story telling—in short, the host of approaches a mother might use to bring up her child. Particularly useful in calming him was body contact, such as sitting on my lap or leaning against me. At first, Adam sought body contact with his mother, whom he had seen tremble in sex play while leaning against her lover. He spoke of being like her, would make a mad dash away from me because for a moment he feared becoming a female like mother. But leaning against me had also felt good. I neither pulled him close to me nor pushed him in any way. I just made myself as available as I could. This neutral openness allowed Adam to recapture some of the gratification he must have experienced when he was an infant. Despite the reports of his being a difficult baby, there must have been times when he was nurtured, when his mother and father held him close and were happy to have borne him. He would not have thrived at all had they always treated him as unempathically as they did now. Mother and father could not bear their inner guilt and ambivalence; they needed to deny and to falsify reality in order to keep their façade intact.

But not all children who have been exposed to the sight of adults having sexual intercourse have parents who are so emotionally fragile as the A's. Lindi is a case in point.

LINDI

The First Interview

Lindi's mother was a mental health professional. She and Lindi's father had been high school sweethearts. She was a cheerleader, he a popular athlete. Their lives seemed to flow along placidly and success-fully until Mrs. B found out that her husband was being habitually unfaithful to her. She was then in her early 30s, a well-groomed, handsome woman who proudly supported herself and her three children after the divorce. An agreement had been reached that permitted Mr. B to spend every other weekend and vacation time with his children. On the surface, everyone had adapted well to the many changes in their lives. Mother and children lived in a small townhouse; father had rented elegant bachelor digs with a sleeping loft. This sleeping loft was a delight to the children, who played house there and also slept there in father's king-size bed.

Mrs. B objected to the boys' sleeping in the same bed with Lindi and threatened to take her former husband to family court if he did not provide more adequate sleeping arrangements for the children. She reported that all three of them came back from their weekends with father "hyper and hardly controllable. He spoils them and lets them do what they want so he doesn't have to pay attention to them. It's particularly hard on Lindi. She's the only female with all those males, and they treat her either as not worth anything or as another boy." It seemed that since the divorce both brothers had taken an inexplicable dislike to their little sister, a dislike that, Mrs. B felt, was stronger than the usual brother–sister rivalries. She suspected that all the children had been present when Mr. B entertained women and had seen sexual behavior. All three children hotly denied seeing anyone but their father during their visits. Mrs. B felt that the boys were being influenced by their father to view females as lesser creatures and, in addition, that the boys might have been frightened or disgusted by the sight of their sister's genitals when all three children slept together. When she confronted this issue with her former husband and the children, all four of them denied anything of the sort and begged to be able to continue sleeping in the same bed while at dad's apartment.

In the meantime, the boys were more belligerent than ever and Lindi developed a slight stutter. She became a remarkably quiet little girl who went around humming to herself so she would not have to hear what was said to her. She gave up doing any homework but doodled on any surface she could find. Mrs. B brought with her to our meeting a napkin Lindi had filled with her doodles (Picture Li1). Mrs. B was sure that the doodles represented penises, and she was highly agitated that her lovely young daughter should have regressed to a point where she no longer drew people age appropriately. Lindi was eight years old and to this time had shown every sign of healthy development. But now her father had teasingly begun to call Lindi "his

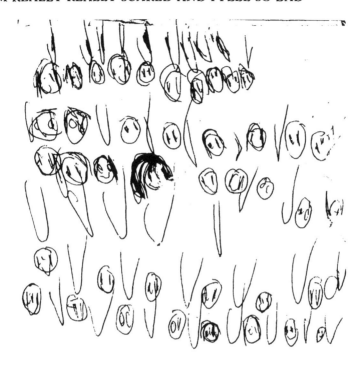

Picture Li1   Symbolic doodles..

little dumb blonde" and enjoyed telling his friends, in Lindi's presence, about her naive "dumb blonde" remarks. When she sulked, or protested being exposed in this fashion, he hugged her and promised her gifts, which were never delivered. Mrs. B tried to reason with him but to no avail. Mr. B continued with his half-teasing, half-seductive behavior until Mrs. B demanded that they go to some sort of family counseling together. Mr. B declined, choosing to go for psychotherapy instead. After the first few weeks in therapy he sent the children home with the message "that he would now stop seeing crazy girls." Lindi thought he meant her and became even more withdrawn, drawing a self-portrait entitled "crazy me" (Picture Li2). It was at this time that her mother brought her to me for treatment.

Course of Treatment

Lindi was as friendly as a little puppy when she came into the treatment room. She happily examined the toys and decided that

Picture Li2 Crazy me.

instead of playing with them, she would like to dance with me. Her mother had been a student of dance in her early youth and sometimes said, "I should have been a dancer." Now Lindi thought she might like to try being a dancer, "But not the kind where you do what other people tell you. The kind where you do how you feel." I later learned that Mrs. B had also taken a course in dance therapy and had tried to help her unhappy little girl by trying to provide avenues of expression for her by suggesting that she "move out her feelings." But this well-intentioned attempt had come to naught. Lindi thought it was silly to dance with one's mother. She could envision herself dancing with her brothers or her father, but not with her mother. And come to think of it, she didn't really want to dance with me either. "Two dames don't make it with each other," she said. I asked her who talked like that and she readily told me, "Daddy." I showed her a self-portrait of herself that her mother had given me and said that it would be very difficult for a girl who drew a portrait of herself without legs to dance. Lindi thought that was a pretty silly statement and began to demonstrate to me that she had strong, sturdy legs, which, however, she considered to be too short. She wanted to be tall, like her father, who was 6′ 2″ tall, or like her brothers Peter and Paul, who were unusually tall for their ages. She thought that it would give her an advantage in wrestling if her legs were long. She gave a vivid demonstration of how she wrestled with her brothers but could not quite show me to her satisfaction what actually had ensued. Finally, she asked me to lie down on top of her so she could show me that her legs were too short to hold me down in that position. She began to perspire and became tearful when I told her that it would not be a good idea for me to lie down on top of her but that we could dance with each other to become calmer and to be close together. With a vast sigh of relief, she allowed me to lead her through a waltz. In the swaying and rocking of the dance she relaxed visibly. It seemed to remind her of being rocked by her mother. Finally, she asked, as a farewell after this first and telling session, to crawl through my legs while I was standing up. I asked her why, and she told me forthrightly that this is how one has babies, between one's legs, and she thought maybe she could be my baby that way.

Lindi's agitated actions in the session had me convinced that Mrs. B was right; Lindi had been traumatized by seeing some sort of primal scene. She was clearly overwhelmed and confused and could no longer report exactly what bothered her so much. Unhappily, her mother's loving presence and actual interventions[4] had not provided a sufficient barrier against whatever instinctual overstimulation Lindi and her brothers had experienced. Over the next three years, Lindi and I managed to put together the puzzle.

Because Mrs. B was in a psychoanalysis herself, she had brought up her children to be aware of their dreams. She had just learned for herself that interpreting her children's dreams might be too intrusive

---

[4]While it is essential that parents involve themselves with their children during treatment, it is also essential that they be attuned to their children and try not to act on their own inner needs. But when they offer interpretive interventions, their parenting functions are in part contaminated. All the child's instinctual, unconscious material becomes focused on the parent. If what the parent says interpretively makes the child feel bad, the child will infer that the parent is a bringer of bad feelings. If the parental intervention leads to good feelings, problems with separating from the gratifier ensue. Overgratification and intrusion can wreak just as much havoc as lack of parenting.

and might lead them to view her as a therapist rather than as mother. She therefore instructed Lindi to tell me of her dreams. She told me the following one: She was in the hospital for two years, missing her next birthday because a child molester had cut her eyes with a knife. She had just learned from her mother that there are bad men, and sometimes bad women, who make little girls do things that are bad for them. She had been instructed never to go with anyone she did not know, to come straight home from school, and to inform mother of everything the babysitter said or did. It sounded to me as though Mrs. B felt very guilty about leaving her children while she went to work. Indeed, she informed me by phone, she now doubted some of her allegations about her husband; she thought that perhaps she had overreacted out of jealousy and despair that she could no longer be with him. In my interviews with Mrs. B she had not struck me at all as overly protective or as paranoid. I concluded that her self-doubt must have to do with a phase in her therapy or that, like many modern women, she had to be superwoman, someone who excelled at the work place as well as at home. In the meantime, Lindi revealed an aspect of herself not previously seen. She took a small ball, stuck it between her legs and entered into a twilight state (Bornstein, 1947), during which she was not aware that I was in the room with her.

When during the next interview I asked Mrs. B if she had ever observed her little girl in such a state, she became very upset and said yes, come to think of it, the boys were unmanageable when they came home from father, but Lindi had lately been quiet and withdrawn, just going into her room to be by herself. She immediately wanted to quiz the child but was able to contain herself when I assured her that treatment would bring to light what had made Lindi withdraw. When, during the next session Lindi again stuck the ball between her legs, I asked her if that felt good. She said, yes, it felt good. I then played a game with her. What feels good? She enumerated any number of things and started to giggle and jump around, holding on to her vagina. Eventually, she commented that it felt good to sleep in the same bed with Daddy. He felt so nice and warm. I asked her if she sometimes wished she were old enough, and grown up enough, to marry him. Oh no, she replied. Daughters don't marry their fathers. She spoke seriously and with great emphasis. Obviously, she had been instructed on proper behavior vis-à-vis her father.

In the same session, she drew a picture that showed children on a couch, reaching for their mother, who is turned away from them and has no arms (Picture Li3). As it turned out, Mrs. B had begun to date again, and all the children were upset about this. Understandably, they thought they would lose their mother. But I asked myself, what are the children doing on the couch? And why did Mr. B take the chance of sleeping in the same bed with his little daughter after he had been warned not to do so? I asked for an interview with him but was refused. His therapist did not want anyone else involved with him, he said. He also indignantly denied that he had slept in the same bed with Lindi.

In the meantime, Lindi had taken up her old preoccupation with wrestling. She wanted to lie on top of me, stretch her legs around my waist, or ride on my back. When I suggested that we do long jumps across the floor to some classical music instead, she complied readily enough and once again recalled that her mother had once wanted to be a dancer. I had hoped for just such a memory to reaffirm itself so that she could identify with her mother instead of with the mysterious event that had excited her so much. Identifying with mother firmed up

Picture Li3   Children on the couch.

her confidence sufficiently for her to admit dad had never slept in the same bed with her, but he had wrestled with her and she had loved that.

Lindi told many tall tales. Her mother was distraught, as was her father. They could not understand why this child, who was always so full of life and laughter, would want to lie. Mrs. B worried because she knew that children make up stories only when their reality is too painful to bear. What was it that Lindi could not bear? Once again, tales of child molesters surfaced. Mysterious men were said by Lindi to lurk behind bushes when she came home from school. Bad boys wanted to pull down her panties, and big, ugly girls wanted to take her lunch money away. Mrs. B at times was convinced that all this had happened. I almost believed Lindi myself, except that she regularly experienced the odd withdrawals when I came close to the subject of where and how she slept at her father's house. Her schoolwork plummeted, and she had trouble reading. Both parents were ready to put her into a class for troubled children when she had a dream that, in my opinion, revealed what was so hard for her to digest. She told me with much agitation:

A giant was going to come. She ran away with me. I had shrunk and become her girlfriend. The giant was going to kill us both, but we had brought enough money for a speedboat. Just as she thought "I hope we don't get into trouble," a waterfall came. I jumped out of the boat and helped her out of it. We went home because the boat was wrecked. She decided to stop up all the holes in her house and hoped there would be no waterfalls in her house.

Once again, Lindi was unable to reflect what either verbally or nonverbally the dream might mean, but she drew a picture for me (Picture Li4). I asked her if she could tell me the story that went with the picture. Asking for a story that goes with the picture is a little device I use to help the children distance themselves a little from their inner feelings. They can then feel safe enough to reveal more of themselves without being swamped by their emotions. Lindi tells me that in her picture a girl named Brigit is in a rocket. She wants to go into space to find a star, which she will then give to her mother. I gently tell Lindi that sometimes girls want to make things better for their mothers when they see that mother is very, very unhappy. "Yes," she answers, "I didn't want mommy to know that dad does *that* to Brigit. I wanted to give my mommy a nice present."

Picture Li4a Brigit in the rocket.

Picture Li4b Stars for mother.

We spent many subsequent sessions talking about how difficult it is to put up with a dad who has a girlfriend who acts like his wife. Eventually, Lindi was also able to acknowledge that my presence in her dream was a sign that "we are really and truly friends. But that you shranked was bad. That means you couldn't help me. But that's bad of me. I know you help me all the time," she said. Lindi thought it was particularly scary to see dad's big penis. It was very big, much bigger than Daniel's or Paul's. Apparently her father and brothers marched around naked in the morning. Moreover, Lindi's father was of the opinion that children should see sexual intercourse, particularly the boys, in order to prepare them for life. He exposed himself and the women he slept with to the children. Lindi was able to recall how frightened and upset she had been when she first came to visit dad and found someone she did not know in his bed. She also knew that it made him angry if she told mother about the woman. When the situation became too painful, she began to make up a world of her own in which she could satisfy her unhappy mother and still remain her father's "best girl." Finally, she was able to see that it was not her job to disentangle her parents' complicated emotional life. Even if she wanted to, she could not do to mother what dad did to Brigit. "Silly," she giggled, "girls don't have a thing like that. They have vaginas." Her last self-portrait (Picture Li5), drawn after two years of treatment, shows a person quite different from the "crazy girl" who had entered treatment. It took another year for her to consolidate her gains and for her parents to sort out their arrangements. Lindi left treatment as a fairly contented child. She no longer told lies, had given up her twilight states, and, happily, related realistically to those around her.

Special techniques used with Lindi were dancing, drawing, story telling, and many hours comparing what she perceived with what might be objective reality. In therapy she did acquire the essential psychological skills of reality testing and frustration tolerance. This observation is in accord with Gedo's (1988) thinking, particularly his ideas about a psychological rather than a neurological, apraxia. Lindi's maladaptive behavior stemmed from a failure to acquire those skills earlier; that is, her dazes and odd responses were not a repetition of something experienced in infancy. With many children, it is sufficient to represent their traumas symbolically. Not so Lindi. Since, in her case there was a developmental arrest, it was essential to sort out cognitively what was reality and what was fantasy. Of course, this

Picture Li5   Self-portrait

sorting and reexperiencing had to be facilitated in a totally nonjudg-mental way. Lindi never would have trusted me if I had not accepted her tall tales as a device that could help her through emotionally troubled times. At first, Lindi was caught in a negative oedipal position; she wanted to rescue her mother as a man could. When she saw her father's conduct with women, she wished she could be like him and her brothers and have a penis. She started to tell lies that made up for her supposed lack. But when her real secret was at long last revealed, she was able to go on to the feminine identification necessary for the oedipal period to continue. It had been interrupted by her father's exhibitionism.

Discussion

Lindi loved both her parents. Deeply attached to her mother, she was angry at her father for deserting them. But there were additional complications. Lindi knew that she was female like her mother. She was aware of her inner body sensations and had a beginning under-standing of her sexual apparatus. She attended to her father in the special way of little girls, hoping to win approval of her femininity from him. She had appropriately entered the oedipal phase. But father overstimulated her unbearably and seemed to prefer the boys and other women. Lindi began to despise herself, both because her father seemed to prefer everyone else and because she could not help her mother. For a while, she seemed to have toyed with the idea that she could satisfy her mother in the same way her father satisfied women. Such an undertaking was obviously doomed to failure. But it is not as pathological a wish as might be assumed. Research shows (Edgecumbe and Burgner, 1975; Fast, 1984; Glover and Mendell, 1982) that little girls regularly go through a phase during which they compete for their mother's attention and admiration. This competition has often been thought of as the so-called negative oedipal phase, in which the little girl vies for her mother's love much as the little boy does in the oedipal phase. But direct child observation and research have shown that during this phase it is not only father who is experienced as a rival; anyone who comes between mother and child is viewed as a rival.

For a child like Lindi, however, overstimulation through the sight of her father's and brothers' genitals, and through witnessing her father in sexual intercourse with women, placed her in an untenable position. She wanted at once to rescue her mother and herself and hold on to her father's affection. The pressure was too much for her. She simply withdrew into a dreamlike state during which she might have fantasized having a penis when she pressed the ball against her genitals. The therapeutic task was to desexualize her cognitive ability and to allow her reality testing to mature, thereby make her world safe for her once more. Difficulties in trusting mother completely were also part of the picture because Mrs. B's well-meaning but inappropriate therapeutic interventions had alerted Lindi to the fact that mother was also relatively helpless and could not always protect her. Indeed, Lindi thought she had to rescue mother. Once this role reversal had been eliminated, trust in mother was reestablished, allowing Lindi to develop her faculties calmly.

Lindi's relationship with her father remained somewhat problematic because it was she who had to insist that he cover himself and see Brigit when he was by himself. I feared that this role reversal would repeat the earlier trauma for now Lindi had to take care of dad, whereas earlier it had been mother who needed her care. But our work together had strengthened her. In some ways, she had become a prematurely wise little girl. Of her father she said, "I hope his therapist tells him it gives children nightmares when he does *that* in front of them."

SUMMARY

I have chosen the cases of Adam and Lindi because they are typical in many ways. Adam and Lindi, although they came from very different environments and had reached different developmental levels, had many symptoms in common. They both had difficulties in perceiving and testing reality. As defenses against overwhelming sexual stimulation, they developed intricate fantasies and inner worlds that protected them from acting even more strangely. In the process of shuttling back and forth from inner fantasy to outer reality, they often became unable to focus on the cognitive tasks required for their school work. Both had difficulty coping with the sexual excitation that followed visual exposure to adult sexual intercourse. Lindi without realizing it, masturbated by placing a ball between her legs. Adam tried to think of ways to prevent his erections. He began to confuse his bodily functions and became both enuretic and encopretic. Seeing the larger genitals of their parents had made them feel inadequate, excited and worried all at once. The behaviors they saw made no sense to them, so they misinterpreted them. These misinterpretations, coupled with the physical excitation they experienced, prompted them to make up pseudoexplanations in the form of fantasized creatures and events. They had no way of dealing with what they saw. Therefore, they fell back on more infantile ways of viewing their environment and tried to control it by the magic of their imaginations. In both cases, the parents' sexual and exhibitionistic needs overshadowed the developmental needs of their children.

This kind of family dynamic was present in many similar cases I have either supervised or in which I conducted the therapy myself. It can be seen that visual stimulation of a sexual nature by an adult can be troublesome and seductive for a child even when no actual tactile genital contact with the body of an adult takes place. Indeed, 97% of Weil's (1989) sample of 100 children who were exposed to adult coitus displayed symptomatic sexual activities after exposure.

Some investigators have suggested that it is the violent nature of what they see, not the erotic aspect, that upsets the children most, and that it is the violence that contributes to or causes the enormous amounts of anxiety these children have to deal with (e.g., Esman, 1973). But Weil's statistical analysis of 100 children shows that

> physical forms of violence in the form of beating or yelling do not correlate positively with the arousal of night terrors. Night terrors did not occur more frequently among the children who had been exposed to a history of beating and punitive yelling. Rather, a history of beatings was associated with a reduced incidence of night terrors. These findings therefore support the formulation that it is not the violent aspects of sexual intercourse which provide a source for the arousal of a child's night terrors [p. 58].

My clinical experience has convinced me that Freud (1938), Fenichel (1945), and Katan (1973) were on the right path when they postulated that visual and tactile sexual stimulation provides the source for pathological sexual excitation in children.

CHAPTER *4*

⊒⊒

I Want to Kick the World to Pieces
Children Who Have Been Beaten

Teachers as well as the general public have lately become alerted to the plight of the physically abused child. But there are many children who do not quite fall into the category of obviously abused children. Among many parents "spare the rod and spoil the child" is still an axiom that all too often masks a parent's uncontrollable temper. Beatings are administered as a matter of course without the parent's being the least bit remorseful, although he or she may exclaim that "this hurts me more than it hurts you." Children from such families seldom complain about their parents. They assume that all parents behave in such a manner, or they are too frightened to tell. Often, they are extremely uncooperative in school and respond poorly to discipline. They seem to love their abusive parents, seemingly because a bad relationship is, to them, better than none at all. Sometimes they make themselves into little Stoics who "can take anything." But their own aggression is heightened when they are beaten. They smolder with resentment and fantasies of revenge. Unable to retaliate against their more powerful parents, they become either bullies or self-destructive, hurting themselves in many accidents. And, of course, these battered children frequently become battering parents. Delinquency is also often part of the picture.

The children I want to talk about here are not so easily recognized as abused children. They come from outwardly nurturing families where nobody "has the faintest idea what got into him [or her]." The parents condemn child abuse and are aghast when told that their behavior can be viewed as in the same category. After all, they do not physically harm their child, they say. They do not understand why, suddenly, the child has become a poor student, yells at everybody, has fallen into sullen silence, and may even be self-abusive, contrary, and certain that everybody is against him. Or a meek, ordinarily smiling child may have taken to terrorizing younger, smaller children. When admonished by his parents, he always promises to do better but he never keeps his word. He is extremely touchy when teachers or any authority figure asks him what prompted him to act as he did. He seems to live a life of quiet desperation until something sets off his temper. Then he viciously, verbally or physically, attacks everyone in sight. Or the pitiful whiner becomes a fire-spitting, destructive little monster.

Once in therapy, these children often produce symbolic material about killing and destruction. From a psychdynamic point of view, clearly they are trying to master the trauma of having been beaten by becoming active administrators of beatings themselves. Cohen (1988) has described similar, apparently unexplainable vacillations in abused children who were placed with foster families or in child care centers. At first, they gave in to a "Golden Fantasy" (Smith, 1977) in which they expected to live in a perfect paradise where everything would be taken care of and all their wishes fulfilled. After a while, their essential hopelessness and despair were evident again. Through projective identification,[1] the children made their child care workers and therapists into the abusing parents and wanted to go back home, where the parents were now seen and felt to be the only ones who could fulfill their impossible wishes.

The children I saw were not in quite the same category as those children, but their behavior was so startlingly similar to that of more severely abused children that I feel it is essential to view their plight as

---

[1]Through projective identification one tries to push one's own feeling responses into another so that the other person, not oneself, can be said to possess those feelings. The identification with the other's feelings enables one to stay connected to one's externalized mental states and unconscious defenses.

a related form of dysfunctional parent-child dynamics. Most teachers know at least one of the kind of child I am describing. To illustrate how this kind of child functions, let me tell Lawrence's story.

LAWRENCE

The First Interview

I really never had a first interview with Lawrence or his parents. A kindly school psychologist who felt very sorry for the family contacted me and gave me much of the information that enabled me to start treating the child. She had even paved the way by asking his parents about Lawrence's early development, which was said to be entirely normal. He ate and slept well, walked and talked at the appropriate times, and was said to have shown no trace of jealousy when a brother was born four years later. When his brother was discovered to have a serious and potentially fatal disease, Lawrence was unfailingly kind, helped his mother in every way, and was considered a good son. Lawrence had always been a quiet child. Therefore, nobody thought it was odd when he retreated to his room frequently and spent many solitary hours playing by himself.

Nine-year-old Lawrence was away at camp when his brother died. Instead of bringing Lawrence home and letting him share the sorrow and grief that now overwhelmed his mother and father, it was decided not to tell him anything, to protect him from the effects of the volatile mourning of his mother and grandmother. This was a decision made primarily by the father, Mr. K, who angrily accused fate and wished he could "beat up the devil or even God, whichever brought such suffering down on little children." After coming home from camp and finding his brother missing, for weeks he refused to go to school, to play with his former pals, or even to talk to his family. He just wanted to lounge around the house, listen to music, or watch TV. He was too tired to do anything else. His concerned parents were sure he was suffering from a depression caused by the sudden death of his younger brother. The younger child had needed a great deal of care, and now the parents blamed themselves for not having paid enough attention to Lawrence while his brother deteriorated. They had been so wrapped up in trying to save the younger child's life that it never occurred to them that Lawrence was also scared when respirators and oxygen tanks became standard equipment in the household.

When Lawrence returned from camp, he was amazed to find that all the medical paraphernalia was gone but at first refused to believe that his brother was dead. Instead he made up a tale that his brother was in the hospital. His mother did not "have the heart to disabuse him" and let him believe what he wanted. The parents began to cater to Lawrence as they had done earlier with their younger child. But they had little success. Lawrence warded them off. When he deigned to go to school at all, he came home hours after he was expected and lied about where he had been. When his mother weepingly begged him "not to torture her" by not telling her his whereabouts, he came up with tales of having been waylaid and beaten by older boys who took his money, his watch, his portable radio, or whatever other valuable possession he had with him. Incensed, the parents decided that junior criminals were scaring their son away from his education and notified the school authorities, who promised to do their best to protect Lawrence. But this protection meant that he had to board the bus when the other children went home, which was totally unaccept-able to Lawrence. He "couldn't get his act together" as fast as his classmates. He declared that he had to "secure" his belongings on his person and in his locker with special tapes and locks before he could go home. This symptomatic behavior seemed understandable enough in view of the family's tragedy. Lawrence apparently wanted to make sure that he would lose nothing else. Losing his brother was quite enough.

The school psychologist, recognizing the compulsive nature of Lawrence's behavior, advised psychotherapy for everyone concerned. Mr. and Mrs. K selected family therapy, where again (as they had been told by the school psychologist) they were told that Lawrence needed his own therapist. But Lawrence did not want to go anywhere by himself. He begged and cried until his mother, before ever meeting me, decided that she would be in the sessions with us. Still, despite the support from both the family therapist and the school psychologist, Mrs. K could not bring herself to actually place Lawrence in treat-ment. It was not clear whether she had, in her despair, fastened on her son as a psychological life-support system for herself or whether she had always in some way symbiotically clung to him. Mr. K thought the whole idea of therapy totally absurd but went along with the idea because it seemed comforting for his wife to have "a bunch of hens to cry with." He claimed that as a self-made man he had no understanding of what "you educated people mean by all that psycho-lingo." Therefore, I did not really expect that my colleague in the school would be able to persuade Mr. and Mrs. K that individual therapy for Lawrence was called for. But then an event happened that changed all that.

Mrs. K, helping her housekeeper with the spring cleaning, found a trove of unfamiliar items in Lawrence's room. There was a relatively large sum of money, toys, two or three radios, pocketknives, and all sorts of odds and ends that children treasure. When she confronted him, Lawrence denied any knowledge of the cache until his father came home and quizzed him. Then it was revealed that far from being the victim of attack, Lawrence had been the attacker; he had taken those things from younger children on his way home from school. The parents were devastated. They immediately called me for an appointment.

When we met, they wondered if Lawrence should be placed in a military school for discipline, sent away to a mental hospital, or just be given up as incorrigible. After the first storm of emotions had subsided, Mr. K, in an exploratory session with me, revealed a startling thought. In a way that he could not quite understand, he was proud that Lawrence had shown such cunning and even physical strength although Mr. K would have preferred that Lawrence had "taken on somebody his own size or bigger." Mrs. K was horrified and threatened to end the marriage immediately if he persisted in such thinking. Mr. K again muttered angrily about Lawrence finally showing some gumption, which, he said, came from his side of the family, and agreed to place his son in my care. Mrs. K now decided that she could not tolerate being in sessions with Lawrence. He had disappointed her too deeply and hurt her worse than the death of her younger son had hurt her. He would have to fend for himself. Lawrence had just turned 10 when this conversation occurred. His brother had died about 11 months earlier.

Nothing in what I had heard would lead me to believe that Lawrence had been an abused child. His symptoms appeared to be caused entirely by the sudden death of his brother. Yet I cautiously assumed that something else must be afoot to have caused Lawrence's reported character reversal and thievery.

Course of Treatment

The first session alone with Lawrence was instructive, foreshadowing what was to come. True to her word, Mrs. K deposited Lawrence in the waiting room and informed him that he was on his own. She was quite proud of this decision and had told me about it on the phone when she called to make arrangements for Lawrence's therapy. She agreed to come in for sessions with her husband "some time when we have coped with our grief better." Both she and her husband felt that talking to yet another therapist after dealing with the school psychologist and their family therapist would be too much and would cause them to grieve uncontrollably. How Lawrence fared in therapy and how they could help him would have to wait for another time.

An emotionally abandoned, pouting Lawrence slouched into my consulting room, whispered that he had nothing to say, and just sat there in the most dejected way imaginable. I told him that I had heard a lot about him from the school psychologist and that I knew how hard life must be for him at the moment. I felt this kind of openness was called for because he had in the past had a strongly adverse reaction to not being told of important events. Lawrence seemed interested but just sneered. I also told him that he was free to play with the toys and the records, and to draw or paint. But unlike many other children who eagerly seize the opportunity to "do something," Lawrence wanted simply to sit and stare at me with accusing eyes. As the silence thickened, he decided to pick up crayons and then presented me with a picture (Picture La1). I asked him if the picture meant that he would like me to help him feel more comfortable. He nodded "yes" and in a whisper told me that he thought a large bouncer (a large rubber ball with handles on it that a child can sit on and ride) that was in a corner reminded him of African people dancing around a pot with a person in it. He had seen a shrunken head in a museum once. "Yukh!" he said. Seeing a stack of records on a shelf, he asked if I had any African music. He found some Afro rhythms, put them on the phonograph, and began to dance a savage cannibal's dance, as he called it. It being the first session, I felt it too early to make a stab at interpreting such violent behavior. I did not want to make him even more anxious than he seemed to be already, but I was alerted to the fact that more than depression was at hand. Lawrence's symptoms did not correspond to what I had been told about him.

Picture La1

In the following sessions he produced more pictures. The first two were confused scratches and scribbles, which he drew while he had a dazed smile on his face. I asked him if the pictures meant anything to him or if he wanted to tell me a story about them. I had noticed that whenever he drew something recognizable, he rapidly obliterated it as though to hide, even from himself, what he was thinking about. Actually, Lawrence did not seem to think much. Rather, he was engaged by a confused and overwhelming tide of feelings that he seemed unable to verbalize (Pictures La2 and La3). Since it was so hard for him to talk about what he had drawn, I asked if he could give his pictures a title. Yes, he answered. That was not too much effort, especially if I was willing to write it down for him. He could not quite decide what to name the first picture, but the second one he named "Big-Mouth-Sharp-Tooth-Sam." I wondered aloud who that might be and received, instead of an answer, the portrait of a woman (Picture La4) who had no hands and was depicted as turned away from the viewer. I wondered who this female could be, and immediately Lawrence answered, "My mother, of course." I commented, "How sad

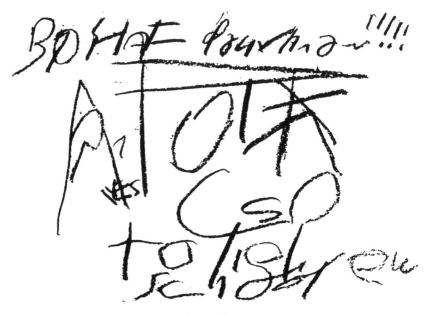

Picture La2

for her that she has no hands." Lawrence had the perfect answer: "But she has sharp teeth." As though to avert any further inquiries, he scampered across the room and asked if we could carve the face on a pumpkin standing on the window sill. I agreed and we carved the face. I was rewarded with a coherent, unobliterated drawing of the pumpkin, which, however, was designated by Lawrence as having come from Mars (Picture La5).

The release of aggression that came about in a structured way during sessions seemed to do Lawrence good. He saw that I was not frightened by his bizarre behavior, and he was able to be more focused after dancing his strange cannibal's dance and carving out the pumpkin. I did wonder, though, when in the transference I would become the mother who had turned away from him, like the figure he had drawn earlier.

Lawrence's depression about the death of his brother and his despair about being emotionally left out was real enough. But what had provoked his image of his mother as a sharp-toothed male, and why did he need to use a carving knife before he could draw in a less confused fashion? Before together we found some of the answers to Lawrence's difficulties, there were many sessions filled with agitated

Picture La3 Big-Mouth-Sharp-Tooth-Sam

recounting of horror movies. As a matter of fact, Lawrence began to identify with some of the characters he saw on TV and in the movies and drew self-portraits depicting himself as behind bars, as being strangled, or as a creature who had hair all over his body, something he had seen in a movie called "The Planet of The Apes" (Pictures La6 and La7). Asked what all this could mean, he said coyly, "I'm the husband of my cat, Cleo, and the father of the two little kittens." He refused to elucidate. I had to wait until the parents' interview for some clarification. The family cat, Cleo, had indeed just had a litter. Mr. and Mrs. K were deeply impressed by how well Lawrence had cared for the cat family. He had not left Cleo while she was giving birth and had once again missed school. But both parents agreed that this absence was not so bad since Lawrence had had the opportunity to "see nature at work and to be the good boy that he really is."

But Lawrence had other ideas. He felt guilty about having spied on the cat and about not going to school. "What kind of parents are they if they let me get away with that?" he asked. I could not help but

Picture La4   Mother

speculate silently about what he had seen his parents do and what he disapproved of so strongly that would make him want to abandon his human identity in favor of being an animal or an animal's husband. He did not immediately respond to interpretive or clarifying questions such as, why don't you think you should watch your cat? I also asked what he meant by his remark about what kind of parents he had. He would not answer other than to adhere stubbornly to his comment that his kind of parents shouldn't have let him watch the cat Cleo give birth. He simply would not answer when I further asked if he had been frightened when seeing the kittens emerge. Yet about a year into the therapy, we had made some progress: he regularly went to school, though he still had poor marks. Although we never openly talked about it, Lawrence had let me know that he no longer beat up other children. Instead, he and some other boys chased little girls with water guns or tried to get into the girls' locker room and shower at school. He pointed out that "all the guys did that" and that there was "nothing wrong with chasing girls." I agreed that it was better than beating them

Picture La5 Pumpkin from Mars

up but wondered aloud what it must be like for the girls to be chased with water guns. Lawrence thought they loved it because they giggled and screamed as they fled. As he told me about these incidents, he usually sat on the floor, pulled the bouncer over to his side, and licked it. He ignored questions about why he did this. He reminded me of a neglected infant mouthing his empty bottle.

Nevertheless, there was some continuity in the sessions. Lawrence no longer related a gruesome story each time but had begun to play with the toys, in particular the soldiers, which fought unending battles on the floor. By this time, he could distinguish between reality and fantasy sufficiently to report a dream, his first: "A guy sees a cave and tries to go into it with a rock in his hand. But it smells, so he doesn't because he thought it was on fire." Lawrence thought this dream very, very funny. He giggled, would not talk about it, and had two of his soldiers wrestle on the floor. Then he threw himself on the floor and, placing the bouncer above his head, began to lick it, mouth it, and stroke it. Then all the soldiers were hit by bombs from a plane and were killed. Lawrence was unwilling to look at either the contents of his dream or his behavior.

When he came for his next session, I had left on my desk some

Pictures La6   Self-portrait

books for children that explain sexuality. My own association had led me to assume that Lawrence's dream of the smelly cave, his identification as the cat, Cleo's husband, and the way he licked the bouncer, all might have something to do with confused fantasies about sexual intercourse or with actually witnessing it. Perhaps the smelly cave represented a vagina, the bouncer a breast. Previous experience had shown me that children who ostensibly have been given correct information about human reproduction did not internalize it if it was given in an unempathic fashion. In the benign atmosphere of the therapy sessions, the children often found it possible to recognize what they had previously rejected and to experience relief by finally accepting cognitively what had been a confused jumble of meaningless words before.

As an opening to a discussion of sexual matters, I have found the use of picture books helpful. Lawrence was fascinated. At first, he called me a dirty lady for bringing such books into my office; then he told me that he already "knew all that stuff." His mother had told him

Pictures La7   Self-portrait

and had helped him to be a man by "practicing with him how a man should behave." If he did not behave like a man, she yelled and screamed and carried on and said she wished she were dead. As it turned out, Lawrence also wished she were dead when she screamed so. In Lawrence's mind, to be a man meant that he was mother's subordinate; that he had to hold doors open for her, fetch, and carry whenever she commanded, and, above all, not to bother her. On occasion, she asked him to come into the bathroom to wash her back. Then he was her "good little man." But Lawrence did not want to be anybody's good little man. He hated having to go to the cemetery with mother or accompanying her on visits to relatives and friends.

After delivering himself of so many observations, he settled down to inspect the books and began to ask me relevant questions. His confusion about what was a sexual and what was a social aspect of being a man was enormous. Slowly, we began to sort out what Lawrence felt and thought when he held open the door for mother and what he thought and felt when he washed her back. In both instances he felt "like a damn servant." But when holding the door, he felt just like a "plain servant," when washing her back, however, he felt "dirty" be-cause he could peek over her shoulders and see her breasts. It now became clear what he had meant by "his kind of parents." He was

angry with both of them for not protecting him from their own
exhibitionistic needs, which Lawrence interpreted as sexual. Father's
shouting was also felt to be sexual because the shouting so often ended
with mother in father's arms. Lawrence could even see the analogy
between a cave and a vagina. He thought vaginas as truly ugly and evil
smelling. He knew because he and his gang had held down a little girl
and taken off her panties. But then they did not know what to do. He
thought this behavior fell into the category of "learning how to be a
man" and was dismayed to hear from me that the little girl was
probably terrified. He certainly hadn't wanted to hurt her. In addition, he could hardly believe that milk could come out of a woman's
breast to feed her baby. Yes, when he licked the bouncer he had tried
to think what that would be like. The cat nursed her babies, so he
knew I was telling him the truth, he said. He wished he could
remember what nursing at mother's breast was like, although his
mother had told him many times that he was an ingrate and a snake
at her breast. Didn't women like to feed their babies? The cat Cleo
seemed to like it, but he had doubts that his mother liked "using her
breasts as bottles."

After revealing so much, Lawrence did not want to come to
sessions any more. Clearly, he was terrified that I would give his
secrets away. His parents, unaware of what had transpired, could not
understand why he suddenly turned against therapy, but they were
willing to go along with Lawrence. After all, he had improved
somewhat. They were, however, with some difficulty, persuaded to tell
Lawrence that he had to continue; they felt it would be too hard on
Lawrence to be "forced" into therapy. When I asked them if perhaps
they were confusing their own struggles in therapy with those of their
son, they gained sufficient insight to assume their parental role and
inform Lawrence that he needed to work things through. I had the
impression that they were surprised that I expected them to act in such
a fashion. Somehow they had come to believe that therapists "spoil"
children.

Before Lawrence came back, he sent me a portrait of me (Picture
La8). In it, I was sitting on a chair, my feet barely touching the ground,
and I had no arms. In addition, he was showing me that he now
thought of me as a bird, a sea gull. The word play on my name is
obvious. Lawrence also spoke to me on the phone. I thanked him for
the picture and told him that I thought we had a lot of work to do. He

Picture La8 Portrait of the therapist

told me that he had begun to feel miserable, had taken to his bed, and refused to get up. After the call a physician could find nothing wrong with him. The parents again became very angry. They insisted that Lawrence return to therapy; Lawrence and I were to deal with the malingering immediately or else. I wondered what "or else" could mean but refrained from asking Mrs. K, who felt no compunction about screaming at me too. Both parents were unwilling to consider the possibility that by taking to his bed Lawrence might be identifying with his brother or that he was calling attention to his own psychological ailment in this way.

As he came to his next session, I could hear Mrs. K yelling as she dragged a limp Lawrence from the car to the door of my house. The minute he reached the door to the waiting room, he straightened up, pushed aside his mother's flailing hands, and marched in. He was now willing to talk. Yes, he wanted a different kind of mother. This one bit, kicked, and scratched him when he didn't behave like her little escort. She also lied to him about everything. One time, on a Sunday morning, he had come to his parents' bedroom. They were "doing it," and his father jumped out of bed and beat him up. He wished his father were dead, too. Then he could go to another world and not worry about anything. He admitted that his father beat him regularly as an educational measure. But when his father beat him, he couldn't see; his eyes became hot and red. He couldn't read when he thought about how angry he was. And he thought about his anger all the time. He was glad now that he had beaten other children and humiliated that little girl. It was better to marry an animal. It couldn't talk back. Why did he not tell me before about all this? I asked. He gave me a pitying look. His mother and father wouldn't listen anyway. Besides, he was not at all convinced that I could or would defend him.

This time, the parents were willing to have an interview. I broached the subject of physical punishment. Both parents were perplexed. What did I mean? Of course they hit Lawrence. How else could you bring up such a stubborn child? I tried to explain to them that Lawrence's behavior was symptomatic, that it might appear to be stubbornness, but he really could not help himself at this point. The idea that inner forces impelled their son frightened these parents. They genuinely thought that "children react differently. They have no responsibility, so how can they worry about anything. If you don't punish them, they don't learn." They simply looked at me in disbelief when I tried to explain that Lawrence might be crying out to be given the same attention and care his brother had received, or that he might be trying to relive a time in infancy when he had been comfortable. In bed also he could forget himself in his fantasies and create a world of his own. But to Mr. and Mrs. K this was all nonsense.

The mother had been an orphan, growing up in a variety of foster homes; the father had been brutalized by his own father. Mr. K thought of himself as a model of decorum in relation to his son: "never drawing blood or even bruising the kid." He described himself as being totally in control when he administered beatings to his son and was proud that he "never allowed himself to hit the kid when he was in a temper." Mrs. K thought Lawrence was "lucky to have parents who were so involved with him." She could see nothing overstimulating or punitive or harsh or demanding or seductive in her behavior vis-à-vis her son. Feeling that he was "too young to notice," she was surprised to learn that Lawrence might actually be sexually stimulated by seeing her naked in her bath. She doubted that I was right, but, since she was paying money for my advice, she said she would refrain from calling her son into the bathroom in the future. In addition, because both their own therapist and I insisted, they agreed to withhold physical punishment "for the time being." Both Mr. and Mrs. K predicted dire disaster and wanted me to take responsibility for Lawrence's behavior from now on.

The ensuing year was a difficult one for us all. Lawrence appeared almost bereft when his parents changed their behavior toward him.

He was able to wonder out loud if they would send him away, as they had sent his little brother away. When I pointed out that everyone had wanted the little one "to stay" but that his illness had killed him, Lawrence was, for the first time, able to cry and tell me how much he feared dying himself. He spontaneously made the link to the many horror movies he had told me about. He watched them and liked them, he said, because then he "had a real reason to be scared." We talked for a while about how we make up explanations that aren't really explanations for those things that happen to us. He stuck his hands under his armpits, flapped his arms, and shouted excitedly, "Mrs. Seagull, flap, flap." This was to continue to be his expression of approval whenever we uncovered an emotional truth.

While in the context of the therapy this was a charming expression of Lawrence's dawning positive feelings for his therapist, the rest of the world saw his similar behaviors as eccentric and bizarre. For instance, he left his classroom without permission to bring a glass of milk to a teacher who was coughing and merely shuffled and grunted when confronted with his impulsivity. Another time, he folded his mother's underwear, found her bras, and asked her if she still had any milk "in there." He stopped playing with his friends and once again spent many hours in solitary contemplation in his room. He neither played his records nor watched TV. His mother, visibly perturbed, reported this to me. Both parents felt that they had done something terribly wrong to cause such a regression in their son. They also were quite certain that I was too permissive with him, whom they now saw as lazy. I tried to explain that Lawrence had many things to integrate; he had lost not only a brother but the kind of parents he had always known. He had to reorient himself, literally to reconstruct his world. On hearing me talk in this fashion, Mr. and Mrs. K wanted to start a course of physical punishment again. They were, however, during our conversation shocked to discover that they really did not want to beat up Lawrence any more. Mr. K felt that perhaps his own father had been a "bastard with a stick in hand" but that this was no reason for him to continue with such behavior. Mrs. K did not know really how a mother was supposed to act. She had no role model and was grateful for her therapist's guidance.

At this point, Lawrence invited me to enter his fantasy life. "Remember when I used to think I was from Mars? Well, I am," he asserted. To prove to me that he was a Martian, he drew a series of pictures to show me how he had come to Earth. He accompanied these drawings with elaborate stories. The first in the series (Picture La9) showed him in a space capsule, getting ready to land on Earth. It was very difficult for him because he had amnesia and couldn't remember who he was. He eyes were in the back of his neck and outside of his body, and he had a lot of tentacles that had to adapt to Earth first. He was full of manic glee when he told me this story. He danced on one foot and flapped his arms and called me Mrs. Seagull. First I complimented Lawrence on his verbal skill. I had never heard him use words like "amnesia" before. Then I pointed out to him that perhaps it was easier for him to have a seagull for a therapist than a human. This way we were both different from the rest of humanity. Lawrence was so thrilled with this interpretation that he made up a ditty:

> There is like here,
> here is like there,
> I like it better when you're here,
> don't be there, be here.

Picture La9   Space capsule

The next picture (Picture La10) was an illustration of how he had equipped his space craft. The craft could also go underwater like a submarine and had Campbell's soup, bay leaves, and a lot of miscellaneous food attached to it. But the food was not inside the craft; it swam outside, alongside the ship. Listening to Lawrence in his excited tale, I had an association of my own. The pictures he drew for me had a vague resemblance to some of the illustrations in the book on sex education that I had provided. I told Lawrence that his drawings reminded me of tiny babies inside their mother's womb. One of them was still so unformed that it didn't even look human, but it already had an umbilical cord and a placenta. Lawrence did not even bother to answer verbally. In rapid succession he drew two more pictures (Pictures La11 and La 12). One showed a space craft and a bomb rapidly approaching the earth. The bomb was going to destroy the earth, but the Martian had already landed, was still connected to his space craft, and could therefore avert the expected crash and destruction. The second drawing showed the "unfortunate family that was

Picture La10   How he equipped his space capsule

Picture La11   World destruction

stuck with the Martian. They wanted to be Martians too but couldn't be. So they invited not only the Martian but a seagull to be part of the family, and that's why nobody has hands or feet."

By this time, Lawrence was able to talk about his pictures even if they were a few days or even weeks old. The illustration of the world-destruction fantasy he had carried with him for so long proved to have other meanings as well. He had included a fairly accurate outline of a penis with tiny people in the testicle. These were called "sperm warfare" and represented his fear of one day having a defective child like his brother. That is also why he had wanted to be the cat's husband. He thought that he could thereby avoid having "a stupid angel for a son who goes and dies while I'm away." All his oedipal longings for his mother now surfaced along with his grief that he was unable to provide her with a healthy son. He was quite certain that his father's potency was impaired "because he had two goofy sons, one who died and one who is like me." Though our work together had progressed well, Lawrence had not been able to sustain himself in school. He was in danger of being left back or of being put into a class

Picture La12 Family

for emotionally disturbed children. The parents did not feel that an increase in the number of sessions would help Lawrence. Quite the contrary, they were still sure that I was "spoiling" him but acquiesced to the treatment because they "didn't know what else to do."

Lawrence, in the meantime, was worried about the size of his penis. The friends whom he saw in the gym shower had big, hairy ones, and he still lacked any pubic hair. He started to spy on his mother and father and discovered that those two sad people spent some of their time crying. He was very startled by this discovery. Just as his parents earlier had been unable to fathom their son's emotionality and inner needs, he had thought of his parents as cold and distant giants. He wondered if he might perhaps ask them to go to his brother's grave with him. After much rumination and doubt, he asked his father if this were a possibility. He reported receiving hugs and kisses from both parents "for the first time in his life." Shortly after this event, he confessed that he "wasn't really a Martian. I made it up."

Mr. and Mrs. K were overjoyed to report the same event at our next meeting. Mr. K could "not believe that the little bugger had that much good in him." He believed that they "were lucky he is such a good kid. Otherwise growing up like that, without any real punishment he'd probably turn into a real louse." Despite his father's continued conflict around the issue of physical punishment, Lawrence now thrived. He attended adequately to his school work, began to "hang out" with his former friends, and regained some of his interest in teasing girls. There was, however, a compulsive note in all this that gave me pause. It did not seem logical that a child who had been in such a depression and so regressed would suddenly turn in to "Mr. Neat and Clean," as Mrs. K reported. His pictures, too, were extraordinarily neat (see Picture 13) at the time his parents decided "it was enough." Lawrence presented me with two farewell gifts, one a self-portrait (Picture La14) "so you won't forget me," and an illustration (Picture La15) of "this is how I want to travel in space. I want to be an aerospace engineer."

Discussion

Lawrence exhibited a number of symptoms typical for a child who had been harshly punished. He was a bully and a tease, a hypocrite, and,

Picture La13   Neat and clean picture

Picture La14   Self-portrait engineer

at times, a liar. He assumed that he was "bad" because he could never comply with either the spoken or the unspoken demands of his parents. They had been so traumatized by first the illness and then the death of their younger child that they did not really pay attention to Lawrence. Although they never said so, my impression was that they felt he was lucky to be alive and that they had really preferred their other, unfortunate child. But even before tragedy befell this family, they adhered to a rigid value system that assumed that they were always right and their offspring always wrong. Mrs. K was on occasion able to protect Lawrence from Mr. K's harsh punitive measures, but even in that she seemed to be more attuned to her own unfulfilled need to be "good" than to Lawrence's needs. She also seemed to have no idea that some of her behavior may have been overstimulating and seductive. Mr. K was even proud of his lack of emotion when beating his son, explaining that this kept him from going "too far" and enabled him to stay "fair." In his need to be always right and to have an immediate outlet for his tensions, he did not consider, or was not aware of, Lawrence's developmental needs and rights.

New York
Airways

Picture La15   Space engineer

Thus, Lawrence was left to construct a universe where dog ate dog, where being an animal himself was preferable to being human. His first game in therapy had to do with killing, with being a cannibal, with eating and being eaten. I saw this as a direct outcome of his dehumanizing relationship with his father. At first, he had no way to connect these disjointed fantasy eruptions with reality. But as his attachment to me grew, he was able more directly to express his anger and disappointment with his parents. Finding them together in sexual intercourse had only deepened his hatred of the brutal measures with which they educated him. He went so far as to wish them dead. But then guilt and fear overtook him. Who would take care of him, who was so desperately different? Although there was no opportunity to deal analytically with Lawrence's identification with his younger brother, I am of the opinion that his fantasy of being a Martian was in part inspired by the younger child's infirmity.

Despite his lack of academic achievement, Lawrence was a clever and creative child. He knew that anger with his father prevented him from learning properly and sought to build his own universe. A crucial element in Lawrence's partial recovery was his father's willingness to stop punishing him so harshly. It is not possible to treat a child successfully if the adults who are entrusted with his care do not change their behavior in this regard. Although his father stopped beating him, Lawrence still assumed that he was bad and had to be punished. But that did not mean to him that he had to accept this badness. He explained it to himself by creating the fantasy that he was not human, that he was a creature from Mars.

He dealt with the overstimulation and heightened aggression he felt as a result of the severe beatings he received by identifying with his aggressive father. He became a bully, thus turning the passive defeat of the beatings into an act of mastery. But all this defensive cruelty was hidden under the massive blanket of mourning for the defective child who had died. Lawrence disconnected himself from everyone in order to protect himself from the same fate. In addition, he had been very attracted to his seductive mother who loved him but was unable to protect him from the punitive father. Both parents at first thought that their educative measures were appropriate. Lawrence had learned to accept the brutality of his life as the norm. Therefore, he did not know how to react when his parents changed their behavior. His universe literally fell apart. He had to reconstitute himself on a new level at which he had the responsibility for his own actions. I suspect that restructuring his life had prompted him to be so extra neat. After being so powerless that he had to make himself into a Martian in order to have any identity at all, it probably felt uncomfortable to have no external structure on which to rely. Continued therapy would have benefited Lawrence by providing him with a less stern conscience; that is, he might then have had a choice in the matter of his neatness.

Lawrence used drawing and story-telling spontaneously to convey his feelings and fantasies. At first he used mimicry and pantomime to express his deepest feelings but soon learned to use speech as the major form of communication. His nonverbal productions were often the most telling ones. Like many other children in his position, he needed to release bodily tensions before he could even begin to structure coherent accounts of what was troubling him. At first, he used a rubber transitional object,[2] the bouncer, to express his deeply

---

[2]A transitional object is a toy or other object that helps a child to remember his

wounded and needy, hostile and despairing self. Eventually, his dancelike transference expression of "Mrs. Seagull, flap, flap" enabled him to show affection and receive it. This small oedipal sign reassured me that Lawrence had entered a more evolved phase of development.

Some years later, Lawrence called me to let me know that, as a college student, he was seeking analysis for his lingering conflicts. Clearly, he had benefited from the earlier intervention sufficiently to free himself from his parents' view of the world.

Another boy, Gordon, was less able to express himself in an art form. His plight was even more desperate than Lawrence's.

GORDON

The First Interview

Gordon's parents were very eager for me to see him. They had heard that I sometimes danced or did exercises with children and thought that movement might help their son, who had been diagnosed as being hyperkinetic. They had read about this syndrome and were puzzled that a single symptom was being used as a basis for diagnosis for their son. They knew that a diagnosis ideally should cover more than one aspect of behavior yet they were clearly worn out from the constant chase after Gordon. He had just turned 12 but felt that he was almost a teenager and therefore entitled to privileges his parents were unwilling to grant him. Some of the experts they had consulted felt that Gordon might be minimally brain damaged, but no evidence had been found other than Gordon's chronic hyperkinesis and, lately, his budding antisocial behavior.

His mother told me with great emotion that Gordon had been quite normal until age three, when he suddenly became "a whirlwind." He passed all developmental milestones somewhat early and was reputed to have a high IQ. Mother was a nurse, father a professional athlete. They had five children, of whom Gordon was the third. They

---

significant others when they are not present. All children go through a period of needing some sort of "security blanket." When the need for such an object remains beyond the toddler stage of separation from significant others, it is seen as a pathological phenomenon.

prided themselves on being "aware parents who provided discipline and a healthy life for their children." All the other children were thriving, according to their parents, who were at a loss to explain what "bugged" Gordon. He had been sent to an educational therapist at age seven where he was given perceptual training. Nothing happened except that Gordon liked this lady and wanted to stay with her. He was then sent to a behavioral therapist, who tried to use aversive conditioning with him. This man tried to enlist the parents' support by setting up punishment and reward rituals, which were to disrupt the entire family. When, in addition, Gordon's hyperkinesis became worse, this therapy was discontinued.

Gordon was now in a special education class where he "sassed the teacher because he can do all the work but can't sit still." Mr. and Mrs. W felt that Gordon was right to want to leave school, because there was no one for him "to pal around with" now that he was in a self-contained classroom. He apparently complained about his classmates' handicaps. His parents sympathized with him in this matter, feeling that he was much too normal to be with a group of "losers." At present, he was under the care of a neurologist, who had referred him to me. At the parents' insistence, Gordon was not medicated.

Mr. and Mrs. W themselves were an attractive, well-dressed couple in their 40s. They gave the appearance of being well informed and well intentioned. The only clue that all might not be harmonious and integrated with them was that neither one admitted to being upset about Gordon's pathology. Mrs. W gave me a state-of-the-art smile and said, "It's all in a day's work when you raise a lot of kids." Both parents had already entered family therapy. I hoped that there they might have dealt with their feelings about Gordon.

Course of Treatment

Gordon swaggered into the office. Attired in the latest fashion, shirt unbuttoned all the way down to his belt, he revealed gold chains and amulets on his narrow chest. Mother had warned me that I would be confronted with a child unable to sit still, someone who perpetually perseverated on the same questions. Instead, Gordon, the junior macho man, collapsed into the nearest chair, nonchalantly twirled a key chain and informed me that he felt exceedingly nervous all the time. He also confessed that he felt he had a problem and that nobody could help him. He hated all his teachers, and they hated him. His siblings despised him, but that was okay because he despised them. I told him that first we would have to become acquainted with each other, and then perhaps we could figure out a way to make him feel more comfortable. He snorted derisively but seemed to have felt my genuine concern for his plight because he replied, "My mother calls my older brother 'son.' I'm just Gordon. Do you think she hates me?" Before I could answer, he took a ball out of his pocket and began to play catch against the wall. He looked at me every now and then as though to provoke a negative comment from me. I asked him if he wouldn't prefer to play catch with me. He declined, explaining carefully that he did not feel ball games to be a suitable activity for women. His speech was so stilted and his manner so stiff that I felt he must be imitating someone. He was quite willing to inform me where he got his ideas: from his father. He also told me that he couldn't always live up to his father's notions of what a man should be like. His older brother David, however, was the paragon of all virtues in the family even though he had been kicked out of a seminary for behavior unbecoming a future priest. The whole family was deeply disappointed about his expulsion but rapidly forgave David his transgressions because he was "brilliant." Gordon was incensed about their easy forgiveness. Unlike David, he was punished for everything, even for "little" things like spitting at his mother or not going to school. I asked him if he wanted to test his parents, to see if they would love him even if he were expelled from school. He roared with laughter at the thought that anyone would love him or forgive him for anything.

It was difficult at this point to ascertain how much of Gordon's paranoid attitude was delusional and how much real persecution he had suffered. Surely it was a difficult fate to be grouped constantly with other children who could not perform on the same intellectual level as he. And how wrong, or delusional, was his assumption that his parents preferred his siblings, particularly David? Did he, like classic sufferers of paranoia, believe that the world was indifferent to his need for love? Did he project his own indifference onto other people? Or was he a child whose neurologic or biologic endowment prevented him from structuring an objective reality for himself? I also wondered if this very young man had to defend himself against possibly homosexual impulses by swaggering so grandly and by showing himself superior to females in every way.

It soon transpired that Gordon was an old hand at therapies of every kind. He candidly admitted that he "knew all about the therapy game," was kindly disposed toward doctors and therapists, and felt they were a vaguely benign, but not very useful, group. After all, none of them had ever been able to help him with his headaches or with the terrible thoughts he had of killing "everyone." He told this tale with the most engaging frankness possible, all the while performing tricks with the ball he constantly carried with him. After several sessions of this kind, he threw the ball closer and closer to my head, obviously looking for a comment from me. I asked him if he wanted to hit me with it. Yes, he did. Why? He hadn't been to school for three days, and he was angry with me because I hadn't stopped him. His other doctors had always kept close tabs on his school attendance, and I hadn't called once about his attendance! I wondered out loud how he expected me to know that he wasn't in school and why I should call the attendance office if he did not tell me about his intended truancy. He was very thoughtful about this statement. Finally, he told me that he just assumed that people could read his mind. Why? Because he always got caught at whatever he did. For the first time Gordon showed some genuine emotion. He collapsed on the floor and told me about the many times he had tried to be good but without success. He was sure that his mother hated him. He finally had figured out that he should act like his father because, after all, his mother liked his father. To be like father was to be loved by mother.

This seemed an appropriate enough oedipal thought. But Gordon's identification with father was unmetabolized by his own psyche. He merely enacted his version of a grown-up without really understanding or feeling what he was doing. It was really a longing for symbiosis, for unconditional love from mother, that possessed Gordon.

In the meantime we had been seeing each other for several months, and I still had not seen any of the reported hyperkinesis. He spoke a great deal about wanting to kill people, to beat them up, and of the unbearable loneliness of being an outsider in a large family. Gordon had an outstanding need to fall down every once in a while. He would literally collapse on the floor, whimper, cover his head, beseech me not to come near him, and then spend the rest of the session curled up on the floor. That behavior was in such sharp contrast to the usual manipulative macho charm that I was certain he was acting out something too painful to talk about. As a matter of fact, he swore me to secrecy about these scenes and forbade me to mention them to his parents.

Though I was very concerned about the paranoid flavor of all of Gordon's productions, his parents were thrilled about his "improvement." They now admitted that he had been a chronic truant but were delighted that his attendance during the last semester had been impeccable.

Shortly afterward, Gordon fell ill. When he returned to therapy, he seemed unable to sustain his former macho persona. He immediately collapsed in his favorite corner and told me of a frightening dream. He had seen himself floating above the kitchen, the earth was moving through the air, and half the moon was also there. He grabbed for it but couldn't get a hold of it. His associations were interesting: it turned out that mother never cooked for the family. Father, and occasionally grandmother, who had come to live with the family, did the cooking. Gordon felt that he did not get enough to eat. As proof, he took his shirt off to show me his protruding ribs. I noticed some odd marks on his back. He explained that "while I had a fever, I fell down the stairs." I did not then have proof that anybody was abusing Gordon, and there was no way of ascertaining what had happened other than to ask the parents. That no one was starving Gordon was clear enough. Therefore I assumed, and filed away as private information, that Gordon was emotionally starved, that possibly the half moon in the dream represented his mother's ungiving breast.

During their next visit, the parents corroborated Gordon's story. But they were uncomfortable about Gordon for other reasons. He had threatened to kill his younger brother Kenneth with a broom handle. Why? Kenneth, afraid of him, had refused to let him into the house. I inquired why Kenneth was so afraid of Gordon. Well, actually, the parents said, they had advised him to lock the door until they got home. Since his physical illness, Gordon had been suffering from the delusion that they were starving him and that Kenneth got his portions of food. I asked why they had not told me this before. They were afraid to share it with me "because I might drop Gordon." Had they discussed this with their family therapist? Oh, they weren't going there any more; they "weren't getting anything out of it any more." I strongly suggested that they resume their therapy and continued to probe. But, like their son, they were unwilling to delve more deeply.

Gordon was not surprised when I confronted him with his parents' allegation. He hated that bastard Kenneth because he got more food, all right, but he also had to admit that Kenneth was a nicer kid. Besides, he was being "mainstreamed," and he didn't want any crazy kid brothers hanging around while he studied. This was the first I had heard of his success in school. I felt inclined to laud him but thought better of it. Gordon still didn't like it when people came close to him, as when they praised him. Instead, I asked him if he would like to have a graduation party to mark his move from the self-contained classroom to a regular classroom. He brightened up at this, and we fixed a date for the celebration, which was to take place in the office and include "booze." I told him it would have to be make-believe booze, and he readily agreed. When the appointed day came, Gordon brought soda, and I ordered a pizza. Gordon was in seventh heaven. He made believe that he was drinking rum and coke, wished that we had beer to go with the pizza, and gorged himself. He let himself fall on the floor with a contented sigh but did not curl up in his usual position. I thought it best not to interpret his behavior; I hoped that the reality of eating to his heart's content in the presence of someone he trusted at least peripherally might do him good. I am not usually inclined to offer so-called corrective emotional experiences to my young patients. I feel that this approach, though well intentioned, is too concrete. In my opinion, it does not aid internalization and growth but offers only immediate gratification. But Gordon seemed to be so unable to remember any sort of gratification that I bent my rules. I was very puzzled about the apparent split in Gordon's behavior. While there were many grandiose and even delusional features in his makeup, I really did not feel that he was truly dangerous or suffered from a borderline condition. There was something candid, even innocent, in his behavior that continued to engage me in a very positive way.

His behavior during sessions changed once he was in "regular class with regular kids." He never stopped talking, all the while imperson-ating all the new youngsters he had met, the new teachers, parents of new friends; his whole new world appeared to overstimulate him. When he finally paused to take a long breath during a session, I asked what was so different in the homes he now visited. Well, they weren't messy, everybody behaved themselves, and the mothers didn't hit the kids. Did his mother hit him? I asked. Yes, all the time. Proudly, he informed me that he "held still when Ma hits. But when David hits me, I run." Why did those two hit him? Just because. Mother, in his opinion, hit him because she thought girls were better than boys. David hit him to protect mother. Did he attack mother? No, of course not! How could I think such a thing?

Gordon now became a veritable storm of excitation. He whirled about the room, kicked at furniture, hit the wall with his fists, and in paroxysm of despair flung himself on the floor, shouting invective at me. He felt he could no longer trust me because I had questioned his behavior. It seemed to me that Gordon was hurt because he felt himself symbiotically tied to me and could not brook the feeling of my being separate from him. His subsequent actions corroborated my hypothesis.

During the next few sessions, he was calmer but could not sit still. After almost a year in treatment, I finally was treated to an exhibition of his famous hyperkinesis. During this frenetic time, both in and out of sessions, he had many minor accidents. He spilled water, broke toys, tore books accidentally, bruised his shins, cut his finger, and, finally, broke an arm. At least once each session, he "collapsed," although now he said he needed to be on the floor and cover his head. Without the inner connectedness to me, he fell back on his former self-destructive behavior, though his cognition did not seem as impaired as previously.

As I watched the scenes of his falling, it had associatively occurred to me that Gordon might be showing me how he behaved during an attack. He certainly looked like someone who was defending himself against being beaten up. Yet, though he was quick to offer to beat anyone at all up, and often spoke of fights between himself and his brother or mother, he never complained about abuse from them other than the imagined starvation.

At this point, the parents decided to see their therapist again. Gordon took full credit for their move. He told his father after every of his own sessions with me, "Pa, you need to have therapy." At first, both parents thought he was again just being a "fresh mouth," but they became worried about his accidents and his constant fighting with David. Thinking that they could not sufficiently control either son, they decided to seek further help. Besides, Gordon had failed English and math again, and they wanted, at all costs, to prevent his being returned to special education classes. It was not clear to them how and why their earlier therapy might have made an impact on Gordon's school career, but it had worked once; maybe therapy would work again.

Confronted by so much magical thinking on the part of the parents, I wondered to myself what other "magic" they had up their sleeves and asked as casually as I could, what, besides going to therapy and talking to him, they did with Gordon when he was unruly. They looked at me with pity. Why, they beat him, of course, they said. I asked if they had discussed the beatings with their family therapist. No, they hadn't, but they would do so.

Matters went from bad to worse. Mr. W accused Gordon of tattling to me and of being disloyal to the family "that had so devotedly cared for him and his craziness all these years." Gordon, outraged by such an accusation, swung at his father and consequently received "the beating of his lifetime." Mrs. W intervened by pouring a pail of water over the combatants with the result that Gordon turned on her. She bit him in the ear, and that supposedly "brought him to his senses." The parents and Gordon told me about this occurrence on the phone and at a monthly family session.

Gordon now sank into an abyss of depression. Nobody in his large family was on his side, he said. There were terrible fights daily. Mrs. W wanted Gordon to be medicated. Mr. W fought this notion vigorously for fear that medicines would "stunt Gordon's growth." Gordon related all this while curled up on the floor of my consultation room. He had given up doing any homework at all. He weakly suggested that his academic failures were, once again, his teacher's fault, but he no longer believed that himself. He was trying to cope with the terrible reality that his parents were indeed abusive and that family life in his household was not as it "should be." Gordon alternated between wanting to kill himself for bringing so much strife into his family and wanting to kill everyone in sight. Eventually he sobbed, "If I had wanted to kill myself I would have done so long ago. I'll stay around just to make everybody suffer."

While the parents were trying to come to terms with their own hostility, suddenly the favored brother, David, began to act out. He was caught trying to sell a small amount of hard drugs. When confronted by the family's outrage and grief, he told them that Gordon had stolen some marijuana from him and sold it. Gordon expected to be "killed" for this past transgression and was amazed and shaken when, instead, the parents tried "to get out of him why he would do such an asocial thing." He could barely deal with this approach. He exhorted his parents to hit him, to beat him so the terrible pain in his head would go away. But the terrible pain in his head was a psychologically determined one. Accustomed for so long to living in a "war zone," Gordon could not at first assimilate another mode of existing. He appeared to need the malevolent internalization of the past in order to make sense out of his universe. In sessions, he would greet me with "Hello-goodbye. Gordon isn't here." He wanted me to bring his mother or his father into our sessions and to confront them for him. He did not believe that in their own therapy they were talking about hitting him.

While he was engaged in this inner struggle over what to believe and whom to love, Gordon for the first time created a symbolic game. He couched it in real enough terms. He had just entered high school, an event he and his parents had dreaded because the transfer from grade school to junior high had been so traumatic for all. But this time, the transition took place without much upheaval. Gordon weathered his first few weeks with some grumbling and then began to examine the new social order in which he found himself. According to him, he had to decide whether he was going to join "the hoods" or "the collegiates." He explained to me that both groups had enormous advantages but that neither quite suited him. He appeared puzzled by the fact that the hoods had rules and regulations of their own; he had heard from his father that hoods were a lawless bunch. The collegiates, on the other hand, abided by all the "old folks'" rules. He certainly didn't want to be dull like that. But most puzzling of all was that his family, who claimed to be among the collegiates, also violated rules and sometimes behaved like hoods. Gordon could not cope with this dichotomy. He kept blowing up long balloons, twisting them, then popping them with as much noise as possible. I was glad that he had resorted to such a relatively mild way of showing his pain until he arrived one day to inform me that he had been really violent that day but would not tell me what had happened. A phone call from mother brought clarification. She had been cleaning the floor when Gordon wanted lunch. When he would not stop pestering her to give him something to eat immediately, she hit him with a broom handle and broke a yard stick on his back. She had often done this in the past but had lately resisted doing so. Much to her surprise, Gordon turned on her and hit her back. Both were so stunned by this unusual inter-change that they both burst into tears. Mrs. W begged me to discuss this with Gordon.

He, however, informed me that mother had lied. He had never hit her; she had never hit him. Instead, he wanted to tell me about the magic, "Catholic magic" he believed in. Wondering what he meant by this, he told me that he "did the thing with his penis and the priest didn't like it." Simultaneously, he grabbed at his crotch. Shame-facedly, he told me that every time he and his mother fought, he had an erection. He didn't know why, but it felt good at first, then horrible. Again, he popped balloons but told me immediately that they represented mother.

He drew a series of boxes and told me that they contained his present, past, and future and held his voice, his coffin, and his shoes. We talked a while about the meaning contained in these symbols. I told him that perhaps he wanted to keep everything in boxes because he might be afraid that his past would spoil his present or his future. But what about his voice, his coffin, and his shoes? Why did he want to put those into boxes? Turning bright red, Gordon told me that he wanted to have a girl, not a crazy girl, a real one and put "his shoes under her bed." I asked if the boxes also represented vaginas. He quickly drew circles and popped a few more balloons. "The women must die," he declared. After much denial and rationalization, Gordon also confessed that he often felt sexually aroused when he was being beaten. Since he had no power to stop the beatings, he unconsciously tried to enjoy them. He was able to make a connection between such a reversal of affect and his clowning in class when he could not tolerate his teacher or the other children. It "felt the same, if I get hit or if I get laughed at or bossed," he said.

Having belatedly arrived at his own version of the Oedipus complex, Gordon began to make rapid progress. Along with being able to talk rather than act out his despair and hostility, he began to recall some of his "outrageous childhood." When he was three or four years old, his dog had puppies. He painted them blue and then got scared and tried to wash them off in the bathtub. When he was caught with this mess, a beating ensued. After a while, the parents tired of hitting him all the time and turned the job over to the oldest boy, David, who "put a branding mark on him [Gordon] with a wire coat hanger." Other childish mischief all had the same result: beatings. But Gordon could not stop himself. In a vicious cycle, parents and son provoked each other into more and more abusive behavior.

Gordon was embarrassed by the erections that plagued him when he spoke of violence. He wanted to be able to control them but found he didn't like "to jerk off unless there were other guys around." He masturbated only in the gym shower or in the locker room when the presence of other boys reassured him that his penis would not fall off. We had to talk many times about how endangered he must have felt by the constant physical abuse that had rained down on him and how hard it was to love parents who were so cruel. He was especially hurt by his mother's failure to soothe him. Apparently she had in the past stood up for him but had eventually "given up and joined the crowd," beating Gordon. At first Gordon thought he wanted to be just a man without women around. But now he began to see that "a man needs a woman" and wanted his mother's approval.

During the sessions he played "oldies but goodies," records he thought his mother must have liked when she was a teenager. At this point, the family thought it was advisable that Gordon join their family therapy sessions instead of continuing his therapy with me. He was eager to do so but did not know how to take leave from me. He and I discussed that it was too early for him to leave but that he had to fit in with his family. He told me on parting that some day he "would like to have a woman who is something special like a therapist."

Gordon kept in touch for a long time, informing me of the long and arduous rehabilitation of his family. He eventually joined the United States Armed Forces, where, I hear, he has become a noncommissioned officer.

Discussion

When Gordon entered therapy he was beset by many symptoms that seemed caused by brain damage or psychosis. His parents' violence had done much damage to this child, who, in retrospect, was probably just a high-spirited little boy who got into a lot of mischief. As with Lawrence, there was a direct correlation between his parents' excessively punitive behavior and his pathology. There was no real change in Gordon's inner world until his parents resolved to curb their hostilities. Yet it was quite clear that despite all that had happened Gordon not only was attached to his family but loved them. He seriously thought of killing himself to remove himself as a constant source of irritation. Only his identification with an almost delusional ideal of a macho man allowed him to withstand the isolation and despair of not being loved enough. He offered himself over and over again as the scapegoat, channeling the parents' aggression toward himself, thus keeping a dysfunctional family intact.

There is no doubt that Gordon was a provoker. Even his clowning in the classroom had a provocative edge. It allowed him to be "on top" of whatever real and imagined misfortune came his way. And the provocations he came up with had an objective: to provide tension discharge for everyone involved. Gordon wanted to love his parents, an obviously difficult endeavor. Instead of progressing through age-appropriate phases, he stayed symbiotically tied to mother as he imagined her to have been when he was a baby. But that mother did not exist any longer. When, in therapy, he came in touch with this longing, he declared that he was being starved.

In addition, he kept himself going by internalizing truly malevolent interpersonal relationships. As long as mother and father were seen as "bastards," he felt entitled to hate them and to provoke them beyond endurance. The only way he could let me know the true state of affairs was by acting out how it was to be beaten. He collapsed on the floor and slowly let me see his despair and pain. When during treatment he began to gain limited insight into his family's dynamic, he psychologically collapsed even further. It was more comforting for him to think that he was all bad and his parents justified in their treatment of him than to realize that they too had problems. When his malevolent introjects finally could no longer hold up, he sank into deep despair. He no longer had a way of orienting himself in his world. He had to build up his own image and that of his family all over again. He began to instinctualize and to sexualize both his own aggression and that of his family until he was finally able to uncover a more evolved kind of longing for his mother.

Although his lurking in the gym shower and the locker room of his school appeared to be homosexual, it was really in the service of refinding his masculinity. He had always felt himself to be supremely male, but this was a false maleness that had little to do with becoming a man. These struggles, too, were brought into therapy and partially resolved. Gordon was unable to symbolize his feelings or, indeed, to think about them, instead of reliving everything, until he began to reach the negative oedipal phase. But in this phase he did not look to his father for identification; father had been too brutal a man for that. Instead, Gordon identified with the boisterous boys he met in school. He brought some of his positive oedipal feeling to me as a parting gift.

Gordon was not really interested in the special techniques I used with the other children. He drew a primitive picture only once, to illustrate one of his infrequent dreams and to show me that he understood my interpretation. He fell on this device by himself because words failed him. He did the drawing at a time when he was just beginning to symbolize rather than act out his conflicts. It was quite a step forward when he began to break balloons symbolically. At one point I fed him, literally, to celebrate his graduation from a self-contained classroom. I did this in order to meet an early and primitive oral need before a true working alliance had formed. I also on occasion associated out loud to his dreams in order to build verbal bridges for him.

SUMMARY

As can be seen in the cases of Lawrence and Gordon, parents must be persuaded to give up their punitive behavior. Most parents are willing to reexamine their modes of punishment only after they have come to terms with the "betrayal" of the child who has told the therapist or teacher what has happened. Prominent child psychoanalysts (Buxbaum, 1935; Fraiberg, 1962; Weil, 1989) have long been aware that their best efforts will come to naught if the parents do not agree that they themselves as well as the child must change. At first this change in the parents is merely external. But it is enough for the child to gain confidence that its life is worthwhile after all. I am of the opinion that children like Lawrence and Gordon are unusually strong to have withstood such abuse. They still have the capacity to change and even to forgive their harsh parents.

I do not know which child suffered more: Lawrence, whose father thought it was his right and his duty to thrash his son; or Gordon, who became the scapegoat for the entire family's pathological rages. Both children nearly lost their sense of reality testing and gave up on themselves. Loss of the ability to test reality is typical of children who must learn to survive in a nightmare world. That they do not become psychotic is probably due to their once, at a very early time in their lives, having been appreciated and loved after all.

Galdston (1981) reports a study of 75 families who in many ways were like Lawrence's or Gordon's family. He noted that the mothers all declared their love of being pregnant and of caring for infants. They did not start to complain about their children until the onset of walking and talking. They could not tolerate the striving for independence and in many ways prevented their children from acquiring the skills for autonomous functioning. These findings are echoed particularly in Gordon's case. Nonetheless, at one time, very early in their lives, Lawrence's and Gordon's mother had nurtured them sufficiently so that there was a small area of health and hope to be reached and worked with.

It is difficult for children who were nurtured only in infancy to give up their present provocative behavior. At first they deny and rationalize their own provocativeness because it is the only way they have of understanding their parents' behavior. If they turned "good" right away, the parents would not know what to do! Or so the children think. Often they are right, and then they have to face, as Gordon did, the uncomfortable truth that mom and dad are far from perfect. Other children hold the belief that their parents need them to be bad, too, but give it up in the course of their development. But because the situations are so desperate for children like Lawrence and Gordon, they defensively hold on to the belief that their parents are always right and they themselves are always wrong.

The most puzzling aspect of these cases is that short-term histories never uncover the basis for all these troubles. Parents and children are united in not seeing and telling about the origins of their conflicts. It is necessary for the clinician to keep a sharp eye out for signs of what is really going on. For instance, there are always learning problems and a tendency to do the opposite of what an authority wishes, as was the case with Lawrence and Gordon. Often the parents report that the children laugh while they are being punished – not that there is ever any talk of corporal punishment. Just "the usual" or other euphemisms. Delinquency is often a factor. The children are characterized by their families and their peers as incapable of appropriate emotional discharge. The children are almost always preoccupied with all aspects of destruction: they think and talk about killing, breaking things, stealing, and robbing. Just as often, they act on these fantasies.

When children have suffered excessive punishment, not only learning difficulties follow. Their negative behavior escalates and takes over more and more portions of their lives. They reverse their affect and do the opposite of what is expected. But these reversals and oppositions do not at all protect them. Instead of being directed against the source of irritation and punishment, their affects and reversals are discharged diffusely, inappropriately, and excessively against everyone. This discharge keeps the internal image of the perfect parent intact. Eventually, this affects the child's cognitive processes so that he turns against even those people who are trying to help. When the adults in authority see themselves constantly defied and laughed at, they, in turn, withdraw. Thus, the myth of the incorrigible and untreatable child arises.

As frightful and as difficult to recognize as the plight of these children is, there is another category of children whose fate is even more disturbing. I am referring to children who have been sexually used by adults.

CHAPTER 5

≈≈

I Don't Understand Anything at All
Children Who Have Suffered Sexual Abuse

Recently, mental health workers have uncovered and brought to the attention of the public the many instances of sexual abuses all too many children are subjected to. This is still a subject that is taboo in many quarters. People just cannot believe that such things can happen in the home of anyone they know. That it could exist in their own families is almost universally denied. Mothers, for instance, are often the last ones to understand what is happening to their daughters. Fathers do not believe that any adult woman would want to seduce and abuse their sons. Homosexual seductions are even more vigorously denied. Yet considerable psychiatric and epidemiologic work (Finkelhor, 1979; Herman, 1981; Mrazek and Kempe, 1981) substantiates that some adults are so sexually dysfunctional that they need to use children to satiate their impulses. Children, of course, have no resources for judging such behavior. There may even have been a pleasurable side to their being seduced by an adult with offers of candies and toys and what appeared to be unconditional praise. The obvious distaste of other adults in whom the child tries to confide discourages disclosure, and so the abuse may go on for a long time before it is uncovered. When children are accused of lying or meet irritation and disbelief when they seek help,

141

their sense of reality and trust is destroyed. They become both fearful and manipulative in the struggle to exist at all. The denial of sexual abuse in families is mirrored in the behavior of society at large.

One form of sexual abuse, incest, was discussed when Freud asserted the now familiar seduction theory of neurosis in his papers "Studies on Hysteria" (Freud 1893 to 1895) and "The Aetiology of Hysteria" (1896). Freud was certain that all his patients who suffered from this disorder had been subjected to sexual seduction in childhood. But a year later, in a letter to his friend Wilhelm Fliess (1897), he renounced this view and concluded instead that his patients were talking of fantasies that had been built on incestuous wishes. Why did he reach this conclusion? He writes, "Then the surprise that in all cases, the father, not excluding my own, had to be accused of being perverse – the realization of the unexpected frequency of hysteria with precisely the same conditions prevailing in each, whereas surely such widespread perversions against children are not very probable" (p. 264).

Freud's monumental discovery of the universality of oedipal wishes proved to be one of the cornerstones of psychoanalytic theory despite his disbelief in the ubiquity of childhood seduction. As clinical and observational research has proven, how a child or adult reacts to trauma and how trauma is elaborated in the psyche can nurture or destroy the inner self. That is, the reaction and fantasized elaboration secondarily emphasize and make more destructive a harmful incident. For instance, a child may not have been physically harmed by an adult masturbating between her thighs, but the remembered pressure of a heavy adult on her chest and the wetness between her legs may conjure up fantasies of monsters persecuting her, with the result that she can no longer learn or play happily. This is so even when the incident itself has been repressed.

Until very recently, reports of early seductions were all too often analyzed as mere fantasies. And, indeed, it takes skill, perseverance, and a very open mind until corroborative material arrives in the form of dreams, memories, and, sometimes, family members' recall. Very often if there has been a seduction, psychosomatic complaints are present. These complaints, in one form or another, symbolize what happened to the patient. But not all patients beset by psychosomatic complaints or who act out constantly have been subjected to incest or other abuse. Where, then, does the seduction theory apply and where does it not? The answer depends on the context in which development of the patient was interrupted, stagnated, or otherwise was impinged upon. But focusing on the fantasy or other symbolic productions of a patient does not mean that in psychoanalytic or psychodynamic treatment one should ignore the influences of actual trauma. Freud himself never was so radical in his assumptions. He said in 1924, "I attributed to the aetiologic factor of seduction a significance and universality it does not possess. . . . Nevertheless, we need not reject everything. . . . Seduction retains a certain aetiologic importance" (p. 168).

It took many years for objective researchers to follow Freud's lead and substantiate incest as a problem in our society. Kinsey, Pomeroy, Martin and Gebhard found in 1953 that 5.5% of a large white, middle-class sample reported sexual abuse by a family member in childhood. A more intensive follow-up conducted by Gagnon (1965) with 1200 women found a 4% incidence of incest. Not surprisingly, psychiatric reports are even more tragic. For instance, Husain and Chapel (1983) found that 14% of 437 girls admitted to a psychiatric hospital had histories of incest.

Despite the reluctant acknowledgment of society that incest is a problem, no direct ways of protecting children have been found. Many schools warn children against going into cars with strangers. Many families try to safeguard their children with warnings as well. But how much can one warn without destroying a child's trust in the world at large, and how can one protect a child from a possibly beloved family member who is sexually dysfunctional?

These are questions for which answers have yet to be found. Child Protective Services are employable only after the deed has been uncovered. Mental health professionals and all individuals entrusted with the care of children are required by law to report all cases of sexual abuse that come to their attention to Child Protective Services. Despite such vigilance, many children still are sexually abused. This happens because the popular picture of the seducer of small children is that of an alcoholic brute who rapes the little one. This can, and does, happen. More often, though, there is a period of seduction that lulls the child while also making it feel guilty. Feelings of grandiosity that it has been chosen to be an adult's playmate alternate with intense agitation and desperate struggles to control overstimulation. When the child does complain, the horror of sexual abuse is often denied on the common assumption that "he (or she) couldn't have done it. She [the child] drove him to it, the slut." The victim is turned into the victimizer, in order to save the third party the need for intervention.

Shengold (1963) studied the impact of seduction by psychotic mothers on their male children. He found that the children needed to deny they had a bad mother and instead fantasized an idealized mother. Thus, the recollection of incest was laborious and had to rely a great deal on psychoanalytic reconstruction, which rests not only on data regarding the clarity of the recollection itself but also on corroborating evidence in the present.

Beres (1958) describes a teenage girl's telling of incest with her father. The girl's immediate response to her own disclosure was

> a mixture of a conscious expression of relief at her confession, a feeling of guilt that she had betrayed her father, and a resentment against the psychiatrist to whom she had revealed the details of her sexual experiences. Subsequently, she manifested a striking, fluctuant type of behavior: on the one hand there was ingratiation, conformity and desire to please, neatness and propriety in behavior and dress; on the other hand there were impulsive outbursts, both of aggressive behavior and involvement in precarious situations . . . [p. 331].

These striking vacillations in a child's behavior can, indeed, be the tip-off that something in the nature of forbidden sexual encounters may be troubling the child. It is also a good phenomenologic description of certain borderline personalities. Marcus (1989) links such behavior to the borderline disturbances and sees a link between incest and the later development of a borderline personality organization. She feels that certain aspects of psychic development cannot take place when incest has occurred. She sees as crucial to the development of pathology the interruption of the establishment of boundaries, which are essential for identity formation. She argues that "in vulnerable individuals, incest impacts on the consolidation of intermediate phases in the establishment of internal/external boundary, whether concurrent or retrospectively; that is, relatively independent of the chronological age in incestuous contact" (p. 204).

Quite simply, incest is injurious at any age. I would like to add that sexual abuse of any kind leaves its deleterious impact. One's most personal borders are disrespected and even destroyed in unwanted sexual contact. For a child, any such contact with an adult who obliterates generational boundaries invariably symbolizes incest and is harmful.

It must be understood that an incestual relationship, and often is not only an event. It involves even one-time sexual abuse, is not only an event. It involves a relationship within a setting, most often the family, which denies the existence, meaning, and impact of the abuse. There is also the influence upon the child of the parent who allows the abuse to occur. Such blindness leads to further distortion and impairs development for the child because it impedes necessary identifications (King and Dorpat, in press).

Therapists who treat sexually abused children have many difficulties. Because of the intensity of feelings involved, the child immediately sees the therapist as a rescuer, but also as an abuser who extracts secrets from their hiding places, as the neglectful parent from whom protection cannot be sought, and as the helpless child himself. The child, unable to control what happens to its own body, can to a certain extent control some of the bodily processes of the abusing adult. All children fantasize that they can be the sexual partner of their significant adults, but their sense of reality and their ability to test this reality keeps them safe. They know they are fantasizing and eventually, when they are teenagers, transfer their affections to someone their own age. But when they have been sexually used by an adult, the childish fantasies are cruelly fulfilled. The child is the sexual partner but not the sexual equal of an adult. Thus, internal and external reality become blurred. The external reality includes the body boundary of the child, which has been intruded upon. The child is often not sure whether or not the event really occurred. In order to escape the painful recognition of inadequacy, betrayal, and helplessness, the child tries to repress, but only manages to suppress from surface consciousness, what has happened. This suppression takes a great deal of energy, leaving none free for age-appropriate tasks. Learning becomes difficult and social adaptation even more so. Precisely because the child's physical boundaries have been disregarded, he or she now also tends to disregard the therapist. How can a stranger help when parents have been so negligent and unempathic? The child withdraws and goes through life mechanically, occasionally erupting into inappropriate, often violent, delinquent behavior. The therapist experiences strong feelings that may prevent him or her from being effective. Revulsion for the adults who abused the child may obfuscate clear thinking. The therapist may harbor thoughts of rescuing the child (who may not want to be rescued) or may wish to be rid of the whole messy life situation that has to be dealt with. The situation can be so devastating that beginning therapists especially would be well advised to seek further supervision or personal therapy. To illustrate what I mean, here is the story of seven-year-old Joanie.

JOANIE

The First Interview

Mr. and Mrs. D were an interesting contrast. Mr. D was round, voluble, and smiling. He wore his crumpled clothing with a certain style. After selecting my customary chair to sit on, he realized he was in the "driver's seat" and affably joined his wife on the settee. He held her hand comfortingly. She, many years younger than her husband, was impeccably and stylishly dressed and very pretty. She seemed stiff and ill at ease. She fidgeted and then sat so still she looked as though she had been hypnotized. Theirs was the second marriage for both of them. Joanie was the child they had "together." Father owned a chain of delicatessen stores; mother was an accountant with a large firm. They were very eager to tell me how they met and why they had left their first marriages but did not say much about Joanie until I reminded them why they had come to consult me. Mrs. D had left two sons with her former husband but had brought her daughter, Ashley-Anne, with her to this marriage. This arrangement had turned out very well for all concerned.

Ashley-Anne, a good girl who made good grades, was the only person who could cope with little Joanie. Babysitters as well as German and English nannies had left the family's employ because Joanie was "impossible." Only Ashley-Anne could put Joanie to bed. But even though Joanie had a wonderful, designer-furnished room of her own she often was found sleeping in her sister's bed. Ashley-Anne did not seem to mind, and so the family had gotten used to seeing the two girls in one bed, in one room, and, in some ways, as one person. Mrs. D thought the girls' relationship was "cute in view of the fact that

Ashley-Anne is 10 years older than Joanie." My offhand remark that Mrs. D did not seem old enough to have a 17-year-old daughter finally made her relax. Father guffawed appreciatively. He thought his wife young too and patted her thigh while she fastidiously pulled back from him.

Both parents reported that Joanie was "devious and a bitch. She lies." Father amended this opinion by saying that Joanie "was a chip off the old block. She is a pain in the you-know-what but strong, really strong, like me and my family. My wife's family are all hypersensitive and aesthetes." Mrs. D was obviously uncomfortable and tried to stop him from going on. Yes, Joanie was a strong child. She had weighed nine lbs. at birth and had been born with some teeth, which the pediatrician pulled without anesthetic. Mrs. D was convinced that this experience had "done something" to Joanie although it had been explained to her that babies cannot feel such interventions. Mr. and Mrs. D then proceeded to argue about the pros and cons of giving a small baby anesthetic for the purposes of pulling teeth. By the time they had sufficiently calmed themselves, the session was at an end. They agreed to come for a further "first" interview. They were annoyed that I would not see Joanie without further information from them. Joanie had lately began to rock herself "on her heels" while crouching on the floor "like a lunatic," as Mr. D graphically put it. The next session was somewhat less emotional. Both parents now agreed that it was good that Joanie was going to start treatment with me because she was in danger "of being the first kid to flunk first grade in the history of the school."

Joanie had been so quiet as an infant that her mother was continuously afraid she might be dead. Mother was sure that Joanie was in shock as a result of her early dental history. She kept looking into the crib to check on the baby and instructed the baby nurse to do the same. When Joanie was seven-and-a-half months old, "things changed. She snapped out of her trance." There was a decided change. Joanie became willful, would not allow strangers near her, and became very attached to her father. Neither parent seemed aware that around eight months of age babies have developed sufficient cognitive and social skills to experience stranger anxiety (Spitz, 1965). When I explained this to them, they seemed confused and did not to want to hear that Joanie had acted "normally." They wanted to tell me that father handled her and bathed her every day. Mother was rejected to such an extent that she sought therapy and eventually managed to "get herself back into Joanie's graces." The child was able to tyrannize the family. Ashley-Anne was afraid of Joanie's temper tantrums, during which she held her breath and screamed until she was "blue and fainted."

Between 15 and 22 months, she became increasingly frustrated, the result, Mrs. D thought, of her inability to communicate. As soon as she could speak, her behavior became more nearly normal, although she continued to have "states," temper tantrums, and screaming fits. The "states" appeared to be twilight states during which the child wandered through the house with a fixed stare, not recognizing anyone, or clinging to Ashley-Anne. Along with this tale of upheaval and unhappiness, the mother told me that babies responded to, and were fond of, Joanie. How did they know? Joanie spent every minute she could find in the company of several young babies who lived on their street, cooing to them and playing with them. Mr. D was very upset with this turn of events. He wanted Joanie to have friends her own age and could not understand what satisfaction she derived from being with infants. It seemed that Ashley-Anne had also taken a liking to babies and now wanted to become a pediatrician, a choice that horrified both parents. They thought she would be better off "finding herself a man and getting settled." They were both eager for the teenager to leave the house but dreaded her absence because then nobody would be there to soothe Joanie. I suggested therapy for Mr. D, but he, in his genial way, refused "for now." It was enough that his "women saw shrinks." On their way out, Mr. D, with a merry wink, informed me that he and his wife had separate bedrooms and that Joanie probably took after his wife. "They are both bitches and strong," he said.

Course of Therapy

It was difficult to recognize in freckle-faced, shy Joanie the-bitch-and-manipulator her parents claimed her to be. Stomach thrust out, feet turned in, she chewed on the hem of her dress, looking younger than her seven years. She answered each question with a barely audible "I don't know." Her mother was in the room with us because Joanie would not come without her. After spending a while sizing me up, she offered me a witch puppet and took one representing a king. She vaguely gesticulated with both puppets until I asked if her puppet felt scared. "No," she said, dropped both puppets, and firmly pushed her mother out the door. Then she informed me that she was not allowed to eat candy, that she was on a diet, and that her mother "didn't miss the boys at all." These cryptic remarks were the only concrete verbal communications I was to receive from Joanie for quite some time.

For the next session, Joanie appeared in leotards and tights, probably in response to the prompting of her mother, whom I had told that on occasion I dance with the children in order to help them express themselves. But Joanie was not interested in dancing. Instead, she plunked herself down on the floor and began to writhe. Looking at Joanie's pudgy body contorting itself on the floor and seeing her pained facial expression, I became very uneasy. I could not then quite admit even to myself that this seven-year-old was acting like an adult woman in the throes of passion, but my unease alerted me to the fact that I should not mirror or in any way join this game. Physical mirroring in dance therapy is a technique to convey nonverbally to the patient that one is aware and accepts whatever the message is. In this case, my intuition informed me that I would be joining in, and perhaps reinforcing, an unholy union with a traumatizing event not yet understood and possibly destructive to the child. Eventually, after Joanie had added some grunts and coos to her performance, we decided to call her game "the Earthworm." In subsequent sessions she would do nothing else. I understood that a tension release was involved for her, and I did not interfere, although at times her behavior had an almost seizurelike quality.

In the meantime, both parents were delighted with Joanie's "progress." She had begun to talk more freely at home; there had been no temper tantrums for quite some time; and at school the teacher, for the first time seemed satisfied with Joanie's efforts. Now the parents wanted me to "work on Joanie's sleeping habits." It seemed the child would simply decline to enter her own bed. Instead, she made a beeline for Ashley-Anne's bed when bedtime came. In addition, she spent hardly any time at home and preferred to "hang out" with the neighborhood babies. Mr. D, feeling the neighborhood ladies were taking advantage of his daughter by having her babysit with no renumeration, was disgruntled. Mrs. D protested, however, saying Joanie was never left alone with the babies and so was not babysitting.

Joanie now embarked on a series of games with puppets and dolls.

Everyone was always put to bed and then shuffled around with much glee. Mothers always asked the doll babies to go to bed. They did not, choosing instead to sleep with their sisters and, interestingly, with their fathers. Despite this game, Joanie insisted that she had never been in her father's bed. When she told me this, she wiggled her little fanny and became coy, again giving me an uneasy feeling that she was hiding a good deal more than she was telling.

At the next parent meeting, the atmosphere had changed entirely. Both parents were very angry because Joanie now not only rocked "on her heels" all the time, she also sucked her thumb, pieces of cloth, or her whole hand. Neither parent could tolerate such behavior; they felt it made their daughter look "retarded." They demanded that I help Joanie stop this behavior at once. I asked Joanie about it at the next session and was treated to an interesting shift in activity. Joanie dropped to her knees and crawled over to the bouncer. She had intermittently played with it but had always seemed ambivalent about it. Now she bounced on it a few times, jumped off, and then sharply hit a metal gong the exact number of times she had bounced. When I asked what she thought about this new game, she rushed to the toy shelves, took all the toys off, and lined them up along the walls of the room. This ritual was repeated many times. Joanie never commented on what she did but played quietly after she had built her fence with the toys. I began to understand that lining the walls with all the toys was a way to make herself feel safe. I said as much and was rewarded by a fairly long story. She informed me that she never slept in her parents' bed but that mother often slept in her bed "because it was not wrinkled." Mother also needed Joanie's bed because father took up too much room in the marital bed. Joanie was not willing to enlarge on this disclosure but also claimed that "nobody in her family ever fought or was angry." I answered that it must be very lonely to be the only angry member of such a peaceful family. She quite agreed but also said that her mother had told her that it was all right to be angry in my room, so angry that she could even scratch her thing here if she wanted to. I asked what she meant by her "thing." With a pitying glance, she indicated her vagina. Joanie had no word for that body part. She listened eagerly when I told her that all females have a vagina and need it for many female functions. At this point, Joanie once again needed to play Earthworm, to crawl and make strange grunts and noises. The same seizurelike quality that had startled me before was there also. I repeatedly imagined that Joanie was enacting coitus. Trying to fill in the sketchy information Joanie had verbally given me, I thought that there must have been fights between Mr. and Mrs. D that so frightened the child that she had to deny them. Perhaps Mrs. D had slept in Joanie's bed while Joanie herself was with Ashley-Anne. In the consciousness of children, coitus and murderous fights are often viewed interchangeably. I thought this confusion might be present in Joanie.

While I was still thinking about how to handle this difficult situation, I received a frantic telephone call from Mrs. D. Joanie was refusing to go near her father, screamed when he came into the room, and hid behind furniture. She had stayed up all night and fell asleep only when Mr. D left for work in the morning. Even Ashley-Anne had been unable to quiet her. Both parents had decided that I must be at fault. I asked for an interview. Only a shaken Mrs. D showed up. Following Joanie's refusal to let her father come close, Ashley-Anne told her mother that Mr. D had approached her sexually many times in the past. But she had enough self-esteem and strength to tell her stepfather to "bug off," he never got close to her. Ashley-Anne had taken it upon herself to save her baby sister from incest and apparently had succeeded partially. When the sisters slept together, neither girl was molested. But Ashley-Anne was disgusted with her mother. She tried to remind her mother that she earlier had attempted to alert her to the danger in the house but had been ignored.

Mrs. D, having suffered through a vitriolic divorce and deeply in love with her new husband, was unable to hear her daughter. "I thought she was oversexed and overstimulated by her own father, not by good, sweet [Mr. D], who took us all in and was so good to us. He would even have taken in the boys if they had wanted to come with me. He is not a terribly sexy man anyway. He is content to cuddle. He doesn't only want sex." Mrs. D did not know what to do. On one hand, she had learned in her own therapy that Mr. D's sexual behavior might indicate a sexual dysfunction of some kind; on the other hand, she did not like sex very much herself and was pleased at not being "brutalized," which to her meant being penetrated during intercourse. Mr. D apparently was not often able to achieve penetration. Mrs. D took her therapist's word for it that her husband's behavior was dysfunctional but could not quite believe it. Yet she wanted to do the right thing for her children. As a first step, she

decided to ask her mother to come and stay in the house so that
neither of the girls would ever be alone either with their father or with
servants. We discussed taking Joanie to her pediatrician for an examination but decided against it because Joanie clearly was very traumatized already. Mrs. D thought it highly unlikely that Joanie could have
been penetrated by her father because "he had a difficult time staying
hard."

Toward the end of the session with me, Mrs. D suddenly remembered that she had on several occasions found Joanie in her father's
bed where the two supposedly had been watching TV while Mrs. D
was at late meetings. Mrs. D had been struck by Joanie's odd behavior
at those times. The child was "in a daze, giggling crazily, and talking
about bad men or somebody chasing her. She also complained about
chest pains." Mr. D had blamed himself for letting her watch scary
movies, and that was the end of it. Mrs. D thought of Joanie as a little
odd and so paid no further attention to the child's complaints. But
now, with this memory, Mrs. D was mobilized. Within the week, she
made arrangements to send Ashley-Anne to prep school, where she
was also to enter therapy. Mrs. D confronted her husband and asked
him to either begin intensive therapy or to get a divorce. Mr. D,
outraged by the accusations, chose divorce.

Joanie missed her sister and her father terribly. She thought it
must have been her bad behavior that drove them away. She began to
accost strangers to ask them if they loved her or if they would take her
home. The mothers of the babies on her street no longer welcomed
her. They thought she had become too "weird" to be around their
infants.

At this time, it was very difficult to be with Joanie. She was shut
off from interpersonal contact like a little autistic child. She seemed to
repel contact, rather than invite it and rocked more fervently than
ever. I saw the rocking not only as a tension release but also as a way
of telling the world that she needed nurturing like a baby. I asked her
mother how she felt when she saw her little daughter rocking in such
a self-contained way. "It breaks my heart," the mother cried, "but what
can I do?" It did not seem to dawn on her that she could take the child
into her arms and rock her.

When Joanie rocked in the consultation room the next time, I put
on a waltz record that approximated her rhythm, sat down in back of
her, put my arms around her, and rocked with her. Before long, she

was cuddling in my lap, contentedly pulling me closer around her. She seemed to want to melt into me. We hummed together and rocked and giggled. Joanie was trying to reconstitute herself. Building on earlier memories of having been bodily nurtured by both her mother and her sister, she now took pleasure in feeling my body warmth and the outline of my body. I thought it was quite a step forward in the much-needed search for the security and comfort that would allow Joanie to trust again. But her mother was of a different opinion. She felt that Joanie had suddenly become a "fiend." Joanie constantly wanted to be near her mother, touch her bosom, and look at her vagina. One day, when the child was very insistent, mother allowed her to come to bed with her. Joanie promptly tried to wiggle her big toe into her mother's vagina while lying down on top of her. Mrs. D felt both disgusted and guilty. She blamed Joanie for being a perverted child and for ruining her marriage. She could not believe that Joanie was trying to tell her what had happened to her.

In the meantime, divorce proceedings were taking place. Mr. D insisted on visiting rights. When he came to pick up Joanie for the first time after the separation to take her out, she screamed and had "a convulsion." Consequently, she was allowed to stay home. When he reappeared the next day, Mrs. D reported, Joanie turned pale and "just looked at [Mrs. D]. There was something in her look that told me that all you said was true. Her father molested her. I didn't let him have her." Mrs. D finally had enough courage to protect her daughter unconditionally.

Fearing public disgrace, Mr. D eventually relinquished visiting rights. But this did not mean that Joanie's troubles were over. She would have good weeks and bad weeks. During the good weeks she acted just like any other child – going to school, playing, and learning. During the bad weeks, she seemed not to know anything. She would play as a very young child does, lining things up or putting toys on top of each other. She would forget what she had learned in school and drive her teacher to distraction with a blank look that appeared to connote stubbornness. At home, she was free to do and be whatever she wanted. Her mother was afraid that any limit-setting would "bring on the convulsion." In sessions, Joanie often went back to her Earthworm game and to her bouncer/gong-striking rituals. There was a significant difference from before, however. After each of these enactments, she would come back to me for rocking and cuddling, but she refused any cognitive acceptance of what both of us knew had happened. Sometimes she would withdraw into her autistic-like behavior and pretend that she did not know me.

During such times, I would tell her that I could understand that she did not want me to know anything about her, that she needed to be all by herself. But, I wondered aloud, perhaps she was also showing me that she was angry at me and her mother for letting all these things happen to her. After this somewhat lengthy interpretation, Joanie usually wanted to be rocked. Little by little—after two years had gone by—she began to respond verbally.

As I had suspected, Joanie was very angry with her mother. Mrs. D's unreliable sense of self and general emotional fragility had not permitted her to nurture her baby daughter sufficiently. As she herself put it, she was so exhausted after her first divorce that Mr. D's willingness to take over for her had seemed like a safe haven where she could give up even the care of her children. She felt more comfortable in the meeting rooms and at the symposia of her profession. Joanie was an unwanted surprise for both Mr. and Mrs. D, who wanted a smooth life without interruptions. Ashley-Anne was a "Godsend." She, along with baby nurses and governesses, had raised Joanie. Mrs. D felt deeply guilty about having virtually ignored Joanie; she had realized during her therapy that babies need all the warmth and care they can get.

Once a connection was made for her between Joanie's odd behavior and the severe trauma of incest, she was unable to comfort the child. She confessed to a loathing for Joanie, as though the child were a junior femme fatale who had ruined her marriage. Although nothing like that was ever said to the child, Joanie acutely felt her mother's coldness and insecurity. Mrs. D believed that she had been able to be a better mother to Ashley-Anne and her brothers because they were not "strange" like Joanie. Caught up in the tragic cycle of projective identification against which Joanie had no weapon, Mrs. D could not sufficiently recognize the emotional needs of her child. She responded cognitively to the catastrophic event of incest and realistically protected Joanie. But there her emotional involvement stopped. She mourned the loss of Mr. D, whom she had experienced as a gentle caretaker.

Thus, Joanie was left very much to her own devices, especially since Ashley-Anne was no longer there to structure and explain the daily happenings to her. Joanie feared my emotional absence as well. She often cried at the end of sessions that she did not want to go home. She wanted to move in with me and constructed a little house for herself in the consultation room. She kept pointing out to me how little space she would take up and how good she would be. Her focus was on her mother's inability to be with her and to nurture her, rather than on the incest with her father. She recalled in play with family dolls how special she had felt when Daddy first invited her into his bed. They watched TV together and Daddy said, "Hold me there." When she did, "there" grew big and "squirted funny juice like milk." Sometimes, Daddy would lie down on top of Joanie and grow big and squirt between Joanie's legs. He always told her that she was lucky because he "didn't ruin her." Joanie guessed that Daddy must have some sort of awful power to ruin people, and she was glad that he loved her enough not to want to ruin her. I gathered that the man prided himself on not penetrating his daughter.

It took Joanie several more years to acknowledge her horror and fear of her father. At last, rage overtook her. She went through a lengthy period of breaking things and having accidents, which she explained away by saying, "I can't help myself. Daddy ruined me after all." She used denial of responsibility for her actions in the here-and-now as a defense against losing the image of her father. Although he had misused her and temporarily stunted her emotional growth, he had been available to her in a way her mother had not been. When not bent on fulfilling his own needs, he did intuit some of Joanie's inner needs and tried to meet them. These contrasting responses were painful truths Joanie had to deal with.

By now a self-possessed and serious eleven-year-old, Joanie asked her mother to send her to Ashley-Anne's former boarding school. "It's no use hanging around my house," she solemnly informed me. "Mother does the best she can, like you always tell me. And I can't live with you. I'm only your patient. I know that now. Maybe I can live with the girls at Ashley-Anne's school. After all, I need someone to live with." In Joanie's inner world, to live with someone meant having someone emotionally available to her. She felt that our therapeutic interaction was at this time "only like my life could be but isn't." She wanted to have me as a caretaker every day. If that was not possible, then she did not want any part of the relationship. Such concreteness was understandable in a child who had been overstimulated, denied, and lied to many times. But I could not dissuade her mother from sending Joanie away. Mrs. D was glad that Joanie had for once said what she wanted. Therefore, therapy had to take a back seat and Joanie had to be allowed "to do what other girls do at her age." Mrs. D was unaware that once again she was interrupting an important process for Joanie that the child herself was unable to grasp emotionally just yet. Thus, at the height of her resistances, Joanie was shipped off to boarding school. Apparently she found a congenial environment there that allowed her to develop. Some years ago, she sent me a card telling me that she had become a teacher.

Discussion

Joanie's case history seems to indicate that the deck was stacked against her from the beginning. Even as an infant she was treated in an atypical way; for instance, when her baby teeth were pulled without anesthesia for medical reasons that were never clear to me. Moreover, she was experienced by her mother as an intruder. I did not find it difficult to believe that a child rejected so early would be "different," given to temper tantrums and denial of reality. The older sister, Ashley-Anne, appears to have kept the child emotionally afloat by her consistent protection. But this protection and nurturance were not the devoted care an average mother gives her baby. To learn about her body, to own her body, to soothe herself, to test reality through her senses, to express herself both verbally and nonverbally, were all difficult psychological skills that Joanie had learned piecemeal and from different sources. Her inner self was like a collage of many lovely pieces of silk and paper. I have often speculated that she loved babies so much because she learned from watching them and their mothers what she had to integrate. Her mother seemed from the time Joanie was born to be unaware of her and unable to cathect[1] her in the way other mothers do, although Mrs. D had been able to be more

---

[1]The term cathexis denotes the investment of the psychic energy of a drive in a mental representation. Mrs. D, for instance, invested her motherly concerns in her other children. Both her love and her hate were actively engaged. For Joanie, there was only intermittent cathexis. She was emotionally aware of her only sometimes. The trouble arose for Joanie when her mother decathected her, or was not aware of her.

nurturing with her other children. Mrs. D seemed at times to forget that she had a daughter named Joanie. It took a catastrophe to bring her to the defense of the child.

Joanie, therefore, had trouble forming an integrated body image. She did not know words for her genitals and, despite her own sexual experience, was surprised that all people have genitals. She did not have sufficient self-esteem or self-knowledge to keep herself out of harm's way and did not know how to fulfill her own needs. All this stemmed from her mother's periodic decathexis of her person and provided the backdrop against which the incest with her father could transpire. Intermittent decathexis is a condition discovered in 1984 by Furman and Furman, who described it as follows:

> [T]he decathexis of parental function is an unusual defense, a very primitive one, that operates in the service of the pleasure principle and is close to primary process. When a parent decathects a child, he avoids a competition between his wishes and the child's needs, avoids the unpleasure of the delay in gratification of his wishes . . . the parents' interest is pursued, the child is treated as non-existent [p. 430].

In Joanie's case history, I have shown how Mrs. D was unable to support her little daughter unwaveringly. It was important to discuss Mrs. D's inability to support Joanie, because the incestuous relationship with the father could not be worked through until Joanie had gained some understanding of what was going on between her and her mother. At first, she was upset and aggrieved that her father had been taken from her. Much as his misuse of her had confused and plagued her, at least he had been available to her and aware of her. Yet she knew that their interaction was forbidden. I do not know whether Ashley-Anne had ever explained that to her or if Joanie knew intuitively that her father's behavior was inappropriate. However she knew, she protected herself by sleeping only with her sister. That some oedipal stirrings were present despite her traumatized state can be seen in her confused statement about her mother's using her, Joanie's, bed and father's taking up too much space in the marital bed. Joanie wanted to be father's wife but knew that was forbidden. Not surprisingly, she stopped paying attention to what displeased and frightened her, gave up learning, and became known as an atypical child. She, more than some of the other children I describe in this book, needed body contact. In a therapeutic regression, she seemed literally to make up for what she had missed.

I would like to point out here that I did not set out to create a so-called corrective therapeutic experience for Joanie. Our interaction grew spontaneously out of her need and my reactions to that need. I tried to stay as neutral as I could so as to enable her to leave me when she was ready. Her remarkable gift for mimicry sometimes taxed my imagination but often provided the door through which I could grasp her experiences. Special techniques used with her included the use of simple dances, music, body movements, and body contact.

In summary, the most important aspect in this treatment was the careful elucidation and reconstruction of Joanie's relationship with her mother until she could understand that her own need to withdraw from contact was "acting like mother" but that she really did not need to "be like mother unless she wanted to." It was only after these aspects of her life were clarified that Joanie could go on to express her rage and disappointment with her father. As a matter of fact, she did not verbalize any detail of her incestuous experiences until the relationship with the mother was more or less understood.

As grievously injurious as Joanie's experience was, Julian-Gregory had even more to struggle with.

JULIAN-GREGORY

The First Interview

Before I ever met Mr. and Mrs. X, I received a bulky envelope in the mail. It contained records of the many tests Julian-Gregory had been subjected to, as well as information about his adoption. Mr. and Mrs. X had already adopted two other children and were "pleased with all of them except Julian-Gregory," who was the youngest. Now almost six years old, he was reported to have been "hyperkinetic" from birth. Although there was no measurable deficit, he had been classified as minimally brain dysfunctional. He was also enuretic. A neurologist had suggested medication, but the parents feared that it "would stunt his growth" and had refused to have their son medicated. Because of his "bright-normal range of intelligence with potential for superior functioning," he was in a regular class. He did not do well there and was disruptive in the classroom. He constantly interrupted the teacher, refused to play with the other children, and was considered a troublemaker. He was said to have poor fine-motor control. Mrs. X was very guilty about these assessments. She felt that Julian-Gregory was very sensitive and had responded adversely to the parents' constant fighting. There had been a trial separation during which time Julian-Gregory's behavior had grown worse. Feeling that the boy was extremely attached to his father, Mrs. X had moved for reconciliation. The parents were now in marital counseling and hoped "to pull it together for the sake of the children."

I wondered what sort of child Julian-Gregory really was. All the reports were full of his physical attractiveness, his intelligence, and his horrendous behavior. For instance, he was said to have urinated in his classroom in front of all his peers but denied having done so vigorously even when his teacher confronted him. Consequently, he was called "delusional" and a recommendation was made for placement in a special class. Feeling that their son might be "wild" and possibly "brain damaged" but never delusional, both parents were incensed at this suggestion. The parents wanted me to work with him because they hoped that my special skills as a dance therapist might help him to be calmer.

Mr. and Mrs. X were a fashionably turned out couple who were very intent on letting me know that they were well thought of in their community. Mr. X had political aspirations and "could not afford to have a hellcat for a son." He professed, however, "to love the little louse" with all his heart. He blamed his wife for being lax with all the children and for being unable to monitor Julian-Gregory's wild behavior. He sheepishly admitted to having been unfaithful to his wife, promised me with great solemnity that this would never happen again, and put his arm around his wife, who did not seem to know what to do with this caress. She then told me that there was little or no affection left between her and her husband. According to her, Mr. X did everything for effect, "without meaning it." She drew a parallel with Julian-Gregory's behavior. She felt that her son was chronically upset by the constant fighting in the house and that he was bedeviled by his efforts to be like his father. Mr. X was "in construction" and could do pretty much everything around the house. Julian-Gregory wanted to do everything also but never succeeded. No matter what sort of project he started, it always ended up in disaster. Often the disasters, according to his parents, were the result of Julian-Gregory's inability to "listen."

I asked about the child's early development and was told that he had passed all developmental milestones well. Mrs. X had brought along a baby book in which she had recorded Julian-Gregory's first laugh at four months, his first crawl at eight months. He walked and talked at 14 months. He had been named after an illustrious and very rich relative who was also his godfather. Mr. and Mrs. X wanted their son to be like this very rich man and were devastated that the child did not fit into their plans. Their counselor had alerted them to the possibility that they might be expecting too much of the child and thus were making him nervous. But they were convinced that they "had to reach for the stars" in order to shape their world, including that of their little son.

Course of Therapy

Julian-Gregory seemed bent on demonstrating to me that all I had heard about him was absolutely true. He sped into my consultation room like a torpedo, scuffed his feet on the rugs until there was an electric reaction, and informed me that he now had to touch a metal rod to give himself more power. I asked what he needed so much power for. The little superman collapsed and told me that he was really a boy named Dandelion, whose heart beat a lot. He invited me to feel his bony little chest. I did so and could feel his heart racing. I left my hand on his chest and told him a story about a child who did not know that his heart was telling him "you are scared." Julian-Gregory was delighted. Really! The boy hadn't known he was scared, but now he knew. There were actually children like himself? How wonderful. He settled down to examining all the toys in the room, picked up a toy hammer, and hit himself all over. I told him that he was not allowed to hurt himself. "Why not?" he wanted to know. Everybody he knew always hurt themselves. His mother threw dishes at his father and then cut herself, and his father kicked his mother. He warned me not to check up on this story because he was quite certain his parents would just say that he was lying. As a matter of fact, he lied all the time, he told me. Why? Because it was "easier that way."

I had read in the many test protocols about Julian-Gregory's poor fine-motor control. Nonetheless, I noticed the ease with which he put together a relatively complicated wooden puzzle and complimented him on it. Oh, yes, he said, when he wasn't "nervous" he could do any number of things. He went on to play with a Lego set and seemed quite contented.

Mrs. X called me anxiously after each session to find out how "the hellion" had done. She did not believe that I found her child quite accessible and that he spent at least half of each session quietly playing. She had noticed, however, that he now seemed to take an interest in the many board games they had at home. He put them on the table and tried to play them by himself. But that was not all of it. He seemed to be able to read the instructions! Mrs. X did not know whether Julian-Gregory had memorized the rules of each game as his older siblings played them or if he could actually read already. Either way, she was pleased to have some corroboration of the superior intellect all the testers had always spoken about. When Julian-Gregory became aware of his mother's satisfaction, he immediately stopped playing with the games. He did not want her to be glad, he told me. She was too mean. She always wanted him to be a big man, but he couldn't be. He could not tell me what it meant to be a big man, but it seemed to have something to do with being obedient. To Julian-Gregory, however, being obedient meant giving up his whole self, or so it seemed to me then.

His favorite play activity in the sessions had become dunking plastic soldiers into a sink full of water. When I asked him why he wanted to give the soldiers a bath, he told me he always got a bath when he urinated in his bed. He pointed to the soldiers' guns and said, "That's where the water comes out, see? They can't stay put in front of the toilet and that's why I have to train them. And you shouldn't have such bad toys like soldiers in your room. That way, children learn about wars before they can understand about it."

I understood Julian-Gregory's game as an attempt to turn the passively suffered toilet training experience into an active mastery and told him so. He was amazed. "You didn't think I was being fresh?" he asked.

Subsequently he invariably directed his fantasy games toward me. A strong transference was in progress. On one occasion, I became a fly that he had to shoo away. I asked whether he had to get rid of me so I wouldn't know any of his secrets. Oh, no, he answered. He had no secrets. It was Daddy who had all the secrets. Another time we were both yo-yos bouncing up and down. He informed me that he would like to be the yo-yo on top, a yo-yo on top of me. During both of these prolonged games I saw how excited Julian-Gregory became. He was sexually stimulated, grabbed his crotch, and could not look at me. Finally, he asked me to marry him. I told him that his offer was very flattering but that I wondered what he really meant by wanting to marry a lady like me. Well, he said, mother was already married, and he didn't like those silly girls in schools. So why not me? Then, he dropped to the floor.

For me, this seemingly charming oedipal interaction had a curiously chilling effect. Julian-Gregory's behavior was not at all childlike. He acted in a knowing, precocious way untypical for him. In addition, he seemed drawn to the floor. Collapsing and falling down was one of his favorite ways of letting me know that all was not well with him. Usually a deliberate fall on the floor meant "pick me up and baby me." He liked being rocked. On that day, it seemed seductive and very sexual. But I also knew that Julian-Gregory liked to imitate his father's behavior. So I asked, "Does Daddy sometimes act like you are acting now?" Instead of answering verbally, Julian-Gregory put the whole doll family to bed. The mother and daughters each had their own bed. But the father and the son slept in the same bed. Julian-Gregory seemed cold and very withdrawn when he played this way. On parting, he told me, "I didn't know I was bad. I learn pretty good when I'm here, don't I?" I did not know what he meant by this cryptic remark.

Clearly, Julian-Gregory was seeking protection and validation from me. At first I thought that he might have witnessed his parents' sex play, but that seemed unlikely in view of their constant fighting. They themselves had told me that they did not even try to hide their fights from the children any more. They rationalized this decision as being "emotionally honest." Why should they make believe that all was well when they despised each other? Anyway, Mr. X thought that it would help Julian-Gregory to become more manly if he saw how a man takes charge in his family. They were deaf to my entreaties to shield their son from their volatility but promised to keep their next monthly appointment. Since Mrs. X called me often, more in the service of ventilating about her son's misdeeds than in the spirit of wanting to understand him, I hoped I would at least be able to empathize with Julian-Gregory in his sessions if I heard from her what the latest marital battle had been about. Julian-Gregory at this point was simply not capable of telling me verbally or even in his games what the daily happenings were. He used his sessions to ventilate some of his distress and to cope with the monsters that now invaded his imagination. He also developed a nervous cough and a facial tic, for which he was taken to many medical doctors despite my pleas that these were psychological, rather than biological, events.

Julian-Gregory had discovered drawing in school and was proud to show me how he could handle the crayons without breaking them. I heard from his mother that his patient teacher had concluded that his fine-motor control was very impaired, and she had spent hours teaching him how to hold a pencil and a crayon. I wondered what Julian-Gregory did in school that made him appear to be so impaired. I asked him. He answered frankly that he had promised mother to be good in school and so made himself "stiff" so that nothing could happen to him. When he was stiff, he managed to sit still and not to get in trouble. Unfortunately, such vigilance also meant that he could not pay attention to what was going on, and this new teacher thought he was "nice but dumb." Julian-Gregory liked being nice but dumb. It was a relief from being thought wild but bright. I told him that he could be both bright and nice if together we could figure out what made him so uncomfortable that he had to get into trouble all the time. He remarked dryly that he was quite aware that I was "on his side." His parents had told him they thought it quite outrageous that I "always took his side."

He then said he would draw two portraits of the "throat monster" that bedeviled him (Pictures J1 and J2), but instead he drew the picture of a "smiling boy with too many teeth." Why too many teeth? So he could do the swallowing instead of being swallowed up. The second picture portrayed a confused, somewhat human image, which, Julian-Gregory insisted, lodged in his throat. In subsequent sessions, Julian-

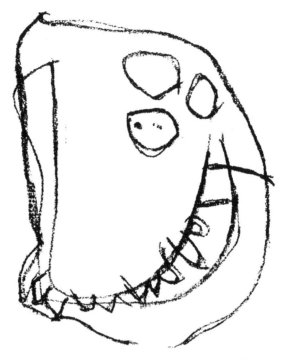

Picture J1   Smiling boy with too many teeth

Gregory put all the dolls, all the toy animals, and all the masks in the play room "to sleep." I noticed that they were always paired, one on top of the other. He was able to tell me that these couples were "doing it." He became very agitated when he told me this and ran to the sink to throw a toy submarine into the water. Then he urinated standing in front of the toilet, apparently without being aware that the door was open. I told him that I had known all along that he could control his flow of urine. Yes, he admitted, he hadn't wet his bed in a long time. But mother hadn't said anything, so he thought he wouldn't say anything about it either. Then he flushed the toilet repeatedly and let water out of the sink. He wanted to make waterfalls, he said. I again said, "Oh, you want to show me how you can control the waterfall and your urine." Julian-Gregory jumped up and down, waved his arms, and seemed nearly to asphyxiate with excitation as he tried to tell me that "something comes off when you're doing it." I grasped that he was referring to the penis inside the vagina and said, "Dad does not leave his penis in mother's vagina. Only sperm stays in the vagina and helps

Picture J2 Throat monster

to make nice babies." Julian-Gregory quieted down immediately and inquired if he was once a nice baby who came out of somebody's sperm. After all, he was only adopted. I told him yes, he had been a nice baby who grew out of a man's sperm. With great seriousness, this small, very unhappy child began to speculate if perhaps the "man with the sperm before his Daddy" was a man who did not fight. He clearly did not want to be like his adoptive father. Apparently he had been given correct information both about his origins and about the sexual act but had in no way been able to integrate this information until he felt safe in the sessions. To have produced such high affect and confusion in him, these questions must have eaten away at him.

Although Julian-Gregory calmed down somewhat and began to act more normally in school, there was still his hyperkinesis and stubbornness, negativism, and sometimes downright hostility toward his mother to contend with. In sessions, Julian-Gregory continued to talk of monsters. There was a new twist to the throat monster. It made him vomit. His mother reported that he did not want to come to sessions any more, that he felt I was wasting his time. When I mentioned to him what his mother had said, he waved contemptuously and said, "You know she lies." Then he fell to the floor. Julian-Gregory was almost seven years old by then and did not want to be held and rocked any more. While on the floor, he told me, "You have to be on my side again. Because people don't eat people. I can't eat people. You can't eat me. People eat animals, but they have to be killed first." All this had to do with his vomiting spells, which were increasing in frequency. Often they occurred just when the family was getting ready to sit down to dinner. Julian-Gregory held my hand tightly, and finally, after telling me so much, fell asleep right in front of me. He woke up friendly and sped out of the room.

His behavior told me that there was more to the story than a possible reactivation of oral-phase cannibalism. Sleeping in my presence seemed to have given him strength. There appeared to have been a temporary memory of good-enough mothering that relieved him when he fell asleep with my hand in his. Julian-Gregory certainly needed such refueling. That need became apparent during his next session. He was in a state of total despair. Clasping his crotch in fear and loathing, he told me that his father had come home drunk, been kicked out of the marital bed, and had come into his bed. Once installed there, "Daddy mixed me up with a girl. He bounced up and down on top of me, and then Mommy heard me and came and took me into her bed. But she said I must be a big man and not make her bed wet." He also informed me that his mother did not want him to tell me what had happened.

Julian-Gregory's symptoms now made total sense to me. Surely this had not been the only time the child had been assaulted. On further inquiry Julian-Gregory corroborated my suspicions. "But," he warned, "they won't believe you. I told them and they didn't believe me." Sometimes, he had had to fellate his father.

I requested an immediate session with both parents and confronted them with the facts. Mrs. X collapsed in tears. Mr. X feebly tried to deny everything, then blamed his behavior on frequent bouts with alcohol. I insisted that he seek treatment immediately and tried to enlist Mrs. X's help. She, however, was overtaken by the social consequences if her husband's behavior became known. Torn between loyalty to her husband, fear of abandonment and poverty, and love for her son, she was paralyzed. Both parents at this point had been referred by the family counselor to individual therapists with whom presumably they had been playing the same game of secrecy as they had with me. Mr. X alternately tried to threaten and to charm me out of believing his son. After a harrowing double session during which he shouted and nearly walked out several times, he finally agreed to discuss with his therapist what had happened.

Julian-Gregory improved somewhat after this disclosure. His school work became acceptable, though his negativism remained. I had every reason to believe that the incestuous behavior of both parents had stopped. But now the expectable sequence consequent to Julian-Gregory's anger at me took place. He did not want to come to sessions and told me that he loved his father and wanted to be just like him. Although freed from his vomiting spells, throat monsters, and tics, he felt that I was trying to make him "crazy" so that he could not love his parents. It was difficult to demonstrate to him that he mistrusted me now because I seemed to have taken an important piece of omnipotent gratification from him. After all to replace mother in father's actions must have meant a lot of power to the small boy. But Julian-Gregory possessed an amazing amount of resilience. One day he took a baby bottle I keep in my treatment room and began to feed a doll. He constructed a bed, put himself to sleep, and once again wanted to hold my hand while he snoozed contentedly. Quite simply, he gave himself the good feelings of a nurtured infant that he needed so badly. He played this game many times and derived great satisfaction from it.

Invariably, he calmed down and was able to tell me what the day had brought. He even was able to own up to some of his "troubles," such as running away from a teacher when she called him and hiding his sister's scissors because he wanted them for himself. He faithfully reported that he slept in a clean, dry bed every night. He relished describing to me how unwrinkled, fresh, and neat his bed now was. He relished even more my pleasure in his accomplishment.

At this time, his favorite sister, Jill, began to act out. She was accused in school of being a pickpocket. Julian-Gregory seemed to know that this had something to do with his improvement. During a family therapy session with another therapist it had become clear to everyone that Julian-Gregory and Jill were inseparable because they felt more secure that way. But now that Julian-Gregory liked being "good," Jill felt left out and alone and took over the function of family scapegoat. Julian-Gregory was very upset about this and began to plot how he could be "both good and bad so people wouldn't blame Jill like they used to blame me." He finally decided that he would like Jill to come and see me as well. His fantasy was that both of them would sleep in the bed that he regularly built in a corner of the room. On further reflection, he decided not to ask his parents to bring Jill because he preferred having me all to himself.

He confessed to playing the same game with Jill that his father had played with him. Jill liked it, he said, when he bounced up and down on top of her. He felt that was particularly nice when neither one of them had clothes on. Lately, they had both begun to have doubts about this kind of fun. Jill felt that "it could hurt her stomach" if Julian-Gregory continued to bounce on her. Julian-Gregory offered to be more gentle but made the link with his own experiences. Maybe what Jill really meant was that she couldn't "breathe right" when he was on top of her. Julian-Gregory also thought that he really did not want to do "that" any more. As far as he could ascertain, none of the other children in school did anything like it with their sisters.

While he had at first had identified with the aggressor, his father, and in this way tried to master passively suffered trauma by becoming an active perpetrator, he was now able to reflect upon his own actions and find different ways of solving his problems. Clearly, the child's reality perception and ability to test reality had become firmer. He was almost consciously looking for role models who would permit him to act in socially acceptable ways. The more Julian-Gregory was able to talk about his experiences and the more his games became expressive of his thoughts, the more he improved. Unfortunately, as he improved, his sister further deteriorated. Since Julian-Gregory no longer acted out for her, she had to do her own "dirty work," as her mother put it. Jill stole and tried to set fire to the house. Through all these upheavals, Julian-Gregory advanced psychologically. Although he was upset about his sister's behavior, he began to make friends and even was invited to other children's birthday parties. This accomplishment seemed a milestone to his mother. None of her children had ever been accepted in the neighborhood, a rejection she had irrationally blamed on their having been adopted.

Later there was a flare-up of symptoms that Julian-Gregory himself related to an incident of father's coming home drunk and occupying his bed. "My sissy pointed straight up and I got my neck wet with urine because I was afraid Daddy would bring the throat monster back," he said. But, he reported further, father also vomited and urinated in bed, so Julian-Gregory was not blamed for it.

I did not have the chance to help Julian-Gregory examine what his erection in the presence of his father's destructive behavior might mean. His unhappy mother threatened suicide and was no longer able to take care of the family. Other family members and paid helpers took over for her. But their responsibilities did not include bringing Julian-Gregory for his sessions. He called me several times to let me know that he was "good." Some years later I learned that he had been able to stay in regular classes although in the slowest track. He had the reputation for being a "cool" kid, whatever that means.

Discussion

Almost all of Julian-Gregory's behavior seemed to be dominated by oral-phase derivatives. Even his so called hyperkinesis had the stamp of pleasure-seeking, like an infant's. While he sped about, he did not have to think and could dispel fantasies about the highly overstimulating, brutal behavior he was being subjected to. After I understood more about his environment, I began to marvel that he functioned at all. His incontinence certainly had to do with tension release, but, more specifically, it also was a symbolic expression of what happened to him when his father approached him incestuously. What seemed like excessively regressed behavior had meaning and function in Julian-Gregory's life as both a defensive and an adaptive mode. The same can be said for his hyperkinesis. When his father's needs reached a crescendo, Julian-Gregory regressed even further. He vomited and literally tried to get rid of the semen that was introduced forcefully into his mouth. I gathered that he had tried on several occasions to enlist his mother's help, but she was engaged in a psychological struggle for survival herself and had not many resources left to give the children. Julian-Gregory, as the youngest, was the least able to stay on an even keel. But just as he used oral defenses to protect himself, he also was able to adapt oral gratifications to help him to survive. When he fell asleep in my room while holding my hand, he appeared to relive the satisfaction of an infant who falls asleep happily in the cozy enclosure of his mother's arms.

Julian-Gregory had a good many ego strengths. They were evident in his ability to withstand the pull to join in the regressive behavior of his sister, who had been his confidante and ally. When the symbiosis with her was dispelled, he was regretful about her regression but tried to solve the problem in various healthy ways. His ability to symbolize was totally intact. At first his hyperkinesis seemed to have been sparked by a neurologic dysfunction; its symbolic function was not visible until the middle of treatment. His adaptability and good nature in a household that chronically abused and misused him was truly amazing.

Special techniques used with him were music and rhythmic body contact, puppet games, and drawings.

In summary, despite grievous injuries to his physical and mental self, Julian-Gregory was able to survive with many ego strengths and psychologic flexibility intact. He was able to curtail regressive behavior and acting out once a positive transference had been established with me. He, like Joanie, used the treatment situation to "grow" trust, rudimentary self-esteem, and the ability to adapt.

The devastating effects of incest are evident in the cases of Joanie and Julian-Gregory. But, as I said at the beginning of this chapter, incest is not the only kind of sexual abuse children can fall prey to. Franky's history illustrates this tragic theme.

FRANKY

The First Interview

Franky's parents called me at the prompting of their son's school psychologist. Franky was five years old, in kindergarten and, according to his parents, "out of control." He had been sent home several times for his disruptive behavior. His teacher had suggested to the parents that perhaps he was not yet ready for the vigor of kindergarten and that he should be held back for a year. But Franky was already the veteran of nursery school and a therapeutic milieu play group. The parents had withheld this information from the school officials in order to give their son "a fresh start where nobody knew him." They had not always found Franky to be difficult. They reported that he had been a good baby and a source of pride to them until he was about three and a half or four years old. Then his behavior suddenly altered. He became encopretic, seemed at times to be "not in this world," did not listen to anyone, and played "weird" games such as pulling out all the flowers in their large garden and starting his father's car. He had nearly "killed himself" when the car rolled out of the driveway into the street, causing a collision. They brought newspaper clippings with them to substantiate their tale.

A wealthy and charming young couple, they clearly had expected their son to be a source of gratification to them. When this expectation was not fulfilled, they turned on each other. Each was convinced that the other had in some way caused their son's deviant behavior. Mrs. K talked of her husband's racing cars and his love of skiing as a wildness that might have infected Franky. She also hinted that she thought Mr. K unfaithful. He, on the other hand, scoffed at all her conjecturing and accused her of not being able to control the child. His marriage to Mrs. K was his second, and I gathered that he had some regrets about having divorced his first, older, and richer wife. Mrs. K was cast in the role of Cinderella, who was to be grateful to this Prince Charming although she came from a wealthy family herself and was well educated. Both Mr. and Mrs. K somehow felt that it was a gross injustice to have had a child like Franky inflicted upon them. In particular, they were upset about his habit of making a friend out of gardeners, handymen, and other occasional helpers on their large property. He preferred the company of these sometimes gruff men and their children to that of the more refined children of the family's friends. Mrs. K thought this propensity was the result of Mr. K's frequent absences and his neglect of Franky. Mr. K, however, felt that he spent "quality time" with the child and accused his wife of leaving Franky too much in the care of maids, housekeepers, and other help. They would not hire a governess because their friends might think they had failed as parents. Their circle of friends apparently had dedicated themselves to providing a different lifestyle for their children than they themselves had experienced. Instead of putting their children in the care of nannies and boarding schools, they wanted to be "traditional but open to the needs of the child."

When Franky showed the first signs of antisocial behavior, he was taken to an expensive play therapy group euphemistically called "I love to play." Franky didn't love to play. He loved to run around, push other children down, and destroy toys. He did not respond to kindness, I was told. Both parents advocated that I be "tough" with Franky. His behavior had become worse since Mrs. K's second pregnancy became visible. He had on several occasions kicked his mother in the abdomen, telling her to "drop her load." Mrs. K understood the link between Franky's encopresis and her pregnancy quite well. "You can see what we are up against," she wailed. "He thinks the new baby is a piece of shit. He wants me to soil my pants like he does."

The expensive private school they had in mind for Franky would not accept him until he was toilet trained. Both parents now wanted me to do that job for them. Both were also opposed to therapy for themselves although they promised to "check out" what their friends thought of the idea. Apparently, there was little regard for privacy among the friends, all of them revealing their actions and thoughts freely. I had the impression that this group was designed to provide the family interactions its members did not have with their own parents.

Course of Treatment

Franky turned out to be small for his age, agile, and graceful. His mother had obviously dressed him in his finest clothes to meet me. He seemed well mannered enough, looking at the toys, commenting on the weather, and asking me if the school psychologist who had referred him was my boss. He thought bosses were very important people. His father went skiing and racing with his boss, and he, Franky, was then the boss of the house. So far so good. Suddenly, Franky asked me why I had to see him; I was "a lady who talks to children who have troubles. I don't have any troubles," he said. Well, I answered, I was glad he thought so. But maybe he wanted to make-believe for me so I would like him better? With this, Franky dropped his well-bred façade, grabbed a rubber toy hammer, and began to hit his head, his arms, and his legs, all the while laughing gleefully. I took the hammer out of his hand and told him that there were certain rules in my room: he was not allowed to hurt himself or me. Shouting "rules, rules, rules," Franky ran around the room and hit the walls with the hammer I had just put down. I watched for a moment and then commented that he seemed quite strong to me and that his arms and legs seemed to work very well. I offered this comment because I thought that perhaps he felt so overwhelmed by meeting yet another authority figure that he needed to hit his extremities in order to feel them and to make sure that he existed at all. Franky thought this over for a while and then settled down to some serious investigation of the toys.

Since it had been reported to me that he had a very short attention span, I noted his concentration and lengthy examination of the toys as a sign that he had some hidden strengths. The toys were not fancy enough for him, he finally told me. They did not "do" anything. I demonstrated to him that my toys were for "doing *with*," that he had to invent the games to go with them. He thought this idea very strange inasmuch as he had become accustomed to being entertained rather than to playing. Nevertheless, at the end of the hour he did not want to leave. Apparently we understood each other quite well. His actions showed that he knew there were problems but that I could be trusted—to a point. I was also pleased that he was able to integrate and to make use of the clarifying interpretations I had offered him. I concluded that perhaps he was not quite so disturbed as his parents and his school psychologist thought.

Franky's mother seemed upset every time she either brought or picked up her son. The daughter of a young friend was also in therapy and that child wanted her mother in the sessions with her. Why was Franky content to be alone with me? Mrs. K wanted to know. I explained that depending on their developmental levels, children sometimes need total privacy during treatment; at other times they need to cling to their parents. Mrs. K was pleased to have this information and in the following parent sessions told me about the many books she was now reading, in particular about children like her son. I again advised therapy for her, and this time, she agreed. It was just too painful for her to "give up" Franky to me without assistance and reassurance of a professional on her side. Mr. K was still unwilling to enter therapy but to please his wife, agreed to go along for counseling sessions. Franky was aware of all this. His parents discussed with him their decision to enter therapy as though he were an adult. He took their move as a sign that he could control them by "wishing on them." He told me that he had wished they would come to see me more often but was quite content that now they had their own "play lady." He had noticed that every time they had a session with me, they were "more nicer" to him. Again, I was struck by Franky's ability to observe, to process the information gathered, and to form a logical conclusion. I thought this remarkable because so much of his behavior seemed driven by instinctual demands beyond his control. That he felt he could instead control his parents did not seem so far fetched; after all, they discussed with him matters no child has sufficient information to judge. In their own way, more benign way than that of the parents of Joanie and Julian-Gregory, they obliterated generational boundaries.

Franky settled into a predictable routine during sessions. He played "nice," calling my attention to his ability to control himself and the toys. One of the scenes he liked to enact was of a storm in the sink where he regularly tried to capsize his father's boat. "I won't drown," he always declared, "But Dad will be sorry he wasn't there. He's supposed to take care of us and he doesn't, not much, anyway." I thought at first that he was talking about his mother's disappointment at being left alone so much, but I delayed talking to Franky about it in order to gather more information first. I did link the storms in the sink to his own irregular bowel and urine control. We seemed to be making headway in that department. Mrs. K reported that Franky was managing to have a dry bed and dry pants most of the time. One day, however, he came in to the session with wet pants, reeking of urine. He told me that mother had poured water on him "to cool him off". I thought this an odd pronouncement and asked Franky what mother wanted to cool off. He proudly said, "Men get wet, too." Then he started to race around the room, pull toys down, and pound the walls in an excess of glee. Eventually, he told me that he had just enacted another story. He plummeted onto his hands and knees, telling me that he was a moose that his father had shot from the back. He played moose-hunting for awhile, then manufactured one of his storms in the sink, during which he pushed a boat in, and in, and in, chanting rhythmically.

From that day on, he soiled himself daily. His mother was ready to remove him from therapy, but his father prevailed upon her to let Franky continue because he saw more "manly behavior" in other areas. For instance, he liked to throw his son up into the air and catch him like a ball. Franky had often shown me this during sessions, assuring me that he was not afraid to play this game because he had a parachute between his shoulders that could grow big when his father threw him in the air. When I told him that his father was very proud of him for being so manly, he blew up a balloon, popped it, and informed me that his BMs were like that. They popped in and out of him. "Yes," I answered, "and when Daddy throws you in the air, that's exciting like trying to keep BMs inside of you." Franky thought this over, wondering aloud if the BMs would pop him, like Mom was going to pop any day now. I tried to ascertain what he thought was inside of his mother, and he quite coolly informed me that it was "shit." He could not imagine any other thing that could swell up a belly this much. His own belly swelled up when he held in his BMs too long, and hurt when they finally came out. Mother had told him that it would hurt her when the "baby shit" came out. He thought this had to do with mother eating too much. Apparently unable to understand what I told him about the reproductive process, he insisted that we were talking about eating and defecating. He became so tense that he bit a puppet "to make it go away" and threw himself at me to bite me as well. I held him tightly and told him that soon we would understand what was making him so scared.

In subsequent sessions, he brought Tootsie Rolls with him. He told me that they were "what comes out of the bottom"; then he ate them gleefully. He also began to use playdough, which he monotonously rolled into long snakes. He was never able to comment about his activities. On occasion, he repeated the episode of biting and being fearful. Body contact always quieted him. He seemed unable to understand that he had a penis or what it was for. Mother reported that he was now depositing his bowel movements next to his bed or in the garden near the greenhouse. When I asked Franky about this, he pointed to his behind and said, "Because that's where it goes in." There was such an odd grimace on his face that I had the momentary association of faun. His games also had an odd quality, of his being overwhelmed, chased, drowning, and out of control.

All interpretations and clarifications regarding the male and female anatomy and the reproductive process had been totally disregarded or fearfully rejected. What was Franky telling me? I knew him to be highly intelligent, yet he acted like a mentally impaired child. I decided to take a chance and asked Franky, "What do you put in there?" He didn't put anything into his anus, he said. But "the man" did. He then acted out with puppets what had happened to him. Midway through the game, he became overwhelmed and defecated. I told him that he need not be afraid. We would find out together what would make him feel better. First on the agenda for him was that mother should not yell at him for soiling his pants. I took him into the bathroom and helped him to get as clean as possible. Then, I explained to Mrs. K, who was in the waiting room, that Franky had had an important session that we would have to talk about immediately. At this point, Franky was clinging to me. He sobbed that he did not want to go home because "the man" was there. Mrs. K was at a loss to understand what all this meant. I told her to keep the child with her until we had a conference. Both parents showed up for a session that night. I told them that I had reason to believe that Franky had been sodomized. Disbelief and horror made them almost incoherent. Franky was taken to a pediatrician who concluded that there were anal fissures and some ulcerations.

While Franky entered the difficult phase of working through, his parents undertood the task of finding out who had misused and brutalized their child. They came to the conclusion that it had been a gardener who was no longer in their employ. Mr. K was so enraged that he wanted to hire detectives to hunt down the man. He entered individual therapy to deal with his rage and helplessness.

I wish I could report that Franky immediately stopped being encoprectic, but he did not. In an effort to master his overstimulation and the brutalization he had been victim to, he often became resistant and recalcitrant. For instance, while playing with finger paints, and making huge messes, he decided to put his feet on the paper as well. He now produced foot paintings that covered much of the floor. But if I put protective plastic under the paper, he screamed. He wanted to make a mess without restrictions. I told him that he could make a great big mess on the drop cloth I provided. He answered that he could do what he wanted and what he wanted was to mess up my room and me too. We talked about this and together concluded that he wanted me to feel like a messy, angry, helpless little boy. He thought I would make a very funny little boy who would be so nice that his parents would always love him. Then he wanted to put paint all over me. When I would not permit him to do that, he kicked me and screamed at me. I told him he could make believe that I was messy little boy but that he could not smear me with finger paints. My body was my own, as his was his own.

We spent many sessions in such struggles to help Franky understand that he could not infringe on or intrude into or use other people's bodies as his had been used. Sometimes he became so angry, he defecated in his pants. By now his patient mother had provided a clean set of underwear to be kept in the room. Franky knew how to clean himself up and how to change without help. As a matter of fact, he would close the bathroom door on such occasions and give me a blow-by-blow description of what he was doing. One day he became very silent. When I asked what he was doing, he opened the door and proudly showed me how he had distributed some of his feces around the sink and toilet. I told him that I thought that it was very nice that he wanted me to see the usefulness of his BMs. Did he mean them to be decorations like the finger paints? No, he said angrily. He wanted to annoy me and was very, very angry that I was such a dirty lady who could think of feces as a decoration.

Apparently, he felt that he could safely be angry with me. By seeing me as a dirty lady, he projected his own "dirtiness" onto me. Once his feelings of being dirty were externalized, he could refute them and hand them to me, so to speak. Concomitantly, this process of externalizing his bad feelings allowed him to get in touch with his positive feelings both for his family and for me. This positive transference then allowed him to remember and to tell me some of the things that had happened to him.

In this session, after thus having shown me that he had accepted the strictures of his family and his therapist to be clean, he was able to tell me about the games he had played with "the man." He was thrown into the air, just as father had done. Then he "couldn't remember but the man chewed on my penis and sometimes got all wet himself." When Franky made in his pants, the man was angry because "he wanted to crawl with a snake into Franky's tooshie [anus]." Franky could by now understand that the man had done a bad thing. He could also accept that nobody, including himself, had the right to interfere bodily with or to coerce another human being. This assertion led to a crisis with Mr. K, who still liked to play the game of tossing Franky into the air. But Franky did not want to play any more and said so. His father accused him of being a sissy. The father's deeply rooted fears of homosexuality surfaced. He was afraid that as a result of the sexual abuse his son had sustained, the boy might become a homosexual. Fortunately, the father's therapist was able to give him at least a rudimentary understanding of the rights of children to own their own body; that is, he understood that he must stop throwing Franky into the air and stop pummeling him.

The central theme of Franky's sessions continued to be autonomy versus dependency, freedom versus license. He graduated from using truly enormous quantities of finger paints and his own feces to using body lotions, which he distributed liberally over his arms and bare legs. His encopresis disappeared. But now another situation arose. He wanted to massage my arms and legs with the lotion. Why? He wanted to make me feel good, as I had made him feel good. I interpreted that perhaps there had been a time when Franky mistook "the man's" handling of him for a nice thing. Perhaps, if he did something like that to me, he would mistake me for either himself or the man. Franky laughed. Not a chance! He knew very well who I was. I even had taught him to go to the toilet "like a man but not like *the* man." Recognizing me as a helper who enhanced his sense of masculinity by teaching him how to toilet himself allowed Franky to stop repeating his trauma in the sessions.

Despite his interest in all things sexual, Franky did not express much interest in his baby sister. Once he had ascertained that she was indeed "a baby and not a BM," he politely listened to his mother when she tried to have him hold the baby or attempted to explain that this was his sister. He seemed either uninterested or suspicious of all the attention mother expended on this aspect of their relationship. I saw this suspicion as the dawning of the Oedipus complex, which Franky found too threatening and warded off almost consciously. It was as though he did not trust his mother sufficiently to love her.

After Franky and I had worked together for three years, his family decided to leave the area. They had, when Franky first began therapy with me, confided everything to their circle of friends. But now, as the initial shock at their son's fate faded and some understanding of their own role in the happenings dawned, they felt unable to "live it down. Franky needs a new start in life." I tried to make them aware of the repetition implied in this statement. But their shame and fear of ostracism was too strong. They stood by their decision to move away. Franky decided he wanted a farewell party with me. He provided cupcakes and his favorite soda himself. We were very sad together, but Franky tried to cheer me up. He drew a farewell picture for me that showed "a mother who lives in a flower but is bothered by busy boy bees who love her" (Picture F1). Some time later, I received a request for Franky's records from a well-known child psychiatrist in another area of the country. I was pleased that Franky was receiving the help he needed.

Discussion

Although Franky's parents were struggling with many issues from their own past and seemed narcissistically wounded themselves, they loved their children enough to avoid major pitfalls in their parenting. Had Franky not met his abuser, psychological difficulties might never have surfaced to such a disturbing degree. As it was, the major issue seemed to be that the parents, like many others, were only selectively

Picture F1   Mother who lives in a flower but is bothered by boy bees

attuned to Franky's needs. They did not watch him sufficiently to prevent his rape. When Franky did try to communicate within the limited verbal range of a three-year-old, they did not understand him. But he kept on trying. His symptoms were clearly expressive of what had happened to him. This does not mean that all encopretic children have been anally penetrated. But encopresis was Franky's way of letting the world know that control over his body had been wrested from him and that he no longer could trust either his body signals or people who were supposed to convey the meaning or uses of such signals to him. His capacity to learn became impaired and reflected a fixation at the anal phase that he did not outgrow until he was in treatment. He could not assimilate the information his mother supplied about her pregnancy. To him, the crucial point of reference was always what could be pushed into the anus and what came out of it. Violation of his anus had precipitated the developmental arrest for him and now he viewed any information given him from that anal perspective. He often was not at all sure that he existed at all. In desperation, he tried to control his environment by overpowering it with his feces. For him this fecal body product was symbolic of the penis that had penetrated him; of the baby that mother carried in her womb; and of himself as the powerless, seduced, and raped body. At first he could not trust anyone and laboriously had to learn about body boundaries, inside and outside, sensations and emotions.

His parents lack of attunement to his emotional needs was perhaps the most detrimental aspect of their relationship with Franky. By this I do not mean they exhibited the outright disregard for his developmental needs that some of the other parents exhibited for their children, but an inability to attune themselves over a wide range of emotions to the needs of their child. Stern (1985) speaks of selective attunement of parents to certain affective states of their children. The child very early signals to the parents what to him constitutes knowable and shareable personal experience. This nonverbal communicative power of selective attunement colors all forms of experience, from overt behaviors to attitudes, tastes, and internal states. Mutual attunement constitutes the infant's first experience of interpersonal relatedness and is said to form the foundation for empathy. The parents' selective inattention, or intermittent decathexis of either an aspect of the child's communication or of the entire child (Furman and Furman, 1984), determines which area of affectivity is downplayed, which acknowledged. Obviously, all parents attune, or disengage, selectively. Because Franky's parents had been attuned to him before his rape, he was able to maintain a semblance of sanity even when they did not understand him and he failed to understand what they wanted of him. In treatment, he regained some of the basic trust and ability to understand what is needed for basic human interaction and interrelatedness. He was able to give up some of his grandiose and desperate efforts at control as well as his symbolic encopresis. When he left treatment with me, he was still unable to appreciate fully that babies are carried in their mother's womb, and he was suspicious of the whole reproductive process. In this crucial area, he remained fixated on the anal and cloacal theories he had formed at the time of his abuse and acted out in the sessions through foot painting and smearing. These highly overdetermined events were expressive not only of his actual trauma, but also of the way he was able, or unable, to elaborate his fantasies. He was not quite able to trust either his mother or his father, the former because she appeared to sometimes forget him, the other because he overstimulated his son.

Special techniques used with Franky were the copious use of finger paints and body lotions to help reestablish actual and internalized body boundaries and to facilitate limit setting.

I would say that Franky, despite his brutalizing experience, fared better than many children in his position. His parents were concerned and involved enough to seek out help. They immediately believed that their son had been brutalized, jumped to his defense, and tried to help. Thus, Franky was spared the painful lack of support both Joanie and Julian-Gregory had to sustain.

SUMMARY

When I reflect on the sexually abused children I have treated, or whose treatments I supervised, the single most astonishing fact is that I was usually the only one who believed the child. Even the therapists who brought me some of their cases did not want to believe that they possibly were in the presence of incest or other sexual abuse. Their disbelief went far beyond the reluctance of theoreticians who speculate about the origins of pathology; their disbelief was even stronger than that of Freudians, who are not sure whether it is the actual trauma that causes the aberrant psychic structure and behavior or whether it is the secondary fantasy elaboration that is at fault. I believe that my supervisees' and some colleagues' reluctance to accept children's overt or covert accusation is a failure of empathic attunement. Their own incest taboos were so firmly entrenched that they could not see beyond the diffuse and fragmented actions of their young patients. In addition, they had carefully been trained to be neutral and objective. To them, objectivity meant that they had to keep an open mind about the presence of pedophilia in parents.

Stern (1985) speaks of three domains of attunement: behavior, affect, and words. The more comfortable therapists are, the more attuned within among these three domains, the more easily they will be able to respond authentically to the needs of child patients. Psychoanalysts and psychoanalytically oriented psychotherapists have always aimed for empathic understanding of their patients. They have always tried to resonate with their patients' unconscious. It is my view that the ability to resonate with patients includes decoding verbally what has been communicated nonverbally. Nearly all therapists learn to decode verbal primary-process derivatives such as metaphors and dreams. But few, even among child analysts, who look at the play behavior of children as free association, try to decode nonverbal communications such as those transmitted through projective identification, acting out, somatic disturbances, and—most important for the children discussed here—body language. In 1965 Spitz began to make the therapeutic community aware of how important the early phases of nonverbal, subjective interactions between mother and child are. He called this mode of intuitive understanding coenesthetic reception.

It can safely be said that what transpired between the victimized children discussed here and their parents, as well as between some of these children and their therapists, was a massive lack of attunement and lack of empathic grasping of the child's developmental needs. In particular the therapists of the parents involved often thought that I was exaggerating. They wanted "more proof" that their otherwise well-integrated patients, such as Joanie's and Julian-Gregory's fathers, were pedophiles or were sexually dysfunctional in other ways. They also did not seem to understand that child abuse is also a sadistic abuse of power. I must confess to feeling irritated, even hostile, when I could not immediately use what had become an obvious fact to me to help the children.

Perhaps I could be accused of undue countertransferential manifestations in my wish to stop the abuse immediately, although by now, years later, it has become a commonplace that the abuse must stop before the child can be helped. Child Protective Services are now in place. Therapists who suspect child abuse but are not sure how to handle procedures can contact such organizations as the C. Henry Kempe National Center for the Prevention and Treatment of Child Abuse or Neglect.[2] There seem to be many more agencies for the treatment of adults who suffered sexual abuse as children than there are facilities for abused children. This situation, of course, reflects the powerlessness of children who are delivered into the hands of primitive and dysfunctional adults. Adults can band together and defend themselves; children cannot. These children all too often are accused of lying, or adults misinterpret their desperate behavior as mental illness or willful mischief. Even professionals often miss the mark.

Children who are assaulted by adults find themselves in an untenable position. They have been taught that they must obey their elders and that they will receive protection and love. But this view of the world is destroyed when the protectors become the persecutors — and I am describing what happens only on a perceptual level. The entire inner development of such children is at stake. In order to exist psychologically at all, they make themselves numb. They isolate what happened from the rest of their inner lives and split off what is giving them so much pain. The brutalization that has taken place, however, is not so easily neutralized. Part of the children's inner strength is used up in keeping the awful secret out of consciousness. Consequently, the children experience twilight states; they lie, steal, and behave in many destructive ways. They often stop learning. Their fantasy life is affected as well. After such traumas, monsters and demons of their imaginings are assumed to be real. The boundaries between reality and fantasy erode, a process that gives to many of these children a near-psychotic stamp. They frequently confuse the inner and outer boundaries of their bodies. They do not feel that they are in control of

---

[2]This organization is located at 1205 Oneida Street, Denver, CO, 80220; Tel. 303-321-3969. It is an agency that focuses on child abuse treatment, training, and research.

their bodies or that they own their bodies. All too often, the adults to whom they turn do not respond supportively. Like Joanie, Julian-Gregory, and Franky, these children become overwhelmed and go into psychologic hiding, all the while hoping for rescue.

Yet unconditional rescue is often not possible, nor is it even desirable because the children must have the opportunity to work through all their negative feelings before they can recover. As the case histories here showed, at first my interventions were felt as unreliable and seductive, just as the abusers had been. A fairy-tale rescue in which the children were seen as all good and entirely without responsibility for their subsequent actions would only reinforce magic thinking and further impede development. Unfortunately, once they have accepted the facts, therapists and educators often do not recognize that love alone is not enough; they give themselves over to their own fear, anger, and frustration by acquiescing to all the child's demands. Franky certainly would not have learned to control his bowels if he had been allowed to smear without limits, and Joanie and Julian-Gregory would have continued to act destructively if they had not had the opportunity to find their body boundaries again. Their symptoms were very similar to those of deeply troubled youngsters, such as borderline or psychotic children. But because all three as infants had enjoyed a brief period when they were loved and appreciated by their families, their development could progress more or less smoothly and they could gather enough strength to let me know what troubled them. Admittedly, their communications were often diffuse and hard to decipher because isolation, repression, and splitting had already taken their toll.

Some children are able to tell straightforwardly what has befallen them. Most, however, are invested in protecting their families and will go to great lengths to keep everything unchanged. After all, their family is the only one they know. Mental health workers and educators must learn to listen and not to dismiss as fantasy a youngster's complaints of abuse, either directly or through symptomology. Often, it is only in treatment that the truth is revealed.

So far, I have spoken about the most emotionally abandoned of children. There is, however, another category of child who comes into the treatment room. These children function extraordinarily well in school, often are great achievers but have no friends and seem to lead little-adult lives. Sometimes they are teachers' pets, a relationship they frequently discourage. They are the socially withdrawn children who do not seem to own themselves because their parents are overly involved with them and, metaphorically speaking, do not let them breathe.

CHAPTER **6**

᠊᠊᠊

I'd Really Like to Kill
My Mom and Dad
Children Who Live Behind
an Emotional Mask

T he children I am about to describe do not often come to the attention to school officials. They are good scholars, are well behaved, and cause no trouble. Occasionally a particularly intuitive teacher may note that these children are too quiet or do not interact with their peers. But, generally speaking, once these children are told that they need to play more with other children, they dutifully do so. They prefer, however, the company of adults, who often adore them because of their ability to verbalize intelligently. The only symptom that can readily be recognized is their usually uncontrollable need to boast and to be the best at everything. They particularly dislike physical education in school but will stubbornly and vainly try to excel even there. Teachers are often touched by their perseverance in the pursuit of learning and fail to recognize that their little bookworms are as desperate in their own way as were the acting out, destructive children I spoke about in the earlier chapters.

These children are quite frequently objects of open adoration in their families. In the eyes of their parents, they can do no wrong. They are encouraged to enjoy and to reach for the very best of everything, whether material goods, schools, or wealth of any kind. Sometimes these aspirations are accompanied by the parental assumption that everything should come easily to their gifted children, who need not bother to reach for rewards to which they are entitled. In other cases, hard work is stressed but always with the assumption that, of course, the children will achieve success. The children never learn to curtail their demands. They remain orally and anally fixated and assume that their demands must be met whatever the cost. Not surprisingly, these children reflect their parents' narcissistic demandingness. As the children mature, they begin to experience dystonic states of detachment, boredom, and even depression. They do not know how to play, either alone or with others, despite their parents' claim that they are unusually creative. Increasingly these children are unable to be alone. By the time they reach latency, they are little adults who cannot play by themselves and are bored in the presence of others. Sometimes they exhibit sleep disturbances or temper tantrums. The parents become distraught and quickly whisk their child off to the nearest child therapist, hoping "it's nothing," "just a phase," or a sudden physical illness. It never occurs to them that they might have had a part in creating this unsatisfied, moody, and suddenly unsatisfactory child.

Brody, Axelrad, and Moroh (1976) attribute such difficulties to a narrow or distorted object cathexis in early infancy. The child does not integrate gratification as connected to caregivers or is disturbed in reaching for satisfaction. Anna Freud (1965) has said that the infant goes from his own body and the mother's body to the toy. Cathexis of his own body and that of his mother facilitates the cathexis of inanimate things, which can bring gratification of a different sort, as in playing. Brody et al. took this hypothesis and built on it in a 10-year longitudinal study of a normal population of mothers and their children. Their major, confirmed hypothesis was that "optimal development of object relations requires the experiencing of a regular sequence of positive cathexis of need-satisfying [part] objects, of people, things and beginning ideas in the first year of life" (p. 3).

They go on to say that children whose families allow for a balance of these factors in their first year will

> in their seventh year, early in latency, and in the period of adaptation to elementary school, show a balance of sound object relations in general and a superior cathexis of ideas and abstract thinking. . . . Conversely, children whose patterns of object relations in the first year are poor and/or deficient and imbalanced will in their seventh

year show poor object relations in general and poorer capacity for abstract thinking [p. 4].

The children I am speaking about in this chapter were well endowed with intelligence and came from "fine families" where the latest books on child rearing were religiously read and followed. But application of principles could not foster for the children the inner representation of a good mother or father who would unconditionally love them. These children understood from earliest babyhood that they were to please the adults around them, no matter what the cost to their own development. In unconsciously offered compensation, they were then overindulged by their parents. As young children, they may have exhibited signs that all was not well. There may have shown an endless need for motor activity or preoccupations with stereotyped activities such as writing numbers or letters without rhyme or reason, all in the service of binding excitation or anxiety. Imaginative play is not within reach despite parental claims that the child is so cute in its seemingly adult pursuits. The child is praised for activities it knows to be empty and is overindulged in other ways that gratify the parents. Thus, the child becomes an imitation grown-up who needs to be entertained at all cost, but in precocious and often expensive ways. But these are inner, mainly unconscious perceptions. Outwardly, the future seems to hold nothing but fabulous success for these golden children. What nobody had reckoned with is that these children in all their imperious and precocious intellectuality do not possess a true self. They are the shadows of their parents' narcissistic needs.

VICTORIA-LOUISE

Mr. and Mrs. Y were an exquisite couple. Dressed in the latest fashion, they might have stepped out of the pages of an expensive and sophisticated magazine. Indeed, Mr. Y was in the advertising business. "On the creative side," he informed me with a smile and immediately took the lead. Having been in psychoanalysis for many years, he felt he understood what plagued his little girl. He saw her, as he saw himself, as a superior human being, endowed with unusual sensitivities that made her unfit for discourse with other, rougher children. He was preoccupied with his own analysis and very angry with his analyst,

who apparently had tried to interpret some of the flamboyant grandiosity Mr. Y exhibited. Nonetheless, Mr. Y, with a sigh, said that he
understood psychoanalytically oriented or psychodynamic treatment
was the only "salvation" for his precious little daughter. He seemed
quite annoyed when I asked Mrs. Y about Victoria-Louise's development as a baby and how she perceived the child's difficulties.

Smiling silently while her husband grandiloquently addressed me,
she was unusually beautiful. She had been an actress but had given up
her profession to do "something useful." She had become a drama
teacher, supporting herself and her husband while he went to grad-
uate school and then established himself in business. Although financially successful by now, they still felt poor, they said. They found it
impossible to keep up with the life style of Mr. Y's clientele but enjoyed
going on cruises and weekends to which they were invited by these
clients. Mrs. Y felt ill at ease with such "conspicuous consumption," as
she saw it. A farm girl from Idaho, she felt that she was an interloper
in her husband's world, though she constantly tried to please him at
the expense of her own wishes. She explained that he "needed her to
make things safe for him." She seemed highly attuned to her husband's
moods, soothing him with a smile or the touch of her hand whenever
he came close to shouting. He clearly experienced Victoria-Louise's
difficulties as his own. Mrs. Y told me in a quiet, methodical way what
I needed to know about the child.

The couple were married for 10 years when, after having given up
all hope, Mrs. Y found that she was pregnant. There had been a series
of consultations and tests with infertility specialists who could find
nothing organically wrong with either partner. Adoption was out of
the question for Mr. Y, who wanted either his own child or nothing at
all. As a matter of fact, he ascribed his business success to his
"everything or nothing-at-all mentality." Both Mr. and Mrs. Y were
delighted with their belated success and were overjoyed when the little
girl was born. They at first could not agree on a name but finally
settled on a combination of "V for Victory" plus the name of an
admired family member. Mrs. Y said labor had lasted for two days
because neither she nor Mr. Y would permit any drugs to be used.
Apparently, the early life of the little family had been ecstatically
happy. The couple took turns taking care of the infant. Mrs. Y vividly
recalled that she had to "push him out of the way" in order to take her
turn with Victoria-Louise. They decided against breast feeding in
order not to spoil Mrs. Y's figure. The infant was complacent and easy

to take care of. They took her with them wherever they went, showing her off like a little mascot. Mrs. Y smilingly told me of the zeal with which her husband on occasion overfed the child, or interrupted her sleep to show her off, or threw her into the air until she shrieked, nobody knew whether with fear or delight. Mrs. Y put a stop to this behavior; Mr. Y felt wounded, although he did give in to his wife. When the baby was two years old, she had some unexplained episodes of breathholding.

Much to their delight, the little girl had talked at nine months and walked at eleven months. I silently hoped that such early ego development had been accompanied with the requisite emotional readiness to function separately from mother. Mr. Y's need to have an exceptionally bright and talented child was so obvious that I wondered if the child had, of necessity, adapted to her father's needs while yet embedded in the separation-individuation process (Mahler et al., 1975). Precocious ego development has long been thought to be detrimental to smooth progression through the various phases of separation-individuation. Mahler and her team hypothesize that "the drive for and toward individuation in the normal human infant is an innate, powerful given, which, although it may be muted by protracted interference, does manifest itself all along the separation-individuation process" (p. 206).

Mahler as early as 1952 warned that some toddlers cannot tolerate a sudden maturational spurt of autonomous ego functions when they are not ready to function separately from mother. A precocious differentiation of the ego occurs when the infant is required at too early a time to assume the burden of adapting to external reality. In Victoria-Louise's case, part of the external reality would have to be Mr. Y's inordinate need to have only the most advanced of children. Victoria-Louise was said to have spoken short sentences at nine months and to be totally fluent verbally by twelve months. Fortunately, Mrs. Y's more level-headed approach also influenced the child. Therefore, I hypothesized, along the lines of Mahler's later thinking, that such early differentiated behavior as Victoria-Louise's speaking and walking was due to the child's inborn precocity of the sensory-perceptive ego nucleus[1] and not because she and her mother had been

---

[1] The ego evolves gradually after birth from an undifferentiated psychic state. This evolution is based physiologically on the sense organs, which are equipped to select only certain stimuli and to reduce the intensity of others. Psychically, certain

inadequately attuned to each other. That there was trouble afoot became clear when both parents recited the woes they thought had befallen their small family. They felt these so intensely that they needed a second interview before treatment of their child could commence.

Victoria-Louise, now nine years old, refused to go to school. Every morning, there was a battle that usually ended with Mrs. Y's driving the sobbing Victoria-Louise to school. Mr. Y felt humiliated and wronged by his daughter's refusal, despite Mrs. Y's more reasonable stance that Victoria-Louise was reacting to a long line of injustices and inequities she had encountered when she entered public school. According to both parents, the child was bored to tears right from the beginning because she could already read and do simple arithmetic when she entered kindergarten. Neither parent thought it odd that their daughter did not get along with the other children and even refused to play with them. They felt that the other children were wild and did not appreciate Victoria-Louise, who was "studious" and had many talents that set her apart. She was then already taking piano lessons and dance lessons and disliked both. However, Mr. Y enjoyed practicing with her and so the two of them had a practice session each evening during which Victoria-Louise received much encouragement and praise from her father. When the family had company, Victoria-Louise performed and was again praised lavishly while the parents basked in the admiring envy of their friends.

In school, no one was impressed that Victoria-Louise was such a star. The other children thought she was "dopey" because she wore designer clothes instead of the ubiquitous jeans and would not participate in their games. The teacher openly favored her and made a monitor out of her. Victoria-Louise, however, resented being made to work collecting the papers and paintings of her classmates. Mr. Y thought her resentment appropriate. He half jocularly declared her chores to be a form of child labor and taught Victoria-Louise to decline politely. Mrs. Y, in a more egalitarian frame of mind, feared for

---

defensive functions also are developed and maintained to protect against awareness of the demands of primitive urges and impulses. In order to function efficiently, certain ego functions, such as perception, motility, intention, intelligence, thinking, speech and language, must mature relatively free of conflict. In the neonate, these undeveloped but existing functions are known as ego nuclei.

her daughter's well-being and advised the opposite. Victoria-Louise was to make herself available to her teacher so as to have her on her side when the other children badgered her. In this exchange, I could see that neither parent considered what Victoria-Louise wanted or thought. They were invested in having their child excel over all others, no matter what.

In the matter of school work, Mrs. Y was as demanding as her husband. Victoria-Louise was to be the head of the class. This goal was so important to her because she felt she had had to marry in order to have "the comforts of life"; she wanted her daughter to have everything "without a man." Mr. Y was incensed at this statement and hoped I would disabuse the child of her mother's "wild" notions. They then discussed at great length that perhaps Victoria-Louise would be better off in a private school but decided against it for the time being because they thought she would not do well away from home. Lately, she had not been sleeping well, appeared wild eyed in her parents' bedroom at night after nightmares, and had been apprehended throwing rocks at some neighborhood children. A therapy schedule of three times a week was agreed upon, with the stipulation that Mr. and Mrs. Y could call for an appointment for themselves whenever they felt troubled. They also wanted Victoria-Louise present whenever they had their session with me. They saw their child, unfortunately for her, as an "equal partner."

Course of Treatment

Victoria-Louise knew how to comport herself. Impeccably dressed, as were her parents, she perched on the nearest chair, straightened her skirt, and told me that she thought she would probably do better in junior high school, when other people presumably would have caught up to her level. I answered that since that was several years in the future, she must be feeling quite alone these days. Oh, she said with a sigh, she was used to that. She was always waiting around for her parents to finish up their work so that they could come and practice with her or take a walk or have a nice talk. I told her that with me she didn't have to wait for anything, that, short of hurting herself or me, she could do anything with her time in my playroom. Despite the suppressed motoric agitation I saw in her fidgeting and hand wringing, and the distress expressed in her white, tense face, Victoria-Louise did not want to do anything. She wanted to talk, having learned from her father that talking is what one did in a therapy session. She punched one hand with the other as she told me that school was pure hell. The boys always pushed and clapped her on the back. They wanted to get her and pull her in the bushes; and after they had gotten her into the bushes, they would just leave her there. Her teacher did not even believe her when she complained, just as I probably would not believe her, she asserted.

I told her that to me she looked like a person who was very angry and did not know how to get rid of the anger. Yes, that was right. She asked if there was a way she could get rid of it? I asked how she felt about the boys who persecuted her. She wanted to push and shove them. I suggested that perhaps she could push and shove something in the playroom. Victoria-Louise, in her little velvet dress and patent leather shoes, selected a large table. Not only was the piece of furniture too heavy for her to push, she did not seem to know how to go about the task of pushing. Together we strained and heaved until the heavy table moved. Victoria-Louise was delighted. She confided, "I don't want to hurt people, but they get on my nerves. My parents get on my nerves, too. They laugh at me when I put the food in my cheek and say I don't know where my mouth is." She then described daily struggles at the breakfast and dinner tables when her parents wanted her to eat although she was not hungry. Apparently, she was required to have impeccable table manners and to eat the quantities of food that her parents felt were right for her. She accepted their saying that she did not know what was good for her, but she did know where her mouth was and she wanted that understood. I promised that I would bring up this controversy at the next session with the parents.

With this promise, I made a friend. Victoria-Louise felt free to tell me about the many impingements on her person and on her space she had to suffer daily. Mother and father fought over what she was to wear. Mother was in favor of jeans with a "nice" shirt or blouses; father insisted on fashionable but unsuitable formal clothing, more appropriate for a party. "And because he gets tense, she gives in," the child confided. On the rare occasions that Victoria-Louise defied her parents—defiance that was almost invariably accompanied by an intake of breath—they told her, "Don't gasp" and made believe they had not heard her complaint. She said that they never listened to her and on occasion told her not to interrupt when she wanted to explain why she would not or could not follow their commands.

But Victoria-Louise was not quite so helpless against her parents as she claimed. In short order, she arrived for her session in leotards and tights, prepared to exercise and push the table some more. She very much liked any activity that made her gasp for breath. She liked this kind of gasping after exertion and differentiated it from the intake of breath when she defied her parents. We ran around the room, played tag, danced to rock music, and made up rhythms on tambourines that then were translated into dances. Victoria-Louise's favorites were Indian war chants she had found among her father's vast record collection. She asked for permission to bring these records to her sessions and was so enthusiastically encouraged to do so by her parents that she nearly gave up the whole endeavor. But being able to use her muscles in whole body exercises was so pleasant for her that she "stopped up my ears and packed away the records."

The child must have been carrying rage and disappointments, frustrations and restrictions with her from a very early age. She yearned for freedom of her motor drive (Mittelman, 1957) and made use of her sessions both by playing and dancing strenuously and telling me about her life. She alternated between acting like a spokeswoman for culture and refinement and a child who was just plain sick of being bossed around.

Her parents commented cautiously that "her creativity was coming back" but pointed out that she was becoming "aggressive." They were quite right. Once she had experienced her own muscular strength, Victoria-Louise attacked those who had tried to impinge on her before and came home with a bloody nose, a black eye, and many scratches. During the session she told me a good deal about what was troubling her. She thought her parents did not mean what they said. They had one set of behaviors for her, another for other people. They made excuses for the wild behavior of friends' and neighbors' children but expected their own daughter to adhere to the standards they set for her. Victoria-Louise thought they were "two-faced."

For a long time, she did not go near the toys in the play room; she was preoccupied and enchanted with her new freedom to move. Then, with many misgivings, she said she wanted to play with dolls. She thought she was too old to play with them yet too young to have babies. But she wanted me to know that she knew all about "that." Her mother had had a "mis." What did this mean? I asked. Mother had been pregnant and, prepared to share some happy times with her, had told her daughter about it. But Victoria-Louise did not want any brothers or sisters. She wished for the new baby's death. When shortly thereafter her mother miscarried, she was not surprised. Her wishes, according to Victoria-Louise, were strong and were always fulfilled! She was not particularly interested in talking about her magical wishes. They seemed to her to be natural. She claimed to know all about the reproductive process but simultaneously announced that she was "too little" to understand it. My impression was that she was trying to ward off cognitive understanding of her parents' feeling states and inner insecurities. Possibly there was also a fleeting identification with the unborn child, whom, Victoria-Louise thought, the mother, preferred.

Victoria-Louise always had a watchful air about her. She always seemed poised at the point of flight. Indeed, she often needed to run around the room to calm herself. Fenichel (1945) has talked about the fact that rage and aggression are frequently held in the skeletal muscles. Watching the cramped pattern of her muscles in action, I half expected some urgent tension release to take place in each session.

During the next parent interview at which Victoria-Louise was still present, I asked how the family felt about bad manners and misconduct of any kind. Victoria-Louise responded: Being "bad" meant giggling during a serious film, making fun of people, or telling lies. Both parents beamed with pleasure when they heard her reply. I asked how they would react to a child who needed to shout and run or to hit someone. The parents were horrified. Why should we discuss such events in other people's lives? I pointed out that, having come home with tangible evidence of fights with her peers, Victoria-Louise apparently was acting like other people now. Neither parent knew what to say. But Victoria-Louise turned pale, started to breathe heavily, and began to turn cartwheels. Then she stood on her head, balancing in a wobbly fashion, until she fell down with a thud. "That's very nice, Victoria-Louise," her equally pale father said. "But that's not how we behave in a therapist's office." "Maybe you don't," she answered, "but I do." Both parents were shocked. I, however, felt that Victoria-Louise's declaration of independence needed reinforcement. I suggested that perhaps the time had come for letting Victoria-Louise have more freedom to explore and express herself. This freedom, I said, included conducting the parents' session without her presence. Her parents were shocked and chagrined to learn that their emotional reactions might be hindering their daughter's emotional growth and individuation. They agitatedly pointed to her good intellectual and artistic achievement and came close to removing Victoria-Louise from treatment, when she asked, "Can't I just be me?"

That settled it. Both parents wanted their daughter to be herself and agreed to further treatment.

In the sessions, Victoria-Louise now took to acting like a much younger child. The favorite theme of her playing was building a house for a family. The house had no door and could be opened only by an electric beam that hung around the necks of the parents. A very stern mother scolded the children and made the children whine. The family in the game was, of course, royal. The king/father was portrayed as being beaten up because he "was like a 100 lb. weakling." Victoria-Louise hastened to tell me that this character was not like her own father, who according to her was "stable, understanding, correcting me when I do wrong things and defends me." In the ongoing play story, however, the father/king was sent out of the country, and the princess/oldest daughter was placed in charge. A witch appeared and set the princess' crown on fire.

I could see how deeply conflicted Victoria-Louise was about her father and mother and how guilty she felt about the strong bid for independence she had made. She feared retribution. Her show of strength – her declaration that she did things differently from her father – also terrified her. On a very deep level she was merged with his narcissistic need to remain one with her. But being one with father meant pushing mother out of her role as father's wife. Despite this seemingly oedipal constellation, I was not at all certain that Victoria-Louise had reached that level. Rather, it seemed to me that her mother was sometimes seen as the provider of babies and of structure. She, not only the father, had the magical phallic beam that opened the house. In this instance, the father was a weakling who was sent out of the country. But while the princess was in charge, an evil witch appeared who set her crown on fire! Again, the female was portrayed in this child's unconscious as the one with the evil power, which is also exciting.

But the fire was not in Victoria-Louise's genital area; it was in her crown. She had identified herself as the princess and rubbed her head vigorously when we discussed the fire in the crown. She seemed relieved when I told her that sometimes we feel forbidden feelings in other areas than those designated for them. She thought her for-bidden feelings were that she wanted to send the father/king out of the country. With this displacement upward of an essentially sexual, exciting feeling and evidence of an erotic attachment to her mother, I saw Victoria-Louise as caught in what Kestenberg (1982) has called the inner genital phase, which, in the beginning, consists of

> a disequilibrium in which pregenital and early genital drives and derivative ego functions vie with one another. The ensuing integra-tion of pregenital and phallic drives and applied ego functions under the aegis of inner genitality is aided by the child's identification with the mother, who acts as an external organizer, reinforcing and guiding inner genitality, the internal organizer at the time. Externa-lization of inner genital impulses is the mechanism which underlies their sublimation into maternal behavior and the wish to be a mother. The former dyadic relationship is now replaced by a triangular "girl-baby-mother" relationship [p. 84].

That Victoria-Louise had advanced even this far must have had something to do with the affection, body warmth, and protection that she did receive from her mother. But internally Victoria-Louise was torn. She knew almost consciously that it was her task, and mother's, to satisfy father's many demands. But she also felt that this responsi-bility was unfair and that she was not equal to the job. Yet staying merged with such a seductive paternal figure gave her gratification and fuel for many omnipotent fantasies, the most prominent being that she did not need anyone else and that she was better than her peers. At the same time, she must have identified with her mother's hidden longings for a mate who was not so narcissistic as her husband. Mother taught her what to say about father, words that reflected mother's own wishes. When Victoria-Louise recited the attributes of her father's behavior vis-à-vis herself, she sounded like a robot. She did not believe what she said. Later she told me that when she sometimes allowed herself to be angry with her father, mother would "teach her" how good her father really was. This "teaching" took the form of admonishments.

To protect her relationship with her parents, the child had

evolved a false self (Winnicott, 1960a), as much as one can speak of an evolved self in a child. Her environment seemed unable to allow her to seek her own internal truth and image but forced her into patterns conceived by her parents without regard for her predilections and developmental needs. Victoria-Louise, then, can be seen to have worn a mask not of her own choosing. Forced by the demands of her environment to develop certain ego functions, she became angrier and angrier. Aggression smoldered within her and could no longer be contained when she first came into treatment. I once remarked to her that she literally had to stand on her head to defy her father. She found this comment pleasing.

In the meantime, the sessions alone with the parents proved to be fruitful. They agreed to soften some of their demands on their daughter. Mrs. Y especially gained a fresh understanding of her daughter's needs. Mr. Y, however, was in a huff. He felt that his wife and I were "ganging up" on him, and he wrote me a note in which he expressed his feeling of injury and declined to come for further sessions. He perceived his wife's more empathic stance toward his child as a defection and wanted to punish both her and me for this. Nevertheless, he began to go easier on Victoria-Louise. She no longer had to perform for company, and the evening practice sessions were sometimes canceled so that she could go outside and play, which at first consisted of her walking to a neighborhood playground and watching the other children. She did not feel welcome and was afraid of them. She once showed a crowd how she could stand on her head but was laughed at "because her underpants showed." Some mean boys began to chase her. Her father thought that they were jealous of her, but Victoria-Louise, for the first time, did not believe him. "Why should they be jealous of me?" she asked. "I have no friends and everybody thinks I'm a freak." Her mother thought that perhaps the boys were showing, in a strange, boyish way, that they wanted to be friends. Victoria-Louise was skeptical but thought she might go back to the playground and see what happened. At this point, two years into the treatment, she had her first dream. Although one of her presenting symptoms was said to be nightmares, I had never heard a word about them. Now she dreamed about Moby Dick. He was real. She and I had to capture him and stand in the water. The tail almost hit her and was right above her. She quickly went back on the ship for safety. The hooks she had would not hold Moby Dick down.

Victoria-Louise thought that this dream was about her wish to "get a chance to sleep with mother in her bed when I can't sleep." Who was Moby Dick? I asked. According to her, it was the boys who chased her who, however, now also called for her on their way to school. In the following session, Victoria-Louise was very distressed. She had proudly told her parents her dream; they often shared dreams with each other. Her father had sniffed and said, "Moby Dick, the great big Dingbat." Victoria-Louise was furious about her father's remark and wanted to scream at him but did not dare. With a pathetic smile, she told me that the dream must be "about hurting and being hurt by someone you love." Her interpretation sounded as though it had come from her parents.

The theme of Victoria-Louise's play now changed. She acquired an imaginary alligator family who licked her and protected her from sleeplessness. After she told me about this fantasy, she also told me that her family did not allow their dog to lick itself. I said that I thought it would be quite difficult for the dog to stop doing so or to be protected by alligators who have such huge mouths and teeth. Victoria-Louise now began to defend her alligators. She enacted each one of them, writhing and crawling on the floor. She made up a joyful alligator dance and often screamed and roared as she imagined alligators would do. After many such sessions, she told me that she had to be a girl alligator because her mother did not like boys. "That's why there was a 'mis,'" she said. Her mother's dislike of boys and men had caused it; her father said so, she claimed.

I began to understand that the child was telling me about actual occurrences in her family, not merely about the symbolic representation of her parents as alligators. When she made the link to her parents while once again writhing on the floor and screaming, she became so furious that she picked up a chair and flung it clear across the room. When it broke, she was horribly upset, turned pale, and hissed at me, "Now you'll give me away." She trembled but would not let me soothe her. I was surprised at the depth and strength of her rage, which I surmised, had accrued from the early pregenital hostilities that had festered in her since early infancy because of the repression and lack of acknowledgement of her personhood. I promised her that I would not tell her parents about the chair until, and if, she felt ready to tell them herself.

Shortly thereafter, Victoria-Louise had another dream. In it was of a combination boy and girl white porpoise. The porpoise felt good to swim with. She decided that it would be good to swim with me, and also with her mother. Her mother and I both had very light hair and the whiteness of the porpoise made her think of both of us. I asked why she thought the porpoise was both a boy and a girl. Well, she said, both I and her mother were very strong, as men were supposed to be. "If you didn't know my father," she said, "you couldn't take to him. He's too strict and wants too much and does unexpected things which are unpleasant for you and pleasant for him." Victoria-Louise had trouble leaving this session. She thought it would be nice stay forever in such a peaceful place as my playroom.

In later sessions, Victoria-Louise talked about the infantile needs that had been expressed in this session and continued to find expression. She spoke in that literate, precocious way that at first had seemed so alien in a child. But by now she was more in possession of her feelings, was less afraid of dissenting, and spoke with true emotion. Some physiologic symptoms now plagued her. She suffered constriction of her breathing pattern and had asthmalike attacks. She was tested, but no allergies were found; nor was there anything wrong with her heart. I treated these symptoms as the expectable accompaniment to anger. This approach brought Victoria-Louise some relief. My interpretation built the semantic bridge that allowed her to say, "I feel furious." Gedo (1988) reports about an analytic patient who used asthmatic attacks in response to the emergence of initially unconscious fantasies of repeating exciting sadomasochistic struggles in childhood (p. 82). But for Victoria-Louise, apparently, the feeling of not being able to breath had even deeper roots. Deep-breathing exercises and a technique I had developed with a colleague (Siegel and Blau, 1978), called Breathing Together, eventually allowed Victoria-Louise to reestablish her normal breathing pattern.

Breathing Together was initially developed in response to the needs of deeply disturbed children whose breathing patterns had never been regulated sufficiently for them to provide themselves with the amount of oxygen they needed for strenuous gross motor tasks.[2]

---

[2]We tested the Forced Vital Capacity of psychotic children with a respirometer after first ascertaining their developmental ages as opposed to their chronological

We hypothesized that although breathing is an autonomous reflex, it also carries the imprint of having been adapted to the mother's breathing rhythms after birth. Blau and I conceptualized the breathing apparatus as being connected with the first body ego and body image. While being held, the baby quite literally feels if mother is anxiously sucking in her breath or if she is peaceful. Mother's innate pattern will always prevail and give the infant clues to how to adapt. To reconstruct the early mother–child dyad without fostering regression, we placed our hands on the chest of the patient while allowing the child to place his hand on our chest. Thus connected, we tried to adapt to the child's breathing pattern and after a while encouraged him to do it "our way." For the children who were our patients then, this procedure produced many changes, including lengthening the attention span. For Victoria-Louise, it quieted her tense affective state and gave her a renewed ability to use her imagination productively. In the steady synchronicity of our breathing together, she again found the nurturing her mother had given her and was able to put aside the physiologically remembered affective states engendered by her exciting father.

Mr. Y had by now returned to the parental sessions with me. He wanted to confront me with the change in his daughter. "You made a psychosomatic child monster out of a wonderful, intelligent, and feeling little girl. She doesn't even want to be with me. She only wants to be with her mother, who also doesn't like me." Explanations about the repressed developmental needs for healthy aggression now surfacing in his daughter were vigorously rejected. I suggested that Mr. Y discuss his own difficulties with his therapist rather than expecting his daughter to carry them for him. His wife once again managed to soothe him and to extract a promise from him "not to take it out on Victoria-Louise."

The child's newest idea was to change her name. She wanted to be called Vicky. I thought this a reasonable request. Not so her parents. They abhorred diminutives and tried to explain to her that she was in some way demeaning herself by choosing a nickname. Vicky now began to signal by the use of her name what sort of mood she was in.

---

ages. We found that they used their breathing apparatus consistent with their developmental ages; that is, if a child was 10 years old but tested like a four-year-old, his apparent use of the Forced Vital Capacity was that of a four-year-old.

As Victoria-Louise, she beat up monsters, screamed, and acted incoherently. She made up a ditty, her "kicking song":

> Sneak up,
> then bite, scratch, kick,
> pounce and bounce twenty times.

She regularly delivered this chant while she was turned away from me and acted it out either with the ubiquitous bouncer or with various stuffed animals. I noted that after each performance she breathed more easily, and I asked her if she noticed that too. Yes, she did. And she clearly understood the function of her ritual: it was to make her feel less helpless. And it had to be performed while she was turned away from me so that it would not hurt me. I understood that the child was trying to cope with overwhelming anger by defensively using grandiose fantasies of the sort that must also have plagued her father. But she did not for long have to use such an infantile way of coping. She now hated her violin lessons, did not want dance any place but in sessions, and was "just sick of being forced all the time." The beautiful tones of the violin did not mean anything to her, nor did the fact that the violin had cost a lot of money. "Let *him* play it," she asserted.

As Vicky, she brought me a dream in which she and her mother were upstairs in their new kitchen when they heard heavy footsteps coming up the cellar stairs. An angry looking man came up and told them to go down. She asked if he would hurt them and he said, "No, I can't be mad at you for not knowing." She thought that "the man came up the steps like when the angriness comes up my throat" and was quite willing to accept the interpretation that the cellar might have something to do with therapy and the unconscious. "But I like what's in the cellar," she declared, "I don't like that my parents think learning is more important than pleasure. They don't want me to have any pleasure."

Vicky was not so helpless any more as she had been. She negotiated with her parents to play her violin one last time at the recital of her school if she would thereafter be allowed to quit. She correctly understood that a sudden withdrawal from the lessons would have heralded too strong a sense of mortification for her parents. At the same time, she was afraid to admit that her breathing pattern had returned to normal. She was concerned about her "kicking song." "I can't go around doing that for the rest of my life," she said.

A difficult time in treatment now ensued in which Vicky tried to blame me for her troubles. She wanted me to protect her more and tell her mother to be more available. She could not believe that her parents would not follow every suggestion I gave them. "They love rules and regulations," said the precocious young miss. Mother, in order to control the now demanding girl, told her that her own childhood had been much more harrowing than Vicky's. But Vicky did not want to hear that. "What do I care if she had to get up at five in the morning? That was then!" she exclaimed. The sleep disturbances reached a new crescendo when she became aware of her parents reacting to each other "like lovey dovies." She felt excluded and jealous and, for the first time, began to wonder if her father had a penis like the boys at the playground who sometimes urinated in the bushes. She had become fast friends with them and took their advice on how to conduct herself in school. Eventually, she confessed being scared by an open door to the hall closet that she could see from her open bedroom door. Why? "I can't call out because Dad might be using it." I pointed out to her that she was taking care of dad rather than herself if she worried about his using the closet. "Yes," she agreed, "but I might be worse off when I complain and don't think of other people's feelings." I tried to learn from her how Dad might use the closet, but Vicky did not know and rejected the thought of a fantasy in which the father urinated.

Vicky was really a pleasure to work with from this point on. She was insightful and every bit as intelligent and creative as her parents said she was. She stayed in therapy until the move to junior high school was imminent. She herself felt that she would like to try to get along without me, provided she could call every now and then or come back when she "had troubles." Her relationship with her parents had stabilized considerably by then, and she had gained enough strength to defend herself when either one of them tried to impinge on what she now knew to be her boundaries.

Discussion

Seeing Victoria-Louise's transformation into Vicky was like seeing development take place *in statu nascendi*. Despite the heavy demands placed on her by her environment, she managed to resume psychological growth once she sensed that I was on her side. Although I did not abandon neutrality, I made it clear to her that her wishes and needs in the sessions superceded commands issued by her parents. Otherwise I doubt that she could have resumed emotional learning. Her father's narcissistic needs especially were so enormous that Vicky often seemed to feel that her own sensations and feelings, affects and emotions had to be abandoned, or else they did not rise into her consciousness at all. To be totally present emotionally was both an unknown and forbidden territory for her. The open message from father was "me first." Therefore, Vicky acted as though all her feelings were useless and worthless. She continued to learn cognitively but could not, in the coercive environment her parents provided, acquire adequate psychological skills. Victoria-Louise at first could not soothe herself, recognize her own body signals, or name her emotions. Grandiose fantasies defended her against the inner knowledge that she was her parents' appendage and not a person in her own right.

Yet the basic core for healthy development must have been there. I believe that during the symbiotic phase Mrs. Y provided good enough mothering, protecting the infant from the excesses of her husband. She did not permit him to interrupt Victoria-Louise's sleep when he wanted to show her off, nor did she allow him to feed the child when she was not hungry or to overstimulate her with exciting physical games. The trouble arose later, when Victoria-Louise was in the practicing subphase of separation individuation. The precocity of her ego development — she talked at nine months and walked at eleven months — left her particularly vulnerable. Yet I do not believe Victoria-Louise to have been a child at risk owing to pre-ego precocities such as hypersensitivity to noise, light, or visual hyperalertness. She was by all accounts a contented baby. Mahler et al. (1975) wrote:

> The more abruptly, suddenly, and prematurely the infant becomes aware of the external world beyond the symbiotic orbit, through such a fragment of pre-ego precocity, the more difficult it seems to become for him to ward off fear of early symbiotic object loss. . . . In such instances . . . it is important that the mother furnish a particularly well-attuned external or auxiliary ego, a particularly protective shield [p. 205].

I believe that Mrs. Y was such a mother, as she demonstrated when she prevented her husband from throwing her infant daughter up into the air too often or rescued the baby from being stuffed when she did not want to eat any more.

Mahler (1966) has made us aware of the existence of phase-specific conflicts that occur regularly although their contents vary from one mother–child dyad to the next. Usually these conflicts do not occur until the second half of the second year. For Victoria-Louise, they arose earlier but were somewhat attenuated by her mother's attunement. This toddler had to grapple with her delusions of omnipotence at an earlier age, during which, I imagine, she was even more vulnerable than the average baby. Generally, the danger is that of narcissistic deflation in the rapprochement phase. Not so for Victoria-Louise. She had a definite sense of her own specialness but suppressed it in order to cope with the demands father placed on her. She felt herself perfect and was told by her father she was perfect. But this perfection clearly eroded and revealed itself unreliable as the child matured. In addition, the child had the heavy task of completing her father's image of himself. He was a perfect father, he thought.

Victoria-Louise ensured her continued psychological growth by isolating those aspects of her inner life that were affected by the primitive needs of her own self and that of her father. She tried to become a child prodigy and, when she failed, grew angrier and angrier. But in her world, there was no outlet for aggression, no place to put her tensions or learn to understand their origin and function. By the time the child was three years old her mother had abandoned her own protective stance and expected her daughter to help her soothe father's many moods. The child learned to suspend her own needs and grew both lonelier and angrier. In treatment, she reexperienced, in a literal way, the impression of being "choked off," when she could not breath adequately. It was her mode of remembering events that had been encoded without reaching symbolic level (Lichtenberg, 1983). Although these events—being thrown up into the air by her father when she was sleepy and the times when her father found it amusing to stuff her with foods she did not want and tried to spit out—were not themselves recoverable in treatment, the affect connected to them certainly was. Vicky could not cope with her hostility. In treatment, there was, at first, a physical tension release without fantasy content. She ran, stood on her head, and screamed like a toddler. Dancing helped to soothe her because of its rhythmic nature. Only later was she able to fantasize and give meaning to her games and her playing. She herself seemed aware of the tragedy of having make-believe alligators for protectors. It cannot be very reassuring to have such jaws so close to oneself!

Parens (1987) warns against the consequences of allowing a child to feel so much unpleasure that it has a temper tantrum. He advises parents to help their children gently to accept limits. But limit setting was precisely what was distorted in the Y household. The healthy boisterousness of a young child was suppressed while intellectualization and rationalization were so forcefully applied that Victoria-Louise became a caricature of an adult. Mr. Y and some of his friends, on the other hand, had no problem giving free vent to most of their feelings. The child both cognitively and intuitively understood that there was an inequity here. In treatment, the expression of her rage both scared and relieved her. Later she expressed rage while turned away from me so that she could not hurt me. In doing so, she both expressed and mastered early infantile omnipotence. With the blossoming of positive feelings for me, she could allow other children into her universe and make friends. Just as importantly, she learned to guard her boundaries and began to defend herself against unreasonable demands by her parents.

In summary, special techniques used with Vicky included dancing and rhythmic activities such as running, hopping, and jumping. A special effort was made not to devalue the parents in this very intelligent child's eyes. No matter how individuated she became, she was still dependent on her parents' actual and psychological availability.

Vicky went on to a prestigious university to which she had won a scholarship. She later became an outstanding performer on the stage. Recently, she sent me the announcement of her marriage.

A case like Victoria-Louise's might be shrugged off as an expectable outcome of narcissistic parenting, a form of parenting that, unfortunately, is all too common. I have had several such cases and know many colleagues who see similar patterns. School psychologists and social workers are also aware of such children but seldom are empowered to refer them for psychotherapy because such children are not conspicuous in school and do not seem to need as much care as their possibly more volatile emotionally disturbed peers. It is not always possible to recognize socially withdrawn children as troubled. They do well in school and their parents are involved with them. While a psychologist or social worker might recognize such children as needing attention, teachers do not call on these professionals to observe such children, most often teachers do not even notice that something might be amiss. There are few clear-cut criteria to alert teachers to the potential of trouble here. Consequently, unless the family feels concerned by their child's solitude, such a child often slips through the cracks in school, only to surface later as the maladjusted adult who makes himself and others miserable with constant, nagging complaints about everything. Matching this sort of childhood experience against that of some adults I have treated, I have formed the impression that so much parental narcissism produces in later life either chronic victims or even more hateful narcissists.

To illustrate how varied, and disguised, the ramifications of parental narcissism can be, let me tell you about Charity.

CHARITY

Her worried parents brought Charity to me when she was almost 13 years old because she had recently begun showing sleep disturbances and had given up some of her favorite pastimes. Charity was a talented dancer who until her 12th year had taken dancing lessons. Her parents had discontinued the lessons, with her consent, because the family was opposed on religious grounds to a career in theater. Recognizing that Charity could probably not simply stop what she had been doing with excellent success up to then, the parents had given their permission for Charity to dance at home as much as she wished. When she in short order gave that up as well, they felt at first overjoyed that their oldest daughter was so mature. Charity's deepening depression worried them however, and they realized that perhaps their daughter had more problems than met the eye.

They belonged to a fundamentalist church that taught abstinence from many of the pleasures most of us take for granted. There were dietary restrictions, which Charity had adhered to even before the required age, and parties, dancing, playing instrumental music, and working on the Sabbath were forbidden. Both parents were officials in their congregation and paid a heavy tithe for the privilege of being spiritually saved. They told me that they prayed often about their "pridefulness," having taken special pleasure in Charity's early understanding of the scriptures and her easy acceptance of the restrictions imposed on her. They were very pleased that she did not make friends with the children in public school because they feared such friendships might be a source of contamination. When I asked them if Charity had made friends in their Sunday school, they seemed puzzled and then admitted that no, their Charity had never been one to mingle with any of the boys and girls she came in contact with. She was, instead, content to play with her three younger brothers but lately she no longer played with them either. Mr. and Mrs. Z thought this change in behavior had to do with her early maturation. Charity's menses had begun when she was 10 years old, and both parents felt that her withdrawal from her brothers at this age was appropriate.

Charity had been a good girl from the time she was born. She had passed all developmental milestones a bit on the early side. She always, even as an infant, seemed to enjoy the services in church and never had to be left in the nursery provided by the religious group. She had a good voice and sang in the choirs both at church and in school. She was an excellent scholar, a help to her mother, and the pride of her father. Her dancing lessons were the only activity that set her apart from the family, and, as far as they could see, she had acted sensibly in voluntarily giving up what could, in the future, become a source of sin. The spiritual leader of the congregation had warned the Z's that Charity would be difficult to wean away from her artistic pursuits if she were not stopped in time. He had also advised them to allow Charity to get dancing out of her system by permitting her to express herself in such fashion at home. Both parents were acutely aware of the sensuous nature of Charity's dancing and agreed that it would be sinful and corrupting for their daughter "to show herself in public." They were opposed to psychotherapy also, but their clergyman had explained to them that Charity's "affliction" was of a secular nature and should thus be dealt with not by him but by a psychotherapist. They resisted his advice until they found Charity wide-eyed, exhausted, and haggard each morning, declaring that she could not sleep. Her schoolwork had also suffered but was still sufficiently good for her to be on the honor role.

The Z's received the suggestion of therapy for themselves with disbelief but promised to consider it since this was "the usual." To them, this meant the usual course of events when a child enters therapy.

Course of Treatment

Charity was an unusually tall girl with long, blond hair. She slouched to hide her early-developed bosom. Hiding behind her long hair, she walked slowly into the room. Her parents had been right. She looked exhausted. She found nothing to say to me, except that her parents and the Reverend Mr. C wanted her to see me; she did not know why. I told her what her parents had said, mentioning her insomnia. Rousing herself slightly, she answered that she did not see how I could help her. She thought she needed sleeping pills but the Reverend Mr. C and her parents were opposed to such "weakness." She said she "tried very hard each night to relax sufficiently to sleep." But neither willing herself to sleep nor prolonged prayer or meditation upon biblical passages soothed her. She barely had enough strength to drag herself to school and to her sessions. She was uninterested in the art materials, music, toys, and games in my consultation room and even less interested in what I had to say. She did not resist coming, however, and appeared like a tall wraith, accompanied by one or the other of her worried parents, who always walked her into the office, deposited her in a chair as though she were an invalid, and then walked back to the waiting room. They always made some sort of comment like "She feels really tired today," or: "She didn't even eat her breakfast today." Both parents were dismayed when I asked them to stop these depersonalizing practices.

They did not understand that a relationship needed to grow between Charity and me before I could help her; instead, they seemed to think of me as some sort of voodoo practitioner who would heal their child by magical means. They were aware that Charity said very little to me and thought they were helping me with their remarks about Charity's behavior. And they most certainly did not feel that they were infantilizing her by walking her into the office although she had shown no sign of unwillingness to enter by herself. They saw themselves as concerned and caring.

Mrs. Z literally wrung her hands when she sent Charity into my office by herself. I understood then that Mrs. Z felt a piece of herself disappearing out of her control. She did not yet trust me enough to leave her daughter with me and merely was following "the usual" because she did not know what else to do. When it was Mr. Z's turn to bring Charity, he hovered near the door so that I had to shut it in his face. There was no comment from Charity, who obediently took her chair and looked at me. Our sessions took their usual, laborious course with me looking for a tiny entrance into Charity's closed-off world, which she tenaciously protected. After her parents had gotten used to letting her enter by herself, something very interesting happened. Charity fell asleep in the sessions! I allowed her to do so but commented when she awoke that she must have felt quite comfortable to sleep in my presence. She simply agreed and for awhile continued her wraithlike comings and goings. I noticed, however, that she sometimes on awakening would glance over to the records and the phonograph on the shelf. At their next interview with me, Mr. and Mrs. Z were overjoyed. Charity seemed more relaxed, had more energy, and, according to them, looked forward to her sessions with me. They were concerned, however, that she did not share with them what we did in the sessions and wanted a full report from me. They were most chagrined that I did not feel free to divulge such information. They quoted the bible to me, trying to prove to me that parents own their children and that they are therefore entitled to know everything about them. I used this opportunity to point out to them that they really needed to know more about the therapeutic process and that the best way to learn about it was through personal exposure to it. They became quite agitated at my "inaccessibility" and in their turn suggested that I talk to their clergyman. I promised to do so, reasoning that since he had been the referral source, he might further influence the family to allow Charity to separate from them.

The relationship with Charity progressed slowly. In time she was willing to discuss her naps during session. At first she thought that no discussion was necessary. She had not slept properly in weeks, so what was so surprising, she wondered, that sleep had finally overtaken her? Wasn't it natural finally to "give in"? I pointed out to her that usually people sleep well not only when they are tired but when, in addition, they feel safe and cozy in their beds. Charity thought that over for a while and then decided that yes it was odd that she slept so well while sitting upright in a chair in my room but not when she was supine in her own bed. Finally, she decided that I must have some sort of power to "keep bad thoughts away." I interpreted this as her beginning to trust in me.

But Charity was very reluctant to trust a stranger. She had been carefully brought up not to trust anyone outside of her congregation. I pointed out that I was hardly a stranger any more, being privy to the family's problems. Now Charity told me what was on her mind. Because I was not of the family's religious persuasion, they all found it difficult to trust me and were amazed that Charity was actually improving. They were distressed and confused that the power of prayer had not been sufficient to heal their child. Charity herself now began to examine this issue. She had assumed that she had done something terribly wrong when sleep fled. She tried to study the scriptures to ascertain where she had failed and had come to the rather sophisticated conclusion that she was an "onanist of the female gender." All her worries about masturbation poured out. Her parents had not forbidden it but had made it clear that she was to stay pure in mind and body if she wanted to enter into matrimony. I asked why, at age 13, she had to worry about marriage. A confused and confusing stream of self-accusations ensued—she was no longer a "clean vessel," having disobeyed her parents and the bible. Charity felt especially guilty because she could sleep in my presence but not when her devoted parents were around. I told her that sometimes, when children grow up, they feel angry with parents who are around too much. Charity flew into a panic. Oh, no, she hoped and prayed that she would never feel that her parents were "around too much"! Children need their parents and cannot grow up without them, she said.

The struggle for separation and individuation was clearly beset by enormous conflict for Charity. She could not allow herself to think about or feel psychological separation from her parents. It seemed to me that Charity did not even feel that she owned her own body. Like a toddler in the separation–individuation phase, she seemed on occasion to feel that others controlled her actions. After all, she perceived her masturbatory activities as hurtful, causing a wound she had somehow brought upon herself. As time progressed, however, Charity began to feel more comfortable with herself. She shyly asked if she could dance for me and was overjoyed when I said yes. It was as though I had made her a gift of her body. I was surprised at Charity's performance. The lanky, bland child became a sensuous woman in total motion as she bent, swayed, and contracted in time with modern, often atonal music. Her choice of music seemed to convey her inner alienation and her struggles to accept her parents' rules. She was highly sophisticated and skilled in the use of dance as an expressive idiom. The loss of this outlet must have been a dreadful trauma to her. I could only hypothesize that she had accepted such a restriction without rebelling against it because she was beset by inner guilt and conflict. Charity was not yet willing to talk about her extreme dependence on her parents and their need to keep her unduly close to them. The one area into which her parents had not been able to intrude with control and demand for obedience was dance. And here Charity excelled. She thrived when teachers recognized her talent but somehow seemed to think it a sin when she succeeded too well. For a while in treatment, she seemed to think that all would be well if her parents would only let her pursue a career as a dancer, but she always stopped herself short of expressing this wish. She knew that her parents might acquiesce but that their religion would not permit them to see performing on a stage as anything but a sin. In their own way, they were as conflicted as their daughter. They felt it was their religious duty to prevent her from dancing, in which they had taken so much pride and pleasure.

The Reverend Mr. C, in the meantime, had been a polite listener when I outlined what the Zs had to contend with. He seemed to understand that there was too close a tie between the parents and their child and that such a tie, if prolonged beyond reasonable expectations, could be detrimental to all concerned. After some weeks, he called to inform me that he had instituted a weekly workshop during which his parishioners would share their experiences and worries about their children. He himself would lead the workshop and keep me informed of the Zs' progress. He wanted me to know that there was no chance of revoking the church ban on performing on stage, but he thought he could influence the Zs to allow Charity more independence.

Charity, meanwhile, was becoming less reserved. She complained about the teasing of other children in school. She had been taught to "turn the other cheek," with the result that, on occasion, she was beaten up by some ruffians. She was incensed but did not dare enlist the protection of her parents because she feared that doing so would make her even less popular in school. Torn between the safe, but

extremely disciplined and constricting world of her parents and that of
the open, but rough-and-tumble one of school, she saw no place for
herself other than in church. There she could sing, and "feel myself
swell up with sound until I want to jump for joy of Jesus." However,
such thoughts had to be kept secret also. No one would have approved
of her jumping for joy of Jesus.

She had been discovered, so to speak, when a famous dance
teacher was for a short while artist in residence at her school. Seeing
her dance among a throng of others, he offered a scholarship when she
was only seven years old. And as long as she had her dancing, she felt
she needed "only Jesus in my heart" to be prepared for anything. Her
parents had not interfered with the lessons and had even watched a
few of the dancing academy's productions. As long as Charity stayed
outwardly a child, her parents were content to let her dance. But now,
with the first signs of womanhood so clearly in evidence, all that had
to come to an end.

But Charity really did not want it to end. She desperately wanted
to continue dancing. I asked her why she had given up even dancing
at home. My question confused her. She became reticent, angry,
resistant in a way I had not seen before. I began to see that there was
more at stake for her than being allowed to dance, that being
prevented from age-appropriate internal separation from her parents
had taken its psychological toll long before the ban on dancing arose.
Charity could not verbalize what was troubling her. Instead, she had
stark anxiety attacks during sessions. Sweat rolled down her face, and
she wrung her hands as she struggled to explain to me what was
"really" troubling her. She no longer wanted to dance. That was too
strenuous, she said, and had nothing to do with what she was feeling.
And, indeed, Charity could not produce the poignant movements
that so many nondancers achieve when they get in touch with the
basic need to externalize affects or memories they have been unable to
communicate verbally.

For Charity, her wonderful technique had been split off from her
feeling of contentment and had served as a tension discharge, pure
and simple. Apparently, she had been able to endure the strict
discipline of her religion with such equanimity because she had a place
to release the stored-up muscular tensions caused by kneeling in
prayer for hours or by the stern admonitions against childish exuber-
ance. She understood the injunctions against passion as censure of her

joyful feelings. Like a medieval nun, she thought of her body as evil and was puzzled by the ecstatic muscular releases it delivered when dancing. She was willing to give up dancing because she thought the sheer physical exhilaration of it devilish.

In sessions, she regressed further, often crying about her sinfulness. She had discussed masturbation with her mother, who was enlightened enough to tell her that it was normal but to be resisted. Charity found she could not resist it. Nightly she thought of elaborate rituals that would prevent her from touching her genitals but chased sleep away as well. Charity found it excruciatingly difficult to talk about her struggles. Haunted by conflicts of loyalty and by sadistic fantasies, she could find no way to soothe herself. If she complained to me, she felt she was accusing her parents. If she recounted her dreams and fantasies, she was giving in to the devil. I finally realized that when talking of her fantasy productions she felt actual physical relief. She linked these body sensations with the release she felt when masturbating. Therefore, I became a transferential devil who tempted and lured her away from the path of righteousness, or so her dreams informed both of us. Eventually, Charity said, "But if I have such dreams and thoughts, I must want them, don't you think?" I agreed that there must be something in her to want such thoughts. But, I said, to me her fantasies sounded like those of someone who desperately wanted to be herself and not just somebody's daughter, or sister, or disciple.

Charity was puzzled and, at the same time, elated. She had always thought that one became a person by using the roles one was assigned to discover life. I traced for her how babies acquire their sense of being a person from the kind of nurturance they receive and how, at first, they can only respond indiscriminately; but that, later on, we all can make decisions about what kind of person we chose to be. Charity asked if, in my opinion, parents should help their children make choices. I answered that parents, like children, are governed by what they have learned. Charity became very thoughtful and wondered out loud if her parents weren't perhaps like children to the Reverend Mr. C. It turned out that she was annoyed with his paternal tone. She felt it demeaning for her parents always to ask his opinion. She did not want such dependence for herself, especially since it had landed her in her "terrible shakes," as she called her anxiety attacks, when she had tried to conform. We discussed the nature of freedom of choice, now that she could decide for herself what to accept, what to discard of the teaching of both her church and her parents. Charity was overwhelmed by the magnitude of these thoughts. She fell silent, was ill at ease, but showed none of the extreme anxiety she had in previous sessions.

The working through process was slow and laborious after that. Charity needed to try out new modes of behavior in her environment. She began to envy boys openly and wrote a ditty:

> There was a fish
> who had a wish
> he wanted to be a boy
> one day his wish came true
> he was a boy with an umbrella of blue.

She had begun to allow herself consciously to acknowledge the difference between the sexes and instead of shunning her brothers, as before, ran after them to see "how they were different." When I asked her if she wanted to see their penises, she giggled long and heartily for the first time. Silly, she said, she knew all about how boys look from long ago! What she wanted to teach them was to leave her alone in the bathroom so she could experiment with new hairdos and a little lipstick. On one hand, her new interests were age appropriate; on the other, they bore the stamp of an earlier developmental time in their voyeuristic insistence and frankness. There was none of the usual preteen coyness or embarrassment in the open way she badgered her brothers. Her sexual interests and her experimentation with personal adornment were forbidden of course, but Charity thought she could "get away with it" if she tried making herself pretty in private and stayed with her brothers, rather than with other males, in her pursuit of their "differentness."

A highly volatile period now ensued during which Charity seemed to be determined to find out everything she could about sexuality and the human reproductive process. Inasmuch as she had been given, and understood, all the basic information, I was puzzled by her obsessional ruminations on the subject. She did not seem to be possessed by penis envy so much as by penis awe. It was as though she had given up dancing—the body as phallus—in order to satisfy an inclination to worship and to admire the male sex and its organs. Greenacre (1953) speaks of penis awe as quite distinct from penis envy, although the two are usually intertwined. She says, "In awe there is intense admiration, a feeling of strangeness, with the sense of the possibility of possession, and sometimes an element of fear. Certainly very strong aggressive feelings are aroused, but are suspended and diffuse, and may be converted presently into worshipful submission verging on the religious, or into states of considerable excitement" (p. 31).

All of Charity's current behavior was described in that passage. She adored, but tried to irritate, the male members of her household. She was rebellious but in a highly sexualized way that turned to breathless adoration of the church as a safe, sublime haven where she was free from "evil" thoughts. Like a medieval saint, she suspected her body feelings to be of dreadful origin and tried to suppress them. She attempted to cope with these phallic-phase derivatives by ignoring them. When she felt like dancing or running, she prayed. When she was angry with anyone (which she often was), she prayed. But what the prayer brought her was a "tingling sensation all over, both wonderful and awful, as though God were both stroking and hitting her."

Greenacre informs us that such phenomena can occur when a small girl sees the penis of an adult man, either in its flaccid state or more especially in a state of erection or of becoming erect. The effect depends on several factors: the child's developmental stage, the frequency of experience, and especially the relation to the man who had been observed (p. 33). Greenacre further speaks of the excitement and exhibitionism that regularly are associated with such experiences. She goes on to say, "If penis awe is established early and decisively precedes the awareness of a contemporary penis, the awe remains the dominant and demanding attitude toward the opposite sex, but may vary from a religious oversubmissiveness to the man, in which the selected partner must seem especially godlike, to an attitude of terror and need for frank masochistic humiliation" (pp. 35–36).

I could clearly see that Charity was caught up in being both overly submissive and overly demanding in her relationships with her father and brothers. But where could a girl who had been as carefully protected as she have seen a naked man? Further, her behavior indicated that she must have seen a man naked more than once. I remembered the severe anxiety attacks she had suffered earlier in treatment, and I set out to watch carefully for memories and dreams that would indicate trauma. In the sessions, Charity kept talking about her father as a godlike creature whose own innocence was dangerous to him. He needed her to protect him – she was not sure from what. Her brothers were now "fun" but so different that she "felt odd with them but good."

As we talked about the habits and behavior of the family, Charity often spoke with great excitement about the prayer sessions that were held daily and sometimes oftener in the family's living room. All family members would openly discuss their thoughts and feelings, addressing them to their God but leaving themselves open to the comments of the others. No harsh censure was permitted, and disclosure was highly prized. In this intrusive atmosphere, Charity held her tongue. She preferred to commune with God in church. Why? I asked. Eventually, she told me that she sometimes nearly fainted with excitement when the family prayed together because her father always had an erection while praying and the boys fiddled with their crotches, evidently because their trousers were too tight, or so her mother had told her when she asked for enlightenment. She was terribly upset by the idea that her father might be experiencing forbidden ecstatic feelings similar to hers while praying. It seemed to her that the whole fabric of the church was constructed to help people conquer their sensuality, and yet, here in her own family, there was no way to avoid such temptation! As Charity talked, her rebelliousness grew.

The parents, alerted by the talk mother and daughter had had, soon discovered their daughter's secret as well. They were ashamed but pleased at the same time, having learned in their group that children must rebel before they grow up. The father acted like a small boy who has been caught in mischief, he hung his head, blushed, and mumbled something about wearing looser garments when praying. Both parents knew intellectually that Charity was belatedly dealing with her sexuality and was trying to separate internally from them. They had even heard of the Oedipus complex and felt resigned to its appearance in their family since that was "the usual." Both mother and father, however, felt that father's erections were so natural and "usual" an expression of "male joyfulness" that they thought their daughter's reaction to it was perverse. They had no insight into the agitation and depression, fear and sensuality Charity experienced. They just wanted her to "stop," though it was not clear even to them what they wanted her to stop. I suggested that, since for Charity the family prayers were so highly charged, perhaps she should be excused from them or they should be discontinued. The father became incensed, fearing that I wanted to break up his God-fearing home. Fortunately, the mother intervened and persuaded him to let Charity pray by herself in her room. He, in turn, feared that Charity would become even more perverse and go so far as to "touch herself" when allowed so much time alone. Nevertheless, prompted by his wife and the Reverend Mr. C, he agreed that Charity's presence at communal prayers would no longer be compulsory.

Charity was nonplussed by her parents' unfamiliarly lenient stance. She now set out to see where her new limits were. Little by little, she gained for herself the privileges other girls in her class had. Strangely, she was not so eager to take dancing lessons any more. Her energy was taken up by a belated struggle for internal separation from overwhelmingly strong introjects. She described how she had to fight for each one of her little freedoms. A new hairdo was discussed, prayed over, and never accepted. A new dress was cause for sighs about her vanity. If a boyfriend dared to set foot in the house, he was quizzed about his religion and that of his parents.

But Charity not only fought her parents, she also identified with them. She had introjected their iron determination to shape life as they saw it. Besides, her years of training as a dancer had given her enormous resilience and stamina. Now she employed these strengths to win a measure of independence for herself. At this point, her excessive devotion to her parents' doctrine gave way to a more formidable phase of rebellion than the relatively harmless preoccupations before. This rebellion, in turn, exacted its toll. Where Charity had previously been able to externalize her aggression and blame sadistic fantasies on devils and punitive gods, she now had to deal with these currents internally. She began to have nightmares that ruined her sleep again. "I think I dream instead of dancing," she said. She began to have thoughts of being robbed and having to report this to the police. She thought these thoughts stopped her from sleeping. I asked her what had been stolen from her. A macramé hanger, she answered. Again, my interpretation that perhaps she meant a penis had been stolen from her brought forth torrents of giggles. Nonetheless, the night after this interpretation, she slept well. She had other sadistic thoughts and dreams: about setting her brother's hair on fire, about revolutions in which her mother was killed or her head hacked off, until Charity could finally acknowledge her anger with her parents, in particular with her mother. "How come she had to make me into a dopey girl and not a boy?" she pouted.

This new and somewhat unruly girl won everyone's heart. Tall and arresting, she looked older than her 14 years. Boys began to be interested in her. Once again, the parents were shocked but this time did nothing to interfere. Charity was allowed to double date but had strict curfews. She knew that it had cost her parents sleepless nights to make such a liberal decision, but she was not grateful. "I stayed a baby for so long because they are babies," she declared scornfully. Her metamorphosis into a teenager had made her contemptuous of her parents' ways. Mr. and Mrs. Z, however, continued their extreme devotion to their church. Mr. Z was offered a small congregation of his own to which he commuted on weekends. Charity was not impressed. "He got that by being a super baby," she declared. "I nearly drowned in all that shit they fed me but he laps it up." Her contempt for the church that had once been her guiding force knew no end. Her parents continued to pray for and with her, but to no avail. Charity discovered the fun of being a teenager and threw herself full force into every extracurricular activity she could find. She rediscovered dancing and with that rediscovery, left treatment. When she left, she coolly informed me that I had "helped her enough. I can now make decisions for myself."

Discussion

The interaction with her parents confused Charity. Although she knew she was loved, the restrictions placed on her were untenable. Although she seemed to have reached the oedipal phase, she was unable to traverse it. She was unable to assimilate the strict value system that her parents, in her particular her father, expounded. To her, he was a great man who could teach and guide, comfort and protect her. He was the kind of man Freud (1939) described as being capable of acting with divine conviction, which may change into ruthlessness. Identification with such a father begins prior to the oedipal phase (Freud, 1921). This may be considered an identification within the ego, though strong superego processes reinforce it until it takes on the imperative quality of morality, perhaps even the kind of moral masochism and asceticism Charity evinced when she entered treatment. For her, the identification with her father had not only made her into an asexual being, it had become so closely connected with instinctual renunciation that failing to see her father as perfect resulted in her feelings of inferiority and even panic. She had to deny her clear recognition that her father, far from being entirely pure and divinely inspired, was subject to sensual sensations and possibly "impure" conflicts. Charity simply was unable to reconcile within herself the punishing and loving attributes of her parents' demands.

While she experienced these superego conflicts, Charity felt inferior because she did not anatomically look like her father. She was in awe of his genitals, wanted to possess them, but could not quite muster the libidinal energy to enter fully into the oedipal phase. She needed her mother's protection too badly to be rivalrous with her. Once we had established Charity's wish to have a penis, she was able to thunder at her mother for supposedly having robbed her. But her anger with her mother did not have the regressed character of some of my other child patients' pregenital fears. Charity was always able to say what she thought and felt after the first phase in treatment. I do not know if she ever gave up the wish for a phallus. She left treatment when she rediscovered dancing, where a phallic and narcissistic preoccupation with her body once again predominated. I could not ascertain if this preoccupation with her body was in response to the demands of her training or if it was a less primary identification with the phallic, narcissistic, and exhibitionistic aspects of her father and his phallus.

It is a curious axiom of mental functioning that, when a parent expresses disapproval or anger, the child knows that she need not fear abandonment. As long as she is bad and deserves punishment, she need not fear loss of contact or protection from the parent. Charity tried with all her might to be a good child, but her attempts backfired. She experienced too many natural body sensations that she had been taught to regard as evil. Her despair became her prison when she saw that her father had to do battle with the same forces and even at his age had not been able to conquer them. She had tried to be like him only to find out that she was indeed exactly like him in her inability to bind or otherwise to cope with sexuality.

While Charity was going through an age-specific phase, her father was undergoing an old, often denied, more often idealized conflict. What was a sin for Charity was the "natural joyfulness of males" for her father. His narcissism informed him that it was good to be erect and potent under any circumstances. The imagined presence of his God gave him license to demand instinctual repression from everyone but himself. Had it not been for the intervention of both his wife and his clergyman, he would have even more decisively protested that it was his daughter who was perverse and narcissistic, not he. Even after many parental sessions he could not see the link between his dread of performing on stage, and his church's injunction against public performances, and the exhibitionism he took as natural in himself.

Charity's ego strengths were as formidable as her talents. Because she was well loved by her mother, she very quickly was able to see me as a protector. She also was able to make use of interpretations early in the treatment and could distance sufficiently from her conflicts to observe her own behavior once the first critical phase of terror and not sleeping was overcome. Her keen intelligence led her to pose philosophical questions not asked by many adults, certainly not by those around her. When she discovered that renunciation of her dancing did not bring her joy but, rather, more pain, she felt despair, remorse, and great anger. She was, however, able to rescue herself rapidly from the many narcissistic wounds she had sustained by refinding within the transference her protective mother. She had to distance from her seductive father and, for a time, had to renounce him as a baby because he was in need of a structure that had become too constricting and harmful for her.

Although I had reservations at first, the interventions of the Reverend Mr. C proved to be useful. Less frightened than his parishioners, he was able to teach and guide them with regard to their children while staying within the tenets of their church. I doubt that the Zs would have acquiesced as rapidly to changes in their family behavior but for his intervention.

Special techniques were not really necessary with Charity. Although she danced in sessions, needing at first the tension release and perhaps my approving glance, this was not a therapeutic intervention that emanated from me. It was not dance therapy per se but a form of muscular tension release only. Charity found her dancing again when she was able to determine more freely and without guilt what direction her life was to take. I was more directive with her parents than with others. They seemed to be singularly unable to imagine any way of treating their daughter than that dictated by their religious vision.

When Charity left treatment, they remained puzzled and resigned to having raised a rebel. Charity has become a teacher of sacred dances. She instructs church groups on how to "dance for the Lord" and is in great demand at sacred dance conventions.

SUMMARY

I have included this chapter despite the fact that children like Victoria-Louise and Charity are not really waifs. If anything, their parents are overly involved with them and do not let them develop freely and naturally. These parents view their children so much a part of themselves that the emotional growth and development of their children is impeded. While this merger between parents and children is similar to some of the other difficulties with parenting I have described, these socially withdrawn youngsters stay by themselves because they feel out of place in the company of other children. They have been brought up to believe themselves too good and too fine for the rough and tumble of ordinary childhood; and because they are loved by their parents as much as the parents love themselves, many of their abilities and psychological functions are highly developed. Often this development is lopsided. The child appears to be highly sophisticated and naive at the same time. They are like miniature adults; they have an "as if" quality about them, as if they were grown up. Because they have been taught that their function in life is to please their parents, they are often rageful. This rage then leads to sleeplessness, further social withdrawal, and isolation while intellectual, and sometimes artistic, pursuits are developed at the expense of the whole personality. The final outcome is frequently a child as spoiled, precocious, and narcissistic as both or one of the parents is. A telling sign of such an inner structure is the utter disdain with which such children often regard their teachers, whose favorites they are nonetheless. After all, their homework is always done and they never make any trouble.

Interestingly, among the cases of such miniature adults I treated, it was most often the father who needed to confine his child to the limits of his own narcissism. He, more often than mother, could not tolerate independence and separation from his miniature self.

CHAPTER 7

Some Theoretical and Treatment Considerations
Mental Representation: The Infant as Active Participant in the Care Giver–Child Dyad

In working with disturbed children, one inevitably asks oneself, how did these children become that way? This question takes on especially large proportions when the young patients do not readily fall into expectable and recognizable nosologic categories. I am certain that every one of the children presented here was born a healthy and normally, or even superiorly, endowed infant. I have in each chapter formulated some psychodynamic assumptions based on developmental precepts that in part explain what happened in each of the cases. There are, however, some further reaching theoretical formulations that allow for more generalized hypotheses about these children. These formulations are useful in identifying the child who does not fit the standard nosologic categories.

Obviously all the children I treated identified with the maladaptive behavior of their parents and then either replicated it or unconsciously strove to distance themselves from anything their parents provided. There is no use blaming the parents; they could not do any better than they did. Thus, the inner representations that evolved in these youngsters' psyches were often unable to support the adaptive psychological skills needed for further psychological growth. Therefore, they often appeared to be desperately mentally or behaviorally disturbed or even psychotic. Nonetheless, somewhere in their early life they had received adequate care. They had inner lives pliable enough to resume psychological growth during and after treatment. Along with the obviously inappropriate and unempathic care they received, they also had been loved sufficiently to acquire at least rudimentary self-esteem and the necessary libidinal supplies to go on living. I am hard pressed to find any other reason for these children's liveliness and creativity, which must have had their origin in the early symbiotic unions with their caretakers. The task of therapy was to liberate this substratum of health.

Because the healthy part of my patients' mental lives belonged to such an early time, comparison with another group of children who often have similar symptoms is warranted. Autistic children also are said to be fixated, or stuck, in the early phase of life. Mahler (1968) places the so-called normal autistic phase in the range of about eight weeks after birth, while the symbiotic phase emcompasses about five months. When I first met some of the children, they behaved as if they were in this early phase. Gino would not speak; Gordon, Julian-Gregory, Joanie and Franky acted as though there were no one else in the room with them. Autistic children also shun contact, are chaotic and egocentric, refuse to speak, and have poor social skills.

As first a therapist and then a supervisor and administrator in a large school for atypical children, I had the opportunity to observe many children who were labeled autistic. The more intelligent ones among them could easily have been peers of my patients at the beginning of treatment, but they did not possess the pliable inner selves of the children described in this book. This lack of plasticity of their mental life, however, does not mean that such children should not receive psychodynamically oriented treatment. Quite the contrary. Often they can reach the functioning level of a nine year old and thus escape expensive and debilitating hospitalization. In psychodynamically oriented movement therapy, for instance, many of these children reorganize their body images sufficiently to leave behind their diffuse or rigid motor patterns. Once their body images are firmer and they begin to perceive the difference between inside and outside, animate and inanimate, they very often learn to speak as well. They even become attached to their therapists and appear to enter a therapeutic symbiosis, complete with mutual affection and physical contact. Unfortunately, only rarely do such children generalize affectionate behavior from their therapist to others in their surrounding. They manage to acquire many skills, but their interaction with others stays curtailed and empty. They can, of course, be taught to hug and kiss family members, but these expressions of affection remain an exercise in emotional futility. Neither parent nor child in such an interaction experiences the warmth and mutual enjoyment that on occasion was present in the children and parents I speak of in this book. In addition, at each maturational step, autistic children appear to experience great distress. They cannot change, and when forced to do so by their own body size and by their environment, they regress. I have often thought that in these somatopsychic regressions lies the purest evidence of Freud's (1920) theory of the death instinct.[1] An illustration comes to mind.

A dance therapy intern was entrusted with the beginning treatment of a very withdrawn, seemingly frightened autistic boy who had shown some positive reaction to music. Therefore, the intern used some soothing classic music that had been shown to help fretful babies to sleep (Murooka, 1974). As expected, the little boy, Jim, responded and allowed the young therapist to rock him. But even on her lap, he liked to curl up in a fetal position. Being trained in developmental psychology, the young woman thought she recognized Jim's wish to return to the womb. On the same record is the sound of a mother's main artery and the blood coursing through her veins, shown to be particularly effective in soothing crying neonates. Reasoning that Jim must have been comfortable someplace, sometime – surely in his mother's womb – the intern decided to play those sounds for him. She wanted to reach his substratum of health. But when she played the record, Jim fled from her in horror, bit his hands, and banged his head against the wall. He apparently had rejected the maternal environment even in utero. How could such a child be expected to reach the next developmental step, or symbiosis? Yet Jim became fond of the young therapist. While in her care, he learned to listen to requests and to comply with them and became accessible to classroom teaching.

---

[1]Freud's hypothesis of a death instinct has provoked much controversy. Biological investigation cannot confirm it. Many psychoanalysts believe, however, that it manifests itself in aggressive, hostile actions directed against self and others. Certainly psycholoanalysts use the concept of aggressive and libidinal drives in their clinical approaches.

But he never found the libidinal energy to relate in any way to his family. With a vacant expression on his face, he allowed his family to care for him. He came to life only in his dance therapy sessions, reserving what little libidinal energy he could muster to enhance his skills sufficiently to stay alive.

The parents of autistic children I have met were of many differing types. Some were loving and increasingly distraught when their children did not respond to them. Others were as distant, unempathic, and narcissistically wounded as the parents of my patients. What all of them had in common with the parents I am talking about is a reluctance to enter therapy for themselves. Therefore, it is difficult to assess what unconscious contribution they might have made to their offsprings' dilemmas. However, among the 50 or so children labeled autistic – indeed, among the 185 labeled atypical – I came across only one case of sexual abuse of the child and two cases of punitive abuse. All three cases were among people whose educational and social strata had ill prepared them to cope with an atypical child. Instinctual overstimulation of the children by the parents, however, was present in all of the cases.

I have digressed in order to emphasize that despite seemingly unsurmountable obstacles among the group of children and parents I am speaking about there were inner avenues of mutual approach open to them. In many of the cases, these did not become apparent until treatment was well under way. I am thinking of Loretta, Gino, Gordon, Joanie, and Franky. They behaved in such bizarre ways that they could almost have been confused with children like Jim. My patients' difficulties arose because their parents' inner lives were so warped that the expectations they transmitted to their children during the symbiotic phase and afterward were usually different from conventional parental hopes and aspirations. Most parents do not expect very much from their infants. They are pleased, even delighted, when the little one simply thrives. A baby usually does not have to do very much more than sleep and eat well. Caretakers are thrilled with the first smiles or the first signs of recognition in the neonate.

Not so the parents I am talking about. Their children were unconsciously expected to provide what the parents had missed in life. The most obvious examples are Joanie, Julian-Gregory, and Victoria-Louise. They were to help their fathers to be mature men. Joanie's and

Julian Gregory's fathers needed a cure for their sexual dysfunction and sought the cure in their children. Victoria-Louise was to be the genius who could heal her father's narcissism. Gordon's parents expected him to fix their dysfunctional family dynamic. It is also striking to note that all the mothers seemed unable to attune themselves to their children. They allowed the fathers to color their judgment of their children's needs and behaviors and never came to their children's defense. Unconsciously, they seemed to expect their children to liberate them from indecision and anxiety. In order to rescue themselves from engulfment by their parents' needs, these sons and daughters often had a preconscious understanding that their parents were not proper models for them. Consequently, the persons of the parents were not identified with. Rather, their behavior was identified with and incorporated; to the children, the parents could seem powerful and meaningful while also being distasteful.

No one can reach a developmental goal without inner representations, even if these representations are based on destructive or incomplete models. How inner representations are acquired is of interest here. Freud (1914, 1920) was the first to assume that unconscious representations correspond to those mental contents to which drives attach themselves and through which drives express themselves beyond the somatic level. This expression includes images and fantasies. Freud's model of the mind ascribed to the infant the capacity to register perceptually, and to store unconsciously in representations, the significant other as distinct from more all-inclusive experiences. Many theoreticians, including Piaget (1976) and Schimek (1975), disagreed with this point of view. They thought that the ability to separately perceive the significant other was developed much later. Ironically, recent research bears out Freud's assumptions. Far from being a passive recipient of whatever handling is meted out to them, infants are now seen as innately endowed with just those capacities that Freud ascribed to babies. Their perceptual apparatus allows them to assimilate and identify with stimuli both from within and outside of their bodies. Infants react to strong stimuli most deeply. Thus, parental behavior can be as strong a stimulus as, or even stronger than, their physical presence and affords the infant the opportunity to identify with behaviors of the parents rather than with the persons of the parents. Thus, Lichtenberg (1983) asks:

How do self and object representation become differentiated within
the first year; how does the infant move from a narcissistic or autistic
stage (without awareness of the object) through symbiosis (with its
merger of representations) to separation from the object and individuation of the self; and how does the infant cope with innate
aggression, envy, and cruelty and achieve concern? [pp. 66–67].

From the point of view of child researchers, differentiation of self
and object exists from birth. But infants' discriminatory activities are
performed at the level of perceptual-action responses. Far from being
helpless, a bundle of destructive instincts, the neonate responds with
eager assertiveness. What is crucial for the discussion here is that
representations of self and object do exist albeit in attenuated form.
Mahler's postulated developmental stages rest on this assumption.
The attenuated, or part object, representations postulated as identification of my patients with their parents' behavior rather than with
their parents' persons have the same origin.

The processes of identification, introjection, incorporation, and
internalization are all crucial in the establishment of inner representations. As early as 1943 Balint contended that identification was the
most important means at the disposal of the infant to deal with the
frightening external world. She said that "identificatory thinking" is
employed by the child for avoiding the unpleasurable and obtaining
the pleasurable (p. 97). According to her, identification is the most
primitive method of recognizing external reality and amounts to
"mental mimicry" (p. 101). Balint implied that the infant needs to use
some form of self-protection to deal with a frightening external world.
She agrees with the psychoanalytic concept that children can and do
gradually construct internal pictures and images of their experiences,
be they cognitive, affective, interpersonal, mental, verbal, or related to
the senses. Jacobson (1964) and Novey (1958) were in basic agreement
but always assumed the infant to be a passive recipient who was hard
pressed to construct an inner picture of the outer world, a developmental achievement that did not occur until somewhere around the
second year of life. In particular, they stressed the inability of the
preverbal child to differentiate self from other.

That the children I describe in this book had particularly frightening external worlds is without doubt. Thus, according to Mahler's
developmental paradigm, which is grounded in psychoanalytic thinking, they should have been stuck at a symbiotic level, with the

attendant difficulties in differentiating self and other, inability to tolerate frustration, and cognitive deficits. They were not. Many were highly intelligent and able to make use of their intelligence, although certainly not in an academic fashion, and were differentiated, but not entirely separated, from the parents. Most did not want to be like their parents. What, then, makes them, with all their emotional and cognitive and interpersonal lags, stay at the developmental level that enabled them to remain flexible enough to resume their psychological growth? I have already postulated that their parents did have some regard for them, but their caring alone could hardly explain the good results obtained in children who hardly had reached the oedipal level of development.

The overlap between traditional psychoanalytic thinking and infant research provides another part of the answer. Infant research supports the idea that interpersonal contact is perceived by the infant from birth. The potential ability to acquire skills, not instinct, is important. In fact, some researchers have posited that the primary characteristics of interpersonal communication are built on capacities that are inborn (Stern, 1985; Beebe, 1986). This view is in opposition to the aforementioned psychoanalytic theories, which hold that drive energies invested in self- and object representations are the motivational force behind development.

Lichtenberg (1983) provides a psychoanalytic view that sees the infant as able to "image" by two years of age and as having the ability to construe an object, including the self, as a discreet, persisting entity whose appearance functions as a sign conveying information. According to him, prior to being able to "image," infants can still perceive an object as separate from the self. Through such a perception, the image of an object is understood to be part of an action sequence. Through such early perceptions Lichtenberg concludes, babies can differentiate much earlier than has been thought possible. Of course, the process of differentiation is not simply a cognitive capacity that unfolds independent of the human environment that surrounds the infant. It has long been understood to entail a mutual coordination of maternal and infant behaviors.

Sander (1962, 1975, 1983) has conducted longitudinal studies in which he delineates a theory of epigenetic stages to describe the early relational world of the infant with the caregiver. He sees the infant–mother dyad as an open biological system. He wrote in 1975:

> The regulation of infant function based on behaviors that have
> become harmoniously coordinated between mother and infant will
> become perturbed with the advent of each new, and usually more
> specifically focused and intentionally initiated, activity of the
> growing infant. Thus, an adaptation or mutual modification on a
> new level is required. . . . The interactional picture is best organized
> in terms of epigenetic sequence in which this progression of relative
> coordination is achieved [p. 135].

This formulation stresses the contribution of the infant as an active participant in whatever differentiation is achieved. It is my contention that although there were without doubt loving and caring interactions among the caretaker–child dyads described here, these early experiences were colored by the inability of both partners to adapt to each other. Thus, optimal growth did not occur. The children's inner representations of their worlds remained fixated at a level that suggests incompleteness, frustration, and destructiveness. These children, however, were not the impulse-ridden, helpless infants of classic psychoanalytic theorizing, nor did they fit the picture of the baby that self psychology proposes. Neonates of self psychology are seen as the passive recipients of narcissistic supplies from mother and as subject to forces outside their control. The children I am talking about, on the other hand, seemed to be actively engaged in interpersonal dialogue and fighting against the proffered victimization.

But because of the skewed internal pictures they internalized despite their struggles to do otherwise, certain essential psychological skills could not be acquired. Nevertheless, these were active infants striving to survive as best they could. They contributed to their parents' distress by not accepting the roles thrust upon them by parental needs. Their unconscious refusal to be swallowed by their parents' frequently nightmarish inner turmoil allowed them to stay actively engaged with self-preservation. Had they not done so, their pathology would have been harder to treat, possibly irreversible. Adam's story is a case in point. He, more than the others, was at the mercy of his parents' unbending emotional demands and therefore was prevented from regaining further mental growth.

These children did not so much identify with their parents' persons as with their parents' behavior. Many of them developed strong defenses against these parental maladaptations. But children's inner and outer experience is limited. Children do not have many psychological tools at their beck and call. In addition, since their inner self- and object representations were curtailed or faulty, many psychological skills could not develop, leading to the asocial and self-destructive behaviors described.

THE ACQUISITION OF PSYCHOLOGICAL SKILLS

Gedo (1979, 1988) noticed among his adult analysands that some appeared during analytic therapy to regress to the most archaic forms of being. These patients did not respond to the usual interpretive mode. Gedo realized that these people had never acquired the psychological skills needed at the age-appropriate time. Thus, their difficulties were not sparked so much by conflict as by a need for external psychological assistance from the analyst. In Gedo's work, we have the rare opportunity to extrapolate from findings about adults to the state in which children with similar difficulties live. What Gedo has called "apraxias" can be discerned *in statu nascendi* in the case histories of the children I am speaking about. Their desperate need to unload tension physically, inability to use their intelligence or to get on with their peers and with adults, poor self-esteem, rudimentary regulation of tension, and lack of accurate self-assessment, all fall within the category of apraxia, the inability to learn psychologically, while cognitive abilities and perception stay relatively intact.

Yet, among the children I have discussed there was a defensive and adaptive quality to many deficits that allowed them to wait, so to speak, until they reached therapy, where they appeared to seize eagerly on the second opportunity to develop more fully. I feel that this is the major expectable gain in these therapies: to empower the children to take the next developmental step and to retain psychological flexibility until they can become masters of their own fate. All the children seemed to reach at least the beginning of the oedipal phase, no mean achievement when one considers the large areas of deficit with which they arrived. They learned to value themselves as persons, to tolerate some frustration and even anxiety. They also were able to assimilate and make use of information about sexuality and reproduction. I have made a particular point of reporting on this issue in almost all the cases because it so clearly illustrates that cognitive presentation of facts very often achieves very little. Rather, it is the combination and confluence of positive personal interactions, including the therapist's acceptance of affectomotor and sensorimotor phenomena, that lead to the beginning of benevolent internalizations. These, in turn, facilitate the laying down of inner representations. Once this has been achieved, the importance of structured cognitive efforts becomes evident and, in these cases, leads to change and growth. Those of my child patients whose lives I have been able to follow after the conclusion of treatment certainly seem to corroborate my formulation.

Gedo (1988) had similar experiences with his adult patients. He writes, "An apraxia can seldom be repaired through direct instruction (especially instruction in some didactic manner). It is almost always necessary first to reconstruct the childhood circumstances that prevented the age-appropriate acquisition of these psychological skills in the first place" (p. 170).

I feel that I need to make this point because in a successful child analysis more inner changes are expectable, and parental curtailment of the treatment does not seem to occur very often. Yet sustaining the psychodynamic mode in conducting these therapies achieves good enough results.

TREATMENT STRATEGIES

Gedo (1988) noticed that the emergence of archaic behaviors in analysis ushered in crucial phases of the treatment (p. 164). This happened only when the analytic situation had become a sufficiently benevolent holding environment. He states:

> In these analyses, the process of working through presents great difficulties because of the humiliation produced by acknowledgment of the deficits in psychological skills screened by the patients' symbiotic adaptation. To achieve success, the analysis must promote the autonomous acquisition of these skills, for this is the prerequisite of overcoming the chronic need for symbiosis [p. 164].

The children I treated were in constant flight from such symbiotic attachments and brought the tumultuous and often chaotic dynamics of their families into the treatments immediately, without first leading up to the chaos through the transference, as adults would do. Of course, children vary greatly in the extent to which they are caught up in their parents' unconscious and in the extent to which they play out their parents' fantasies, wishes, and fears. Part of these children's inner survival strategies had to do with turning away from their parents' unconscious emotional influence. Nevertheless, like all children, they were subject to their parents' projective identifications and consequently were in conflict not so much with themselves as with their settings. Thus, unlike adult patients, who deal with symbolic, internalized parental imagos, children bring their every day world and interactions into the treatment room. Much can be discerned about the interactions with parents from what goes on in the waiting room as well as when the child is brought for sessions. One sees personal history in the making. But this also has its pitfalls. The therapist is presented with two conflicting pictures of the child patient: (1) how the child is presented by the parents and (2) how the parents actually experience the child. These two versions are often widely divergent, as the First Interview sections of the case histories show. This divergence then leads to the issues of projective identification between parent and child.

As I explained earlier, projective identification is an interactional process in which unconscious fantasies and introjects are projected from the maker to the recipient. The concept was first discussed by M. Klein (1946). She used the term to describe the development of preambivalent early object relations in which the bad or hated part of the self is split off and placed into the mother and other significant others in order to protect the infant against its own dangerous and aggressive parts. This conceptualization sees the infant as an active participant in social interactions as well, though "active" here means on the mental, not the behavioral, level. Klein saw projective identification as an entirely normal developmental occurrence that permits the child (or adult) eventually to incorporate and identify with his or her own aggression, thus achieving a sense of power, potency, and strength. This process was evident in the case histories when the children began to be more autonomous and were able to make decisions about themselves. I am thinking in particular of Lindi, Joanie, and Gordon, though all the children reached a level at which they were able to meet the developmental task of integrating bad aspects of the self and reclaiming them from the significant other in whom they had been deposited. Issues about the loving part of the person are tied up in projective identification as well. If projective identification is excessive, as was the case in many of the young patients presented here, good parts of the personality are felt to be lost, and overdependence results, accompanied by lack of concern, care and empathy. Parents and children alike use projective identification to cope with each other.

Although many psychoanalysts feel that transferences in the treatment of children are tenuous and to be viewed warily, I found that my young charges, after an initial period of distrust, eagerly seized on the opportunity to regard me as their "good lady" or as being "on their side." I came to view these early times as periods of intense negative transference and the later ones as times of rebuilding and restructuring inner and outer worlds in tandem with the children themselves. Again, these positive times would not have been possible if, somewhere along this line, there had not been nurturing emotional interchanges between parents and children. An autistic or schizophrenic child who for the first time reaches symbiotic or other positive interaction responds quite differently and without the immediate ability to generalize and to make use of the new skills.

By the time we reached these positive phases, we had as a common goal the alleviation of suffering not previously recognized as such and the rebuilding of the objective reality of the youngsters' everyday world. This rebuilding was achieved by carefully preserving and building on whatever the children regarded as lovable and useful in their parents. Genetic interpretations[2] are not useful to children. Children resist them because they must live day to day with their parents and know from bitter experience that they do not have the power to change anything at first. For the same reasons, children are invested in protecting their parents. After all, their parents are the only caretakers they have and know. However, I did not find the children resistive to exploring the here-and-now happening in the sessions. Often, this exploration led to insight and to the children's forming their own conclusions about who their parents were and what

---

[2]Genetic interpretations are concerned with showing the connection between past and present mental states. Reconstruction can be considered a form of genetic interpretation but is not the same thing. The therapist reconstructs an event but interprets meaning.

was growth producing for them. It was amazing to me to see children who were brought up in generally unempathic ways able to respond empathically to their distressed parents. This empathic behavior again corroborated my early hypothesis that, at least at the earliest times, there must have been mutual gratification in the mother–child dyads. However, the ability to read their own affects correctly, sometimes even the ability to name them, was often missing. This lack, of course, always revealed itself as a defensive measure that allowed the child to stay connected to a parent or sibling who had seriously distorted reality. Ted and Loretta are good examples.

Because of all these difficulties with projective identification and the need of the children to stay connected with their families, I most often contented myself with pointing out obvious discrepancies in the familial constructions of reality, commenting warmly when a child was hurt, and, above all, participating as a benevolent observer when sensorimotor discharge was necessary. I am referring here to the many times these children needed to express themselves through their bodies and with movements. I will return to this important aspect later. Here it is important to underscore the necessity to emphasize and to comment on behaviors brought into the treatment room as though all of them were transference manifestations, yet to keep in mind that they are not examples of a frozen past but a fresh occurrence, personal history in the making.

In addition, much of what I said to the children had educational value. I often offered suggestions about how it might be possible to circumvent a dangerous situation or reinforced the ability to say "no," as in the cases of Lawrence, Julian-Gregory, Joanie, Victoria-Louise, and Charity. I also discussed openly what "we needed to work on" after I was sure that the children trusted me and were able to use my interventions.

Gedo (1988) has constructed theoretical formulations that aid in setting up the frame for an appropriate holding pattern for the type of patient whose difficulties are not caused by conflict but by developmental deficits, as they were in the children I am describing. This holding pattern includes:

> (1) pacification, (2) unification, and (3) optimal disillusionment. The types of intervention differ in their therapeutic aim and involve an infinite range of specific activities on the part of the analyst. The aim

of pacification is to deal with difficulties in tension regulation; that of unification is the development of a coherent program of action; optimal disillusionment is intended to assist the analysand in accepting the realities of his existence without being traumatized [p. 168].

Thus, the interpretive mode with children who are in internal flight from their parents' maladaptation includes extratransferential and cognitive elements not usually included but excludes genetic material.

ART, MUSIC, AND DANCE THERAPY

Almost all the children I worked with had a need to "do" something besides talking and playing. The traditional tool of play therapy was often so coldly disregarded that I wondered if the children had somehow been told that playing could be a self-revelatory activity. After gaining confidence in the setting and in me, they almost all chose to draw, sing, or dance.

The drawings were for many of the children a bridge that allowed them to talk about what had until then been unspeakable. The drawings gave both me and the children a focal point from which to explore coherently the children's unconscious. Lawrence's case also saw a clear progression from fragmented and unstructured, to more reality-oriented, perceptions. Although Adam's external world did not yield an inch during or after our interaction, his drawings nevertheless expressed a recognition of himself as a person rather than as a monster. Just as often, these drawings served no other purpose than for us to spend pleasant, quiet, affectionate time with each other. I have not been trained in the use of art and music therapy, so perhaps I did not do these two adjunctive tools sufficient justice. Their use arose spontaneously because the children felt more secure drawing, singing, or listening to records with me than talking and playing.

I have never worked with a child who wanted to bring in an instrument or asked for one, although many have wanted to sing or move rhythmically to some record of their choosing. Of course, this choice may have to do with my not having available a piano or instruments other than percussive ones. Some small flutes I have were hardly ever touched, nor were finger cymbals. I also keep a tambourine, drums, a gong, and maracas on the shelf. I do not include these as the use of music because the children usually picked up these instruments to beat on them angrily or to signal to me that they hated someone or something. There was no accompanying melody or striving for the aesthetic or the gentler emotions embedded in music, just a reflection of their inner turmoil in rhythms. I welcomed these expressions of hostility because once these instruments were accepted, the angry jumping about could become an Indian war dance, the furious howling a rhythmic chant accompanied by the drums, and so on. Sometimes the tambourines were used for the accompaniment of hopping and jumping, with some sort of explanation by the child about what this could mean. For instance, it was instructive to hear a child tell me that jumping furiously about the room while beating and shaking the tambourine felt good. It was as though in these instances, the children had to have validation of their aggressive energy as a source for positive feelings for me. If I could accept all of the feelings, I was okay. I sometimes suggested the use of these percussive instruments to children caught up in helpless anger, but this did not work as well as when they themselves decided to "beat out" the rhythm of their hostility.

Poems, some of which I have quoted in the book, also burst forth. These phenomena constituted the beginnings of the interpersonal relationships that eventually led to changes in the inner lives of the youngsters.

An outstanding feature of the behavior of all of these children was that they were full of bodily tensions, fears, anxieties, and fantasies that did not allow them to concentrate on anything. Many of them knew that they should "sit still" but simply could not comply. Some had even been diagnosed as hyperkinetic. The use of dance-movement therapy seemed more than once to be indicated. But these youngsters sneered at the usual tools of mirroring and the therapist's dancing to the child's rhythms. They were do-it-yourselfers with a vengeance.

Individual dance-movement therapy follows no set program. It tries to resonate with the patient, following the patient's lead, just as any other psychodynamically or psychoanalytically oriented therapy does. But its emphasis is on the nonverbal communication. The dance therapist watches her patient's nonverbal behavior and then offers either verbal or nonverbal interpretations of what she has seen. She does not necessarily dance with the child, but at times mirrors, in a dance of her own, what she has seen. A pas de deux can, but does not have to, ensue.

In contrast, traditional dance-movement therapy with emotionally disturbed children is conducted in groups and very often looks like a dance class. There is a warm-up period during which the therapist watches for a common "theme" to emerge. Such a theme could be anger with a classroom teacher, sadness at having lost something or someone, or any other human emotion. Actual situations of having fought with each other, of clinging to one another, or of merely being too cold to move are also visible in movement. The dance therapist scans the group and tries to grasp both observationally and empathically what is offered by the patients. She mirrors the sad, slow motions of depression, for instance, and watches to see if there is a change in the group's or individual's dancelike behavior in response to her nonverbally expressed understanding. If there is, she makes larger or smaller gestures, steps, or rhythms in a dancelike fashion.

Patients often show their emotions through body movements that are not yet dances but are dancelike. The writhing of emotional pain or the bent shoulders and slow gait of depression are examples. It is the affective state of an individual or a group that the dance therapist addresses. Her treatment consists of here-and-now experiences that either bring to consciousness, illustrate, or make accessible to verbal interpretation unbearable or hidden aspects of the patients' emotional life. The focus is first and foremost on affect as a bridge between psyche and soma. Building up the body image through the conscious use of body parts or to aid relaxation by deep-breathing exercises is also a part of dance-movement therapy.

One can say that dance-movement therapy helps to recreate the harmonious whole of psyche and soma by facilitating more adequate physical functioning. Catharsis is part of the process of exploring the past nonverbally. Patients' preferred patterns of movement are always integrated. Improvisations are seen as free association and as stepping stones toward autonomous functioning. All these aspects are part of Basic Dance, as Marian Chace, one of the most influential originators of dance therapy in the USA, called it. She saw Basic Dance as "the externalization of inner feelings which cannot be expressed in rational speech but can only be shared in rhythmic, symbolic form" (quoted in

Chaiklin, 1975, p. 203). However, Chace advocated Basic Dance as an adjunctive group therapy. Since her day, much clinical work and research have shifted the theoretical basis to be more inclusive of differing psychological structures and of widely divergent populations. There are also some dance-movement therapists like myself who work individually and as the primary therapist. Thus, Schmais (1974) speaks for dance therapists today when she states that movement itself reflects personality, that interpersonal relationships established through movement with the patient support and produce change in functioning, and that significant changes occur on the movement level that may affect the total personality.

My approach differed in that I conceptualized my observations more rigorously than many other trained dance therapists. Additional training enabled me to do so. I adhered to psychoanalytic developmental theory and the findings of child research as a base from which I could observe behavior and then intervene both rationally and empathically. I needed to understand both cognitively and empathically what was happening to my young patients when they exhibited the movement behavior of either psychotic or neurologically impaired youngsters during individual sessions. Particularly puzzling were the chaotic, temper-tantrum-like behaviors that appeared to be outside of their control.

Watching so many of these children, I came to the conclusion that their unfocused movement events must have meaning. I conceptualized this behavior as a type of regression to a sensorimotor phase that occurs between the 15th and 18th month. It is marked by intentionality, means–ends relations, and formation of affective objects, all of which imply true representational thought by the child. This sensorimotor stage continues to exist under more dominant modes of thought throughout life (Spitz, 1965; Dowling, 1990). Dowling maintains, "These sensorimotor behavioral memories occur prior to fantasy and are influential in determining repetitive behavioral enactment" (p. 93).

It is my opinion that even before they can verbalize, children fantasize about their world. As with any other early childhood fantasy, verbal fantasies can involve children in conflict, both externally with their caretakers and in their inner life when desires and expectations are not met or are subjected to distortions through parental misguidance or selective attunement (Stern, 1985), which skew the infants' perceptions affectively toward what the parents can best tolerate.

In addition, I have conceptualized (Siegel, 1980, 1984) motility as an indicator of developmental levels, as an expresser of internal conflict, and as a receptor that is imprinted with all past and present experience. Given all these properties and the fact that it can be influenced, motility can be viewed as another tool for therapeutic intervention. Therefore, I viewed the movements of my young patients not as symptoms but as an incomplete attempt to express themselves and to enlist aid. I responded as a mother would to the "look-at-me" phase in her child. I did not dance with the children except when my participation was indicated by the story that evolved out of the child's experience. Primarily, I remained on the periphery of the happenings as the interpreter of meaning and affect. The *naming* of what the child saw, did, and felt was the important bridge between affect and somatic expression to cognitive and emotional recognition that allowed for the structuring of more evolved interactions and eventually helped the child to reach the next developmental level.

Though many dance therapists dance with their patients, I generally do not. Even when cast in the motherly role, I do not wish my more evolved movement pattern to overlay or distort that of the child. After all, I am not a dancing teacher, though Loretta and others certainly saw me as such. It is also easy, in dancing, to unwittingly arouse seduction fantasies or to foster abreaction of emerging memories before they have reached consciousness. Therefore, I keep my movement interaction with my young patients to a minimum, though I welcome all their movement productions. There is hardly another way to recognize and to diagnose the past as readily as through the observation and use of body expressions. Change can also be effected readily, in that the patient kinesthetically and cognitively reduces tensions and changes passive trauma to active mastery in a very concrete way.

The use of physical affection becomes an issue here. Sad children often need to lean against their therapists, to sit on their laps, or in some way to be physically close. I believe this need to belong to the same sensorimotor phase I spoke of before. Very early, in our mothers' arms, we learn how our own bodies feel, what is inside and what is outside, and where our own periphery is. If mother was habitually

tense, or unempathic or vacillated in her caretaking functions, recti-
fication is needed (Spitz, 1965). For children at an early developmental
level, there is no other way to transmit and to receive emotional
warmth. But here, too, caution is needed. Too much contact can
become addictive for both therapist and child and can prevent the
child from seeking and accepting another source among his family, in
school or wherever else well-meaning adults are available.

Although the activities I have just described can be construed as
playing, I saw them as a precursor to play. In nearly all the cases, I have
cited a period in which the child almost consciously sneered at the idea
of playing. I think that playing was so thratening because true playing
includes the ability to forget oneself, to be preoccupied, not to be on
guard. Of course, this inner freedom was not possible for youngsters
who came from such fearsome worlds.

Play itself goes through various stages. At first, one's own body is
the only plaything; then mother's body is included. From this place of
safety, soft toys are accepted and become the well-known transitional
objects (Winnicott, 1953). The children I treated first needed to accept
the treatment situation and me as a safe haven before they dared to
play again.

Winnicott (1982) has noted that preoccupation characterizes the
playing of infants. According to his observation,

> the content does not matter. What matters is the near-withdrawal
> state, akin to the concentration of older children and adults. The
> playing child inhabits an area that cannot be easily left, nor can it
> easily admit intrusion. This area of playing is not inner psychic
> reality. It is outside the individual, but is not the external world [p.
> 51].

He goes on to trace how the child uses this created space as a
repository for objects and phenomena from inner and outer experience. Thus, playing becomes invested with meaning and facilitates
development from transitional phenomena to playing, from playing to
shared playing, and so on. But playing involves the body and excitement. The children I saw had to show me, and their families and
teachers, their forms of playing and expression through often unstructured "wild" behavior that in treatment became a "dance" with purpose and meaning.

Another, more illustrative way of looking at this developmental phenomenon is shown by A. Freud and Burlingham (1944). They noted that around the beginning of the second year many children behave as though the sole activity of interest were their need to conquer space by any means at their disposal. Of the Hampstead Nursery population they say, "Sometimes for an hour on end the whole population of the Junior Toddler room is on the move, circling, crossing and recrossing like people on the skating rink" (p. 16).

Peller (1954) views this phenomenon as the expression of a compensatory fantasy that temporarily heals the anxieties that accompany this phase; inner structures are still labile. There is no accompanying story-telling fantasy, just hazy images of grandeur and perfect harmony. Winnicott (1982) corroborates this observation when he states that "play is immensely exciting. It is exciting not primarily because the instincts are involved. . . . The thing about playing is always the precariousness of the interplay of personal psychic reality and the experience of control of actual objects" (p. 47).

Clearly, to my patients, their uncontrollable behavior was anything but meaningless. It was the one way they had at the beginning of our interaction to release tension, express unformed wishes and fantasies, and stay in imagined control of their environment. When they were able to include me in their hazy and turbulent world, their motor activity could be channeled into dancelike choreographies of emotion and shared experience. From there, we could move on to more conventional play therapy or simply talking to each other.

COUNTERTRANSFERENCE

Few studies have been devoted to the uses of countertransference in the therapy of children. Indeed, countertransference in the analysis of adults has only recently become somewhat more respectable as an indicator within the analyst of what is going on inside of the patient. In the treatment of children, countertransference is still viewed with suspicion. In particular the use of countertransference as a way to hold the child empathically has received little or no attention. Various reasons are offered for the paucity of information. Lombardi and Lapidos (1990) see the history of child therapy itself reflected in these oversights. They report that the original impetus for child therapy came from the child guidance movement in Europe (Aichhorn, 1925/1963) which concerned itself with the poor and with the emotionally disadvantaged. Its influences were educational with the emphasis on learning, substitute parenting, and the development of moral and ethical values, admixed with injections from the newly evolved psychoanalytic theory . . . the culture characterized children as having beast-like natures which come to be tamed through the civilizing effects of society. The language in Hugh-Hellmuth's (1921) pioneering article on the analysis of children expressed such attitudes through references to children as "young creatures" (p. 287) as did her advocacy of such educative analytic goals as the imparting of moral and aesthetic values [p. 98–99].

It is interesting to note that in current behavior modification programs of the more benign type, similar values and concepts are espoused although clinical research and direct child observation have long disproved the educability of the human psyche by purely cognitive and rational means. This rationalizing attitude, however, seems to have left its stamp on current child analysis and psychodynamic therapy despite Melanie Klein's (1973) pathbreaking discovery that playing is the free association of the child.

Another reason why the uses of countertransference have been neglected, disavowed, or denied may be that there is often "too much of it" (Marshall, 1979, p. 598). Frightened, angry, or pathetic children arouse many feelings in the therapist, not all of them having to do with the child's needs. Children present themselves with all their difficulties exposed in their everyday life in a much more direct way than adults, who have some measure of defense and ability to cope. Particularly in the case of abuse, the therapist cannot help but be angry with the parents and wish to rescue the child immediately from its internal and external wars. But such rescue is neither desirable nor possible. Even after "rescue," the child must live with the internalized image of the abusing parents, or the neglectful parent, and in his or her young psyche find the generosity of spirit to forgive often serious transgressions after working through anger. Therefore, immediate or, worse, impulsive, action on the part of the therapist does not serve anyone.

I came to the conclusion that even justified anger at the parents and the wish to rescue the child had strong countertransferential components (notwithstanding that anyone would feel this way upon

uncovering such hurtful events). Reflection and self-observation informed me that therapeutic utilization of negative feelings depends on
how one uses one's anger and rescue fantasies. Merely feeling justified
rage and disappointment does not suffice for intervention because
they tend to skew one's judgment and can lead to more disruption.
Once I learned to distill my anger, so to speak, I managed to find
interventions that were useful to parent and child alike. I have found
it easier to dissuade parents from hitting their children than to
persuade them to give up sexual exhibitionism or to admit incest.
Lawrence's and Gordon's parents thought I was much too much of a
"softie" in my treatment of their sons, but they also regarded me as an
authority on child rearing. In addition, their own therapists had
managed to help these parents gain some comfort from their own
harsh consciences. An eye for an eye and a tooth for a tooth were
maxims they had lived by but could relinquish as guiding principles
when their children's welfare was at stake.

Nevertheless, Adam's parents and Lindi's father could not be
persuaded that their sexual exhibitionism had influenced their children adversely. They considered such ideas old fashioned and too
restrictive. Their inner lives were so impoverished that they could not
give up exhibitionistic sexual gratification even for their children.
Joanie's and Julian-Gregory's fathers claimed to love their children,
and they did. But their love was so primitive that it did not include the
ability to constrain their sexual wishes toward their children. They at
first denied that they had committed incest and threatened me
repeatedly either with lawsuits or by their demeanor.

If I had given free reign to my own anger, disgust, and wish to
punish, I would not have been able to help anyone. I learned to weigh
my inner responses carefully. This often meant that I had to suppress
discomfort when I was told how bad the child was and how they, the
parents, were blameless. My inclination was to blurt out, "You did it.
Now stop it." I wanted to act like a strict probation officer who deters
her probationers from further criminal actions. But the parents needed
as much empathy as the children. This was a painful lesson to me, but
it was also a fruitful one because it allowed me to find the right words
to promote peace in the families and growth for the child.

Equally unacceptable is the attitude that one's countertransference constitutes an indulgence that could lead to inappropriate gratification of the child. I have found that my countertransferential

understanding of a child's developmental needs often opened the door to the right kind of interaction, interaction that would not have occurred had I allowed only psychoanalytic interpretive technique to inform me. While remaining grounded in psychoanalytic developmental psychology, I tried to figure out what a given child was sayinig to me with words, games, dances, singing, or any other spontaneous production. I tried to understand the child's warding-off behavior and defensive, hostile, and aggressive actions. If I had not accepted the children's anger and acting out as necessary under the circumstances, I could not have helped them.

Given all those considerations, I regard countertransference as a way of responding both consciously and unconsciously to the child patient in a manner that includes all of my responses. I accept that this means I too have to work on whatever conflicts are aroused in me, that is, that the child's parents or significant others as they are represented in the child's psyche will affect me (Racker, 1968). I have clinical evidence (Siegel, 1988) that even the evocation of previously repressed inner conflicts can be of help in solving the child patient's turmoil. My discomfort in the face of unrelentingly infantile or hostile parents has often put me in touch with my own childhood dramas and has allowed me to rethink the tragedies of those who were entrusted with my care. This rethinking and refeeling has enabled me to be more closely attuned to the children I treat and is in accord with the scant reports about countertransference in therapeutic work with children. Milner (1955) speaks of her resistance to discomfort and the difficulties she experienced in being used therapeutically by her patient. Her unease fled when she understood that rather than witnessing a regression, she was in the presence of an attempt by her patient to make contact between his inner and outer worlds.

Ekstein's formulations (Ekstein, Wallerstein, and Mandelbaum, 1959) are perhaps the most useful. He emphasized that in work with children, the therapist faces countertransference to the child–parent unit he encounters in the present, but also that from the past. His position is supported by "the observation regarding the extent to which beginning workers with children commonly evoke fantasies of magically rescuing the child from the wickedness of his parents. Such fantasies can be said to reflect the defense against archaic guilt and anxiety generated in reaction to the fantasied replacement of the child's parents, and 'parents' more generically" (p. 188).

In my experience, it is really true that the child therapist is forever reworking her own inner representation of caretakers so that she herself can provide solutions to problems experienced as unthinkable and unspeakable.

The idea of incest or physical abuse is so abhorrent to most of us that we do not even have a mental formulation of what our response would be. The child-care worker who comes into contact with such behavior must nevertheless face it, deal with it, and state an opinion about what has been observed. Outrage is most often expressed. It seems impossible to meet child abusers with anything resembling understanding or kindness. One wishes to punish them—certainly there is no similarity between such people and oneself. But have we never felt so angry with our own children that we thought, "I could kill that child"? On the other side of the coin, did we not find our children to be the most beguiling of all? There is, however, a vast difference between having such feelings and acting on them. Nonetheless, there is a common root to such feelings that makes understanding possible. Once such thoughts surface, it becomes possible to tolerate, to be helpful, to find a common bond that yet preserves the boundaries necessary between parents and children, between professionals and those who seek their help.

Besides such generalities, there are specifics that each therapist must work through. For instance, supervisors are of the utmost importance when one becomes a therapist. Because of their assumed superior knowledge and experience, they are often idealized by beginning therapists. I was no exception. Yet my supervisor talked about the psychic elaboration of incest and how the child who had been punitively abused fantasized about beatings. While I recognized this way of thinking as extremely important during certain phases of the treatment, it was of no use at all when I was confronted with the reality of Joanie's father, for instance, who insisted that I was filthy minded and wrong and that he had never committed incest. The man's denial seemed set in cement. I was faced with the task of mobilizing Joanie's mother to protect her child, but when I reported my interaction with Joanie's mother, my supervisor talked of the mother's narcissistic personality disorder and the empathy she needed. Her intrapsychic problems were secondary concerns for me. I finally came to understand that my supervisor, though kind and understanding and completely correct in his theoretical formulations, had no tools to help me meet the immediate demands placed upon me. I had to make up my own style of intervention as contingencies arose.

This realization was at first a tremendous blow to my inner world. I felt betrayed by psychoanalysis as a theory applicable to the psychodynamic mode I was working in. I felt betrayed by my supervisor, who wanted to talk about exquisitely precise psychic determinants when a child was being abused. After much introspection I recognized that I was reliving with my supervisor, and in the treatment of children like Joanie, my own dependency needs. I wanted a recipe for dealing with seemingly impossible situations and when none was forthcoming, I was as angry as a child who does not yet have coping mechanisms of her own. I began to understand that the burden of understanding was on my shoulders. To reach the place where my supervisor's recommendations would apply, I had to break new ground. This scared me because it destroyed the notion that I could lean on someone else when in trouble. When I discussed the situations with colleagues, they were equally distant. They had solutions ranging from imprisonment of the parents to five-times-a-week analysis for acting out individuals like Gordon's mother and father, who were rigid in their thinking and could barely tolerate the interventions of their family therapist. My colleagues by rationalizing and intellectualizing, distanced themselves from my quandary, leaving me again to find my own way.

Eventually, I learned to stand on my own psychological and professional feet. I included in my treatment approaches whatever was helpful to my young patients as long as I could justify what I was doing along developmental lines. Psychoanalytic psychology and some of the findings of child research once again became my guiding principles. This synthesis did not take place until my own inner turmoil surrounding long-hidden dependency needs were resolved. Along with this conflict resolution, I could face and at least in part demolish another sacred cow: the myth of unfailingly perfect parenthood, that is, that parents automatically know how to parent when their child is born. Ideally, I would like to see classes for men and women in how to parent as soon as a pregnancy makes itself known. They would have instruction not only about the crucial times directly after birth and during the first few years, but also on how to deal with recalcitrant underachievers, bullies, youngsters who do not want to eat. There are any number of relatively benign situations that can nevertheless make life impossible for parents and children when advice and guidance are not available. I don't know if such classes would help parents to love their children more, but at least the classes would give structure to their parenting.

Reworking one's inner assumptions in connection with each new youngster who came into treatment with me brought rich rewards despite some of the shortcomings in outcome depicted in this book. Not all of the children emerged entirely free of their conflicts, but all of them seemed to have benefited sufficiently to take further developmental steps. In reworking my own conflicts, I became able to empathize more closely, to understand, and to help. In short, countertransference in the work with children is as helpful as it is in the treatment of adults if used with caution. In addition, the transference–countertransference dyad provides the matrix that parallels the mother–child dyad, thus facilitating the mutuality and intimacy missing in approaches that are not psychodynamically oriented.

References

Anthony, E. J. (1957), An experimental approach to the psychopathology of childhood: Encopresis. *British Journal of Medical Psychology*, 30:146–175.

Balint, A. (1943), Identification. *International Journal of Psycho-Analysis*, 24:97–107.

Barkley, R. A. (1985), The parent-child interaction patterns of hyperactive children: Precursors to aggressive behavior? In: *Advances in Developmental and Behavioral Pediatrics*, Vol. 6, ed. D. Routh & M. Wolraich. Greenwich, CT: JAI Press, pp. 117–150.

Beebe, B. (1986), Mother-infant mutual influence and precursors of self-object representation. In: *Empirical Studies of Psychoanalytic Theories*, Vol. 2, ed. J. Masling. Hillsdale, NJ: The Analytic Press, pp. 27–48.

Beres, D. (1958), Vicissitudes of superego functions and superego precursors in children. *The Psychoanalytic Study of the Child*, 13:324–335. New York: International Universities Press.

Bornstein, B. (1947), Hysterical twilight states in an eight-year-old child. *The Psychoanalytic Study of the Child*, 2:229–255. New York: International Universities Press.

Breuer, J. & Freud, S. (1893–1895), Studies on hysteria. *Standard Edition*, 2. London: Hogarth Press, 1955.

Brody, S., Axelrad, S. & Moroh, M. (1976), Early phases in the development of object relations. *International Review of Psycho-Analysis*, 3:21–32.

Buxbaum, E. (1935), Exhibitionism and onanism in a ten-year-old boy. *Psychoanalytic Quarterly* 4:61–189.

Chaiklin, H. (1975), *Marian Chace, Her Papers*. Columbia, MD: American Dance Therapy Association.

Cohen, Y. (1988), The "golden fantasy" and countertransference: Residential treatment of the abused child. *The Psychoanalytic Study of the Child*, 43:319–337. New Haven, CT: Yale University Press.

Coren, H. Z. & Saldinger, J. S. (1967), Visual hallucinosis in children: A report of two cases. *The Psychoanalytic Study of the Child*, 22:331-356. New York: International Universities Press.

Cunningham, C. E., Siegel, L. S. & Offord, D. R. (1985), A developmental dose-response analysis of the effects of methylphenidate on the peer interactions of attention deficit disordered boys. *Journal of Child Psychology and Psychiatry*, 26:955–971.

Dowling, S. (1990), Fantasy formation: A child analyst's perspective. *American Journal of Psychoanalysis*, 38:93–111.

Edgecumbe, R. & Burgner, M. (1975), The phallic-narcissistic phase: A differentiation between oedipal and preoedipal aspects of phallic development. *The Psychoanalytic Study of the Child*, 30:161–180. New Haven, CT: Yale University Press.

Ekstein, R., Wallerstein, J. & Mandelbaum, A. (1959), Countertransference in the residential treatment of children. *The Psychoanalytic Study of the Child*, 14:186–218. New York: International Universities Press.

Esman, A. H. (1973), The primal scene: A review and a reconsideration. *The Psychoanalytic Study of the Child*, 28:49–81. New Haven, CT: Yale University Press.

Fast, I. (1984), *Gender Identity*. Hillsdale, NJ: The Analytic Press.

Finkelhor, D. (1979), *Sexually Victimized Children*. New York: Free Press.

Ford, C. S. & Beach, F. A. (1951), *Patterns of Sexual Behavior*. New York: Harper & Row.

Fraiberg, S. (1962), Technical aspects of the analysis of a child with a severe behavior disorder. *Journal of the American Psychoanalytic Association*, 10: 338-367.

Freud, A. (1946a), *The Ego and the Mechanisms of Defense*. New York: International Universities Press.

_____ (1946b), The psychoanalytic study of infantile feeding disturbance. *The Psychoanalytic Study of the Child*, 2:119–132. New York: International Universities Press.

_____ (1963), The concept of developmental lines: *The Psychoanalytic Study of the Child*, 18:245–265. New York: International Universities Press.

_____ (1965), *Normality and Pathology in Childhood*. New York: International Universities Press.

_____ & Burlingham, D. T. (1944), *Infants Without Families*. New York: International Universities Press.

Freud, S. (1896), The aetiology of hysteria. *Standard Edition*, 3:189–221. London: Hogarth Press, 1955.

_____ (1897), The Complete Letters of Sigmund Freud to Wilhelm Fliess, ed. J. M. Masson. Cambridge, MA: Belknap/Harvard University Press.

_____ (1900), *The Interpretation of Dreams*. *Standard Edition*, 4/5. London: Hogarth Press, 1953.

_____ (1905), Three Essays on the Theory of Sexuality. *Standard Edition*, 7:135–243. London: Hogarth Press, 1953.

_____ (1906), My view on the part played by sexuality in the aetiology of the neuroses. *Standard Edition*, 7:271–279. London: Hogarth Press, 1953.

_____ (1908), *On the Sexual Theories of Children*. *Standard Edition*, 9:205–226. London: Hogarth Press, 1959.

_____ (1910), The future prospects of psychoanalytic therapy. *Standard Edition*, 11:139–152. London: Hogarth Press, 1957.

_____ (1913), The disposition to obsessional neurosis. *Standard Edition*, 12:311–326. London: Hogarth Press, 1958.

_____ (1914), On narcissism: An introduction. *Standard Edition*, 14:73–102. London: Hogarth Press, 1957.

_____ (1915a), The unconscious. *Standard Edition*, 14:159–216. London: Hogarth Press, 1957.

_____ (1915b), Instincts and their vicissitudes. *Standard Edition*, 14:109–140. London: Hogarth Press, 1957.

_____ (1916), Introductory lectures on psycho-analysis. *Standard Edition*, 15. London: Hogarth Press, 1963.

_____ (1917), Introductory lectures on psychoanalysis. *Standard Edition*, 16. London: Hogarth Press, 1963.

_____ (1920), Beyond the pleasure principle. *Standard Edition*, 18:7–66. London: Hogarth Press, 1963.

_____ (1921), Group psychology and the analysis of the ego. *Standard Edition*, 18:67–144. London: Hogarth Press, 1955.

_____ (1924), Some neurotic mechanisms in jealousy, paranoia and homosexuality. *Standard Edition*, 18:223–232. London: Hogarth Press, 1955.

_____ (1925), Some psychical consequences of the anatomical distinction between the sexes. *Standard Edition*, 19:243–258. London: Hogarth Press, 1961.

_____ (1931), Female sexuality. *Standard Edition*, 21:225–243. London: Hogarth Press, 1961.

_____ (1933), New introductory lectures on psychoanalysis. *Standard Edition*, 22:112–135. London: Hogarth Press, 1964.

_____ (1938), An outline of psychoanalysis. *Standard Edition*, 23:144–207. London: Hogarth Press, 1964.

_____ (1939), Moses and Monotheism. *Standard Edition*, 23:3–137. London: Hogarth Press, 1964.

Furman, R. A. & Furman, E. (1984), Intermittent decathexis—a type of parental dysfunction. *International Journal of Psycho-Analysis*, 65:423–434.

Gagnon, J. (1965), Female child victims of sex offenses. *Social Problems*. 13:176–192.

Galdston, R. (1981), The domestic dimensions of violence: Child abuse, *The Psychoanalytic Study of the Child*, 36:391–414. New Haven, CT: Yale University Press.

Gedo, J. E. (1979), *Beyond Interpretation*. New York: International Universities Press.

_____ (1988), *The Mind in Disorder*. Hillsdale, NJ: The Analytic Press.

Gelles, R. J. (1975), The social construction of child abuse. *American Journal of Orthopsychiatry*, 45:363–369.

Gil, D. G. (1975), Unraveling child abuse. *American Journal of Orthopsychiatry*, 45:346–356.

Glover, L. & Mendell, D. (1982), A suggested developmental sequence for a preoedipal genital phase. In: *Early Female Development: Current Psychoanalytic Views*, ed. D. Mendell. New York: SP Medical & Scientific Books, pp. 127–174.

Greenacre, P. (1952), Penis awe and its relation to penis envy. In: *Emotional Growth*, Vol. 1. New York: International Universities Press, pp. 31–49, 1971.

Hartmann, H. (1958), *Egopsychology and the Problem of Adaptation*. New York: International Universities Press.

Henker, R. & Whalen, C. K. (1989), Hyperactivity and attention deficit. *American Psychologist*, 44:216–223.

Herman, J. L. (1981), *Father–Daughter Incest*. Cambridge, MA: Harvard University Press.

Husain, A. & Chapel, J. L. (1983), History of incest in girls admitted to a psychiatric hospital. *American Journal of Psychiatry*, 140:591–593.

Jacobson, E. (1964), *The Self and the Object World*. New York: International Universities Press.

Katan, A. (1973), Children who were raped. *The Psychoanalytic Study of the Child*, 28:208–224. New Haven, CT: Yale University Press.

Kempe, C., Silvermann, F. N., Steele, B. F., Driegemueller, W. & Silver, H. K. (1962), The battered child syndrome. *Journal of the American Medical Association*, 181:17–24.

Kestenberg, J. (1982), The inner genital phase-prephallic and preoedipal. In: *Early Female Development*. ed. D. Mendell. New York: SP Medical & Scientific Books, pp. 81–127.

King, K. R. & Dorpat, T. L. (in press), Daddy's girl: An international perspective on the transference and defense in the psychoanalysis of a case of father–daughter incest. In: *The Inner World of Women*, ed. E. V. Siegel. New York: Bruner Mazel.

Kinsey, A. C., Pomeroy, W. B. & Martin, C. E. (1948), *Sexual Behavior in the Human Male*. Philadelphia: Saunders.

———— ———— Gebhard, P. H. (1953), *Sexual Behavior in the Human Female*. Philadelphia: Saunders.

Klein, M. (1946), Notes on some schizoid mechanisms. In: *Envy and Gratitude*. London: Hogarth Press, 1975, pp. 1–24.

——— (1955), The psycho-analytic play technique. In: *The Writings of Melanie Klein*, Vol 3. London: Hogarth Press, 1975, pp. 23–164.

——— (1973), *The Psychoanalysis of Children*. London: Hogarth Press.

Kohut, H. (1971), *The Analysis of the Self*. New York: International Universities Press.

Kovacs, M. (1989), Affective disorders in children and Adolescents. *American Psychologist*, 44:209–217.

Lester, E. P., Jodoin, R.-M. & Robertson, B. M. (1989), Countertransference dreams reconsidered. *International Review of Psychoanalysis*, 16:305–314.

Lichtenberg, J. (1983), *Psychoanalysis and Infant Research*. Hillsdale, NJ: The Analytic Press.

Loewald, H. W. (1986), Transference-countertransference. *Journal of the American Psychoanalytic Association,* 34:275–287.

Lombardi, K. L. & Lapidos, E. (1990), Therapeutic engagement with children: Integrating infant research and clinical practice. *Psychoanalytic Psychology,* 7:91–103.

Mahler, M. (1952), On child psychosis and schizophrenia: Autistic and symbiotic child psychosis. *The Psychoanalytic Study of the Child,* 7: 286–305. New York: International Universities Press.

_____ (1966), Development of symbiosis, symbiotic psychosis and the nature of separation anxiety. *International Journal of Psycho-Analysis,* 47: 550–560.

_____ (1968), *On Human Symbiosis and the Vicissitudes of Individuation.* New York: International Universities Press.

_____ , Pine, F. & Bergman, A. (1975), *The Psychological Birth of the Human Infant.* New York: Basic Books.

Marcus, B. F. (1989), Incest and the borderline syndrome: The mediating role of identity. *Psychoanalytic Psychology,* 2:199–216.

Marshall, R. (1979), Countertransference in the psychotherapy of children and adolescents. *Contemporary Psychoanalysis,* 15:595–629.

Masson, J. F. (1984), *The Assault on Truth.* New York: Farrar, Strauss & Giroux.

McLaughlin, J. T. (1981), Transference, psychic reality, and countertransference. *Psychoanalytic Quarterly,* 50:639:664.

Mead, M. (1928), *Coming of Age in Samoa.* New York: Morrow.

Milner, M. (1955), The role of illusion in symbol formation. In: *New Directions in Psychoanalysis,* ed. M. Klein, P. Heiman & R. Money-Kyrle. New York: Basic Books, pp. 82–108.

Mittelman, B. (1957), Motility in the therapy of children and adults. *The Psychoanalytic Study of the Child,* 12:284–319. New York: International Universities Press.

Money, J. (1987), Sin, sickness or status? Homosexual gender identity and psychoneuroendocrinology. *American Psychologist,* 42:384–399.

Mrazek, P. B., & Kempe, C. H. (1981), *Sexually Abused Children and Their Families.* New York: Pergamon Press.

Murooka, H. (1974), *Lullaby from the Womb.* Hollywood, CA: Capital Records.

Novey, S. (1958), The meaning of the concept of mental representation of the object. *Psychoanalytic Quarterly,* 27:57–59.

Parens, H. (1987), *Aggression in Our Children,* Northvale, NJ: Aronson.

Pelham, W. E., Bender, M. E., Cadell, J. E., Booth, S. & Moorer, S. H. (1985), Methylphenidate and children with attention deficit disorder. Dose effects on classroom, academic and social behavior. *Archives of General Psychiatry,* 42:946–952.

Peller, L. E. (1954), Libidinal phases, ego development and play. *The Psychoanalytic Study of the Child,* 9: 178–198. New York: International Universities Press.

Piaget, J. (1976), *The Grasp of Consciousness: Action and Concept in the Young Child.* Cambridge, MA: Harvard University Press.

Racker, H. (1968), *Transference and Countertransference.* New York: International Universities Press.

Róheim, G. (1958), The Western tribes of Central Australia: Their sexual life. *Psychoanalysis and the Social Sciences,* 5:221–245. New York International Universities Press.

Roiphe, H. & Galenson, E. (1981), *Infantile Origins of Sexual Identity.* New York: International Universities Press.

Sander, L. W. (1962), Issues in early mother-child interaction. *Journal of the American Academy of Child Psychiatry,* 1:141–166.

_____ (1975), Infant and caretaking environment. In: *Explorations in Child Psychiatry,* ed. E. J. Anthony. New York: Plenum Press, pp. 129–166.

_____ (1983), Polarity, paradox and the organizing process in development. In: *Frontiers in Infant Psychiatry,* ed. J. D. Call, E. Galenson & R. Tyson. New York: Basic Books, pp. 315–327.

Schilder, P. (1951), *The Image and Appearance of the Human Body.* New York: International Universities Press.

Schimek, J. G. (1975), A critical examination of Freud's concept of unconscious mental representation. *International Review of Psychoanalysis,* 2:171–817.

Schmais, C. (1974), *Dance Therapy in Perspective. Focus on Dance,* 7:7–13.

Schur, M. (1953), The Ego in Anxiety. In: *Drives, Affects, Behavior,* ed. R. M. Loewenstein. New York: International Universities Press, pp. 67–103.

_____ (1955), Comments on the metapsychology of somatization. *The Psychoanalytic Study of the Child,* 10:119–164. New York: International Universities Press.

Shengold, L. (1968), Child abuse and deprivation: Soul murder. *Journal of the American Psychoanalytic Association,* 27:533–560.

Siegel, E. V. (1972), The phantasy life of a mongoloid: Movement therapy as a developmental tool. *American Dance Therapy,* Monogr. 2. Columbia, MD: American Dance Therapy Association.

_____ (1980), Integrating movement and psychoanalytic technique. In: *Expressive Therapy,* ed. A. Robbins. New York: Human Sciences Press, pp. 258–279.

_____ (1984a), *Dance Movement Therapy: Mirror of Our Selves.* New York: Human Sciences Press.

_____ (1984b), Severe body image distortions in some female homosexuals. *Dynamic Psychotherapy,* 2:18–28.

_____ (1986), The connection between playing and adult love: Reconstructions from the analysis of some homosexual women. *Dynamic Psychotherapy,* 4:53–67.

_____ (1988), *Female Homosexuality: Choice Without Volition.* Hillsdale, NJ: The Analytic Press.

_____ and Blau, B. (1978), Breathing together – a preliminary investigation of a motor reflex as adaptation: Variability of forced vital capacity in psychotic children. *American Journal of Dance Therapy,* 2:35–42.

Smith, S. (1977), The golden fantasy. *International Journal of Psycho-Analysis,* 58:311–324.

Sperling, M. (1978), The role of the mother in psychosomatic disorders in children. In: *Psychosomatic Disorders in Childhood,* New York: Aronson.

Spitz, R. (1965), *The First Year of Life.* New York: International Universities Press.

Stern, D. (1985), *The Interpersonal World of the Infant: A View from Psychoanalysis and Developmental Psychology*. New York: Basic Books.

Stoller, R. (1964), A contribution to the study of gender identity. *International Journal of Psychoanalysis*, 45:220–226.

_____ (1984), *Presentations of Gender*. New Haven, CT: Yale University Press.

Weil, J. L. (1989), *Instinctual Stimulation of Children: From Common Practice to Child Abuse*, Vol 1. New York: International Universities Press.

Winnicott, D. W. (1953), Transitional objects and transitional phenomena. *International Journal of Psycho-Analysis*, 34:89–97.

_____ (1982), *Playing and Reality*. New York: Basic Books.

INDEX

Elaine V. Siegel, Ph.D. is supervising and training analyst at the New York Center for Psychoanalytic Training. A Member of the Academy of Dance Therapists, Registered, she served for 14 years as director of the motor development unit at Suffolk Child Development Center, a research facility of the State University of New York at Stony Brook. Dr. Siegel maintains a private practice in Long Island and lectures widely both in the United States and Europe. She is the author of Dance-Movement Therapy: Mirror of Our Selves *(1984) and* Female Homosexuality: Choice Without Volition *(The Analytic Press, 1988).*